The Amazing Journey of the Kickapoo Kids

—∭—

A Novel based on a Personal Experience

Paul Lagan

ISBN: 1503224465
ISBN 13: 9781503224469
Library of Congress Control Number: 2014920952
CreateSpace Independent Publishing Platform
North Charleston, South Carolina

Reviews

A "novel based on personal experience" that follows the postwar legacy of baseball in a small Wisconsin town.

As the story opens, a man named Bones is attending an old-timers' reunion, reminiscing about the glory days of the 1940s and '50s Millersville High School baseball team in Wisconsin's Kickapoo Valley. The rest of the book is a flashback to how that team developed after originating in Bones' hometown of Sterling in 1946-47. Debut author Lagan paints an alluring picture of the rural Midwest, from the simple pleasures of nature and farm life to an idealized family culture: "We were taught values, and we knew that if problems arose, our parents would be there for us—no matter what." Nevertheless, the town has its pitfalls—moonshine, violence, rough company—and it's partially for these reasons that the town's parents convert a planting field to a baseball diamond and get the boys started on the basics. The first two-thirds of the book interweave the story of the rise of the baseball team with tales of life in Sterling, including a visit by "gypsies," a time that local kids put an outhouse on the roof of the bank, a harsh winter and a big flood . . .

Lagan tells of the Kickapoo Kids going to the state championship three years out of four, playing against schools 10 times their size, and of five team members being drafted by Major League teams. Still, there are some memorable moments . . . when Dad and Preacher dry off the field by setting it on fire, or when Shane uses a beefsteak to pad his glove so that he can play as catcher. These times will evocatively remind readers of how baseball, in its early days, was a country boy's sport. The bones of a great American baseball story . . . **Kirkus Reviews**

Reviews

Lagan takes us back to a time when boys played baseball before and after their chores.

In the epilogue of *The Amazing Journey of the Kickapoo Kids*, author Paul Lagan stands in a now-empty field where his Millersville High School baseball teams of the late 1940s and early 1950s played their home games. "I shake my head, and wonder how many people know just how good this team actually was," Lagan writes. "Or if they even know the team existed." Securing the teams' place in history is the obvious goal of Lagan's labor of love. A charming glimpse at small-town Wisconsin life as residents adjust to life after World War II is a welcome side dish.

The first-person account follows Lagan—referred to throughout the book only by his child hood nickname, "Bones"—and a group of baseball-loving friends as they come of age in the small villages in the Kickapoo Valley, located midway between Milwaukee and Minneapolis. When they get to tiny Millersville High School, their team goes on three *Hoosiers*-like runs deep into the state tournament, beating teams from some of the state's largest schools in the process.

In fact, swap basketball for baseball and Indiana for Wisconsin and *Kickapoo Kids* has a very *Hoosiers*-esque feel. Lagan even borrows from one of its most famous scenes when he describes a coach noting the "distance from pitcher's rubber to home plate" at the state tournament location is the same as back in Millersville. It's notable, however, that these Kickapoo Kids had a combined record of 32-2 in 1952 and 1953, one year before little Milan High School inspired one of the greatest sports movies of all times by winning an Indiana state title.

Kickapoo Kids won't be confused with a glossy Hollywood script . . .

But the joy of the book lies in the knowledge that Lagan wrote it based on sixty-year-old memories that he and former teammates shared. And that, as Lagan notes in a disclaimer at the end of the book, "color has been added and license taken on many occasions to bring wonderment to the reader."

Whether or not it's superfluous wonderment, sports fans will enjoy tales of the Negro Major League's Kansas City Blue Birds barnstorming trip through town, and of a local pastor giving up a portion of his valuable farm land to give the kids a place to play ball. Beyond baseball, we meet moonshine runners, evangelists, and gypsies. We experience the proliferation of atomic bomb shelters, polio, and rock n' roll. We live in a time when fathers work the field, mothers mend clothes, and boys play baseball before and after their chores.

It's a good time and place to live—***Foreword Reviews***

Reviews

When I sat down to begin reading *The Kickapoo Kids*, it didn't take me long to become interested in the story... *The Kickapoo Kids* is an engaging story that evokes the best kind of nostalgia, taking readers on a journey back in time to experience the coming of age of some boys who made baseball history . . . you will have one heck of a tale on your hands— ***Word Alive Press***

Reviews

Paul Lagan's book, *The Amazing Journey of the Kickapoo Kids,* turned out to be a lot more than a localized version of the movie "Hoosiers." Kudos to Paul Lagan . . . In writing the book Lagan said that he mixed "accuracy with mysticism and wholesomeness" in a blend to create the "reality of life." It worked and you should read this book— ***Crawford county Independent-Scout***

Dedication and Acknowledgments

M any people are responsible for the idea, imagination, research, and completion of this story. I cannot list all of you. I send best wishes to my teammates and classmates whose lives were intertwined in their recollection of "the good old days."

Most of all, memories are with my wife, Susan, 8/11/46 – 2/10/13, who helped edit my blundering mistakes, and who with love, patience, encouragement, and understanding spent time alone while I was glued to my computer. She will always be the love of my life, best friend, ministry partner and my hero—I miss her!

Intent and Disclaimer

Most of this story is based on personal experiences as seen through the eyes of the author and as he remembers. Information was also obtained through face-to-face interviews, tales, personal documents, historical data, newspaper clippings, and various other articles and sources.

Color has been added and license taken on many occasions to bring wonderment to the reader. Some names of actual participants and towns have been changed so as to not reveal their real identity. Additionally, some characters' actions, along with various happenings, are totally the product of the author's imagination.

Our intent is to not only prevent the accomplishments of these young men from being lost somewhere within the archives of history, but also to inspire, encourage, and suggest areas of positive change for the future.

About the Front Cover

The road on the front cover is from Sterling to Preacher's farm where the Kickapoo Kids played Oriole's baseball.

Prologue

"From what I've been able to find out, those Millersville High School baseball teams you guys had back in the 40s and 50s would have kicked some butts today," the sharp-looking gentleman said to a group of us old-timers sitting around a banquet table. We were attending a sixty-year reunion for our high school baseball team. The gentleman making the compliment was the master of ceremonies and a retired, famous sportswriter from a Madison newspaper.

"I've been doing some checking for this banquet. You guys were amazing, to say the least." The sportswriter strolled to a table where more of our players were deep in chatter.

And that we were—amazing.

The columnist was referring to a courageous group of underdogs from a small rural high school in southwestern Wisconsin, who were unaware they were playing a part of history that may never be repeated.

There are divisions in Wisconsin high school baseball today, but at the time of this story there were none. Playing against schools with enrollments upwards of twenty-five hundred students, Millersville had a total enrollment of one hundred seventy-seven students. Seven starters on the Millersville championship team were selected from twenty-one boys in our senior class. After school, five were offered pro contracts. Three played on a 1957 Soldiers Grove team that won the Wisconsin Baseball Association Championship, and two were members of a 1971 Madison team that won the AABC National Stan Musial World series.

It wasn't long before the gentleman passed my chair on his way to the podium to begin the ceremony. He paused for a moment. "I use what you guys did to encourage kids," he said. "Ever think about writing a book? You'll have one heck of a tale to tell."

"I just might do that," I replied.

So here's my story, much as I personally lived it . . .

The Amazing Journey of the Kickapoo Kids

A Novel based on a Personal Experience

THE SCENE

September 1946

Sprinkled along a twisting one hundred twenty-mile stream from the northern part of Wisconsin, south to the Wisconsin River, is the world in which I live, the Kickapoo Valley. Once inhabited by Kickapoo Indians, the land (located about half way between Milwaukee and Minncapolis) has given way to small villages occupied by residents who are almost oblivious to the trials of everyday life evolving around them.

My great-grandfather homesteaded the rolling, one hundred twenty acre wooded area we live on five miles west of Millersville, a town next to the Kickapoo River.

He obtained his property in a land grant from the U. S. government. The town was named after the first grain and sorghum molasses mills in the area.

"For the first few years, he and your great-grandmother lived as hobbits in a dugout, which was little more than a hole dug in the side of a hill," Dad said as he pointed out the location to Sunny and me when we were haying in the field one day. "On that location, my grandfather and grandmother built the home they lived in. I was born in that house," he said. "Today, there is nothing left except a lilac bush and a patch of field lilies."

Many nights I sat in our kitchen during the winter months next to an old Round Oak wood-burning stove while Dad repeated stories told to him by my grandfather. Dad's eyes brightened when he started, and by his hand gestures I could tell he enjoyed telling us the tales.

"Indians camped on a back portion of our farm when your grandpa was a boy—their campfires glowed at night," Dad said. "When something killed one of the cattle, or one died from some ailment, we let them take it away for food. They thought of what we did as an act of friendship. Their family and ours passed each other sort of like ships in the night—neither of us hardly knew the other were there. We didn't bother them, and they left us alone."

"Why did they camp there?" my brother, Sunny, asked as he moved his chair closer to Dad.

"I guess there was a spring coming out of the ravine back in our woods at that time," Dad replied. "You know where those wild apple trees are on the hill back there?" Dad pointed over his shoulder. "And where those walnut trees and berry bushes are? Well, I guess there was even more back then, like mushrooms and wild strawberries."

Almost every year, Sunny and I found arrowheads turned up by the spring plowing.

—⁓—

Our country was starting to recover from many years of rationing and sacrificing during World War II. Although there still remained a certain amount of nostalgia for the prewar era, wages were rising in our area and the emphasis was on having more advanced machinery, appliances and automobiles. Prior to that time these pioneers, who for their families were forced to accept life's hardships—were the last generation of American sodbusters who literally dug a living out of the earth with a team of horses and their bare hands.

The older generation in our area did not benefit as much from the postwar financial explosion because many had never recovered from the loss of their savings during the Great Depression. The average sixty-five-year-old had nothing but a small Social Security pension for an income.

"Your Uncle Jim lost everything he had in the bank," Dad said, "and never got it right again. He turned to the bottle, and died from a fall down the hay shoot in our barn!"

"We ate lard sandwiches mixed with salt for lunch during the depression," Dad told us. "Sometimes hot water mixed with bacon grease for soup. Your grandmother called it poor man's soup. We ate chicken necks with most meals. Anything left over was thrown into a pot and called 'slum gum.'"

—⟨⟨⟨—

The pace was slower here, the terrain well cared for, and responsible people (who were proud of their property) occupied the farms and homes within the small villages. Barns were freshly painted, weeds cut, machinery maintained, and brightly colored tractors roamed the field.

Socially, almost everyone knew everyone else and we always referred to each other by our first name, or a nickname. It was almost an insult to address another person you were acquainted with by their last name, unless, of course, in certain times of respect, or proper or unusual circumstances. People waved from their car while meeting and passing each other on the highway. Just about the only time neighbors got together was during church, shopping, grain thrashing, corn shredding—and baseball games. Hard work was our inheritance and baseball our legacy. Every town of any size had a local team, and some of the talent was exceptional—ours was no different.

The Kickapoo was built around families and kids came before carriers. Grandparents lived with their children and grandchildren, and passed down valuable knowledge and experience. There were almost no divorces—husbands and wives needed each other to survive in this frontier environment. Almost all meals were eaten together as a family. There we discussed everything that happened at home, school, and in our local community during the day including news on the radio. We were taught values, and we knew that if problems arose, our parents would be there for us, no matter what. Everyone's mothers were home when their children returned from school. We were expected to behave. To be sent to the principal's office was mild compared to what awaited us at home if we misbehaved in school. The idea of parents bailing us out if we broke the law was unheard of; they actually sided with the law.

—⁓—

Hands on the clock didn't turn as fast here as in some other parts of our country. Holidays were celebrated traditionally. Christmas was no exception. Decorations, carols, and roasted chestnuts and popcorn balls were everywhere. Our Christmas tree was decorated with ornaments handed down from my mother's family; I've never seen replicas.

On Christmas Eve, shortly after we were finished with the evening milking, Sunny and I would rest for a few minutes in the soft straw of a manger along with a dozen or so purring cats. Body heat from the cows and horses kept us warm—perhaps much like that evening 2000 years earlier.

After we returned to the house, I remember falling asleep behind the old wood cook stove in our kitchen. It was warm there. The spicy smell and crackling sound of the wood burning tranquilized the moment. We had no electricity; oil lamps were used in our house and kerosene lanterns lit the other buildings. A strange sort of shadow was cast throughout the areas they occupied. Our coal furnace often could not compete with the near zero temperatures so Mother would heat a brick or stove iron and wrap it in a paper sack and place it under the covers at the foot of our bed to keep Sunny and me warm.

—◊—

My brother and I received our elementary education at a grade school in Sterling, from first through eighth grades. Our school played ballgames against a few other small schools. There was one bat, one ball, and no gloves. We walked to a school our team played against that was about three miles away. Our parents took turns driving us to play two other schools that were a few miles farther.

We attended a small Catholic church. The decor was beautiful. The rector knew his parishioners personally, and if someone did not attend for a week or two, he paid them a visit. There was a relationship between him and the pastors of the Lutheran, United Methodist, and Congregational churches. When something happened that was detrimental to the community—they united and organized against it. We never locked our door after leaving home. I never recall Dad or Mother signing a contract for anything; a handshake was enough. They never missed an opportunity to vote.

"There will never be a Black Sox scandal here, not in our valley," Fr. Tom Murphy said during Mass one Sunday at St. Mary's Catholic Church in Millersville. Fr. Murphy and Pastor Gus Johnson of the Sterling Lutheran Church seemed to be the best of friends, and they always sat side by side at baseball games. "Bleacher bums," they called themselves. Neither wore a religious collar outside of church services and dressed no different than the rest of us. These two men of the cloth were by no means pompous stiff-necked individuals. They would take Sunny and me fishing at times, and at other times one or the other would stop by our farm and help with the haying. Most of the time at ball games they were more vocal with the umpires then the parents of the players. Fr. Murphy was the "shaker" of the two, and Pastor Johnson the "hugger." Fr. with a handshake and Pastor with a hug.

Although people did not wear their spirituality on their shirtsleeves, most attended one of the churches in the area. People prayed before meals. One of my most vivid memories of my youth is observing Dad and Mother, on their knees each evening in our farmhouse kitchen, leaning on old wooden chairs— in prayer. They would then climb the stairs to their second-floor bedroom, each evening ending the same, with the sound of Dad and Mother exchanging kisses.

"God have mercy on us," Dad sighed. They had labored almost nonstop, side by side from four in the morning until ten at night. Finally there was rest . . .

—⚊—

Mother scrubbed our dirty clothes on a washboard with homemade soap and then cranked them through the wringer on our *Speed Queen* washing machine. It seemed like our appliances never broke. Our clothes smelled fresh after drying on the clothesline that ran from a tree to a corner of our house. I remember Mother listening on our Coronado battery radio to programs like Stella Dallas and Ma Perkins as she did the washing. I could usually hear her humming a southern gospel song by Roy Acuff, "The Gray Speckled Bird." *Makes me feel sort of good all over.*

"I know she's happy when she's humming that song," Dad said. "A woman that hums while working is a happy woman."

On Friday nights we sat spellbound, listening to boxing from Madison Square Garden in New York City. Boxing was big in the valley and names like Dempsey and Louis were as popular as Ruth and DiMaggio or Blanchard and Davis.

The four of us hand-milked sixteen dairy cows every morning and evening, no vacations! Our family drank whole milk, meaning it was not pasteurized. Each cow had her own stanchion in the dairy barn and knew exactly where to go when entering.

Very little was bought from the small grocery stores in the area, except coffee, flour, sugar, and some spices. We didn't even buy toilet paper; prior year's Sears Roebuck catalogs were used for that venture. There was no indoor plumbing in my earlier years so an outhouse served the purpose. Facilities were shared with spiders that weaved sticky webs throughout the enclosure. I guess our family was a little higher up in modern conveniences than most of our neighbors, because ours was a four-hole. The less fortunate had just one or two.

Millersville had a telephone office, and everyone shared a party line. Telephone numbers were composed of a number of sounds or "rings." Ours was two long rings and one short ring. People would do "rubbering," meaning they would pick up the receiver on the telephone and listen to the conversations of the other people on our line. Many people got very angry at the rubbering and verbally let those listening know how they felt about the invasion of their privacy.

But all most of us kids wanted to do was play baseball.

Chapter 1

THE BUS AND THE BLUE BIRDS

As the sun began to break the darkness in the eastern sky, the large gray bus with big dark blue lettering on the sides, "Blue Birds Baseball," moved along Highway 171 through the hilltop orchards. The passengers inside glanced though the side windows as it rolled past apple trees whose branches stretched almost to the ground from the weight of ripened fruit. Carefully the bus jolted over the curving, steep dirt road that was lightly covered with gravel to keep the dust down and entered the valley that lay below.

Startled, Sammy, the owner of Sammy's Grocery, and the early morning shoppers inside his store, paused in their activities, mouths falling open as the large vehicle they had heard and read so much about passed. Two young lads who were playing catch in front of the store stopped and stared. Our neighbor, Delbert, who we called "Preacher," told me about it.

"It wasn't so much the bus that was impressive," Preacher said, "but what it represented—the Kansas City Blue Birds Professional Baseball Team."

"So that's the team," Sammy said to Clyde. Clyde just kept staring . . .

"Well, I don't think they'll beat our boys by as much as most people think," Sammy said as he walked quickly across the room to stand beside Preacher. "What do you think?"

"I think they'll do whatever they want to do," Preacher replied.

Creeping ever so slowly, it proceeded along the main street of this small southwestern Wisconsin town and came to a stop at a large sign posted at the far end. Pausing for a few moments to allow time for the driver to read the words "Crawford County Fair," the bus turned in the direction the arrow pointed and continued south on Highway 131, past the Millersville High School and to its intended destination.

With each touch to the accelerator emitted a loud blast, creating a ruckus equal to a dozen John Deere tractors exited its mufflers, and breaking the silence on this Saturday morning in the fall of 1946.

As the bus moved through the fairgrounds gate, early morning workers could notice a burst of blue smoke trailing from its exhaust pipes and the stink of engine oil burning. The bus rumbled across an open field, pulled behind a concession stand next to the ball diamond, and, with a screech, accompanied by a burst of air from the brakes, came to an abrupt stop! Aroused from their sleep, a flock of pigeons roosting on the concession stand roof burst into the air with a loud flapping sound and circled the field.

The Kansas City Blue Birds, from the elite Negro National League, had arrived at the annual Crawford County Fair in Millersville to take on a group of all-star players from teams throughout the Kickapoo Valley of Wisconsin.

—∾—

The bus remained stationary for the next few hours, no sound, just motionless. Nobody got out. It was almost as if a space ship had landed on earth from somewhere in the outer limits, its doors closed, waiting for something to happen!

People congregated around the field, talking in low voices, hands gesturing in broad sweeps that encompassed both the bus and the ball diamond. Eyes darted to the bus repeatedly. Frowns began to deepen.

The Millersville High School baseball team was playing a forenoon game against another school, La

Farge, before the main attraction of the day started. This was a decisive game to determine the league championship. As usual, things were not going well for the Millers. Additionally, neither team seemed able to keep their concentration on the game, apparently waiting for the elite Blue Birds to make their appearance.

By late morning, the high school game ended and the local players making up the all-star team arrived at the field to begin loosening up for the big game.

"What do you think they're doing?" one player asked another.

"Don't really know . . ." A worried frown accompanied the reply. His eyes darted to the bus uneasily. It was obvious his unseen opponents had already intimidated him.

"Maybe they're just trying to spook us," one said to another. "I've heard of that tactic."

"They're starting to do a pretty good job of it," replied another. "Ever think about who we're playing?"

Suddenly, the door by the driver's side of the bus snapped open and a slim athletic-looking black man stepped out into the fresh fall air, followed by his teammates. Getting their land legs under them, they looked around surveying the area. They stretched, yawned and slowly walked toward the infield. Some of the players paused for a few moments to reach down and examine the rock hard dirt of the infield, which had been unsuccessfully disked and dragged, and the height of the outfield grass that had been bleached by the hot summer sun.

They appeared rested, not what you would expect from a team that lived and ate on a bus, avoiding hotels that might not allow them to stay. They also appeared relaxed, and why shouldn't they? After all, they were the best in the land—and they knew it!

—w—

I remember tossing and turning in bed the night before, dreaming about what was to transpire the next day. The images were so real that every time I awoke I was sure what I was dreaming had actually happened. Disappointment washed over me when I realized it had not. Each time, before drifting back to sleep, I scanned the room to see if a crack of light was beginning to appear through the window of the upstairs bedroom I shared with my brother, Sunny. It was impossible to tell what time it was because my pocket watch was downstairs by the radio.

Finally—it happened!

An orange glow gradually crept across the floor . . .

"Let's go," I said, nudging my brother in the back. "Do you think they're here yet?" Sunny grunted something that was not intelligible.

I was so anxious I wanted to scream. By the time my skinny legs propelled me downstairs the house was empty. Judging from the large round clock hanging on the wall over our kitchen stove, Mom and Dad were already in the barn and half done with the milking. Although I was only eleven and my brother twelve, we were expected to help with the farm chores. I felt a little guilty for oversleeping. *I should have been there to help them.*

As I bolted to the barn, I could hear the squawk of a blue jay and the *rat-tat-tat* of a red-headed woodpecker nearby, pounding out his morning meal from the side of a rotted oak tree. Ben, our Plymouth Rock cock, crowed with assurance to announce the new day. *A sunrise will never escape that rooster.*

"How long before we can go?" I asked when I joined Dad and Mother.

"About a couple of hours or a little less if you'd help," Dad replied. One of us had left a gate open by mistake the night before, and the dairy herd had strolled out into the woods. It wasn't long until they were over the hill toward a neighbor's farm. Dad rounded them up shortly after he found the cattle missing at 4 a.m. The back woods were *silent, fresh,* and peaceful then, just before dawn. It was black out—pitch black—allowing the width of the sky to be illuminated with the glittering dust of mega millions of stars. This was always his favorite time of day.

As I hurried to help with the milking, barn swallows made a flight in and out of the barn in their back-and-forth trips to their straw-and-mud nest atop of the entrance door.

I thought about the teams I'd seen play at the fair and fanned my imagination about the Blue Birds. Last year it had been the House of David, a Jewish professional traveling team from a town in Michigan. All their players wore long beards. The year before, it was a team from the US military base at Camp McCoy in central Wisconsin. At the time, the military team was bursting with major and minor league talent that their country had drafted into the service. The Milwaukee Chicks, the champions from the All-American Girls Professional Baseball League, was the competition the year before.

The Blue Birds will be even more exciting to watch, I thought. Besides, most of us kids had never seen a black person before. Many of their players were better than a lot of the major leaguers, and they made more money traveling around the country playing exhibition games than they could if they were playing in the major leagues.

I imagined myself out there someday, playing against teams like the Blue Birds. *I hope I'll get the chance*. Milking done, I paced around the yard. My parents seemed to be taking forever to finish up in the house. Impatiently, I picked up a stick that Sunny and I used for hitting rocks, and it became an impromptu baseball bat in my hands. It felt awkward and heavy as I hefted it, picturing the crowd of thousands that traveled every year to the fair. I imagined their faces filled with excitement as they watched me, one of the local all-stars, step to the plate. In my mind I was PJ, the local legend who hit a towering home run just last year at the fair against the House of David.

"Why you doin' that?" Sunny asked.

"Just warming up."

I swung the phantom bat hard, imagining the ball flying high over the stunned players of the opposing teams and over the snow fence that encircled the outfield. Why city kids played games like football or basketball I couldn't tell. Nothing felt as good as this—nothing!

"Bones, you coming?" Sunny, called to me. Bones and Sunny were nicknames we picked up almost from the time we were born. Mine was because of my skinny frame. I never knew how Sunny picked up his. I can never remember either of us being acknowledged by any other name.

The stands in my imagination disappeared as my brother called me. I dropped the stick in my haste to rush to the car. Sunny was already standing beside the vehicle, his Cubs baseball cap positioned neatly on top of his head.

At least I wasn't the last one there. Sunny hopped from one foot to the other, looking beyond me as I reached our blue Plymouth. "Hurry, Mom," Sunny yelled.

"Be sure you've got everything." Mom entered the passenger side of the car with a smile. She laughed at something Dad said, the color high in her cheeks as she settled herself in the seat. *She enjoys this, too.* Mother glanced up at the sky; the clouds were becoming more numerous in the west. "Toss your jackets in the trunk in case it rains."

"Will do."

"I'm excited," I said as I got in next to Sunny. "I hope some of the other guys are there. Keep your eyes open."

"Where'd you say you'd meet them?" Dad asked, as he settled himself behind the large blue-colored steering wheel and adjusted the rearview mirror.

"Behind the backstop," I responded.

"Well, okay, let's go then."

With a *thud,* Dad slammed the door on his side of the car, stepped on the clutch, and shifted it into gear. My heart was already hammering in my chest. Riveted to our seats, we drove away.

—⁓—

In a few minutes, which seemed like an hour to Sunny and me, we drove the five curving miles from our farm in the hill country to the Kickapoo Valley.

As soon as we arrived at the fair ground entrance, officers from the Crawford County Sheriff's Department directed us through the open gates and we proceeded to look for a place to park. Cars were everywhere with people scurrying between them toting overloaded wicker picnic baskets.

At least two thousand families from all along the Kickapoo Valley drove many miles each year to be a part of the excitement. Baseball was what drew the crowds—and this day was one everyone had been looking forward to all year. The Crawford County Fair provided an opportunity for the local all-stars to match their skills against some of the famous professional traveling teams of the era.

Dad drove past the parking lot to a space beneath a group of wild apple trees. Either the red bottom apples had fallen or the animals had eaten them. The big full ones that hung from the top branches glistened in the sunlight. "We need to get away from the heat of the parked cars," he said.

Families were already spreading handmade blankets and colorful quilts sewn from discarded clothing on the green grass of the outfield. Several were beginning to eat picnic dinners.

We were situated among a patch of red clover and some dandelions that were in seed. Their puffs blew around like snowflakes in December. Nobody ate like a bird. Mom had packed a cavernous basket filled with fried chicken, potato salad, lemonade, biscuits with jelly, and chocolate cake, and she laid each portion out in front of us in carefully prepared order.

Once in a while an adventurous ant or a fly would get in the lemonade, but we'd just scoop it out and continue. Smoke from campfires kept pesky mosquitoes at bay.

"Now don't eat too fast or it'll all come back up," Mom cautioned with a severe look at the amount of potato salad on my fork.

"I won't, Mom," I blurted with my mouth full.

After gulping our food down, Sunny and I jumped up. "Can we be excused?" Sunny asked.

Mom looked at our empty plates and sighed. "Okay, but don't forget, I warned you about eating too fast."

We ran full out to the ball field, our feet churning in our black-colored Red Ball tennis shoes like the blades on our windmill at home. I wiped the chicken grease off my hands on the overalls I was wearing as I ran.

"Slow down!" Sunny yelled. "You're gonna burst a gasket."

The flat cap I pulled down on my head blew off in the wind. I paused, and caught my breath. When I saw Sunny pick it up and realized he was chasing me, I continued running. In my haste, I stumbled over the dead branch of a maple tree that a storm destroyed years ago. *Holy tamale, the field must be more than a half mile away.*

A snow fence encircled the outfield, marking the distance for a home run, and when I got to it, I could see there was only about four hundred feet to go before I reached the backstop. Red, white, and blue banners attached to the fence waved occasionally in the slight breeze as we raced by. I noticed the billboards in left, center, and right field. Chesterfield, Old Gold, Camels, Lucky Strike, Pall Mall, Raleigh, and Phillip Morris were a few of the cigarette advertisers. Blatz, Schlitz, Pabst Blue Ribbon, Hamm's, Budweiser, Old Style Lager, and Miller High Life were most of the beer signs.

"THERE IT IS!" I yelled at the top of my voice. "That's their bus—look at it." I pointed to the bus parked beside the concession stand. "It says Blue Birds Baseball—that's the Kansas City Blue Birds!"

Chapter 2

PREACHER

As soon as we reached the infield, I realized the players were finishing their batting and infield practice, and the starting pitchers were beginning to increase the velocity of their pitches as they warmed up along the first and third base sidelines. At first, I wondered what the *smacking* sound was until I realized it was a fastball striking the catcher's mitt. *Wow, that must hurt.* A stray ball bounced my way. I nonchalantly picked it up and threw it back to the infield. *I'm part of the game.*

I watched as a player from the Blue Birds bent down and tightened the shoestring on one of his shoes. He picked up a wooden bat from an assortment of various lengths that were leaning against the backstop and flipped it up and down to make sure it was the right weight. Unlike helmets in football, the cloth cap he was wearing was the only protection he and his teammates had against a smack in the head by a stray pitch.

The players' shoes lifted clouds of dust into the air as the Blue Birds sprinted past me on their way to the field, the metal spikes from their shoes *glinting* in the bright sunlight.

The local stars wore the same uniforms they did all season. The names of the various teams they represented stood out across the front of their jerseys. I immediately recognized some of the players. Brad, Red, Bob, Mike, Dick, and a few others looked out of place from where I usually saw them in shops or out on tractors. On the field, however, they lost their workday persona and became something more than farmers, shopkeepers, teachers, and laborers. These men were very talented baseball players. I felt that ache again in the pit of my stomach.

I want to be like them someday.

A couple had played professionally before the war. There were others who simply preferred the relaxed life of the Kickapoo as compared to the bright lights of the large cities—they were content living here after the hell some of them had been through in service overseas. Besides, if they reached the big time, the most they could hope for was about six thousand dollars per year, which, although twice as much as they could make here, they didn't have to put up with the hassle that would be involved.

On the other side of the field, decked out in uniforms that were gray, baggy and wool, with blue on the bills of their caps and on the lettering of their jerseys, the Negro team looked impressive. A blue stripe ran down the sides of their pants, and their socks were solid blue.

Players for the Blue Birds had names like Jingles, Sweet Billie Grimes, Smokin' Roy Bell, Le Roy, Closer, Coop, Three Fingers Jack, Willie, Black Jack Jefferson and Wishbone. They were entertainers as well as players, performing tricks with the baseball like that of the 1934 Gas House Gang of the St. Louis Cardinals or the Harlem Globe Trotters in basketball. Their ease with the ball, the way they made it appear and disappear almost at will was magical. "Shadow ball," they called it. I glanced toward Dad, who was bent over with laughter, while we kids looked on in amazement.

As advertised in local newspapers, the Blue Birds had pitchers that threw overhand as well as sidearm. They even had a young woman that pitched underhand. One man threw both left and right handed, and an outfielder had only one arm. They played one inning barehanded and in grass skirts while the catcher sat on a rocking chair catching their pitcher. The team usually played one inning using only four players, pitcher, catcher, shortstop, and first baseman. *I hope they will do the same thing today.*

In their travels they faced teams from every walk of life. Dull eyed factory workers with grime under their finger nails, and reddish colored leather skinned farmers—tough men who long ago may have wished for something better before the Depression and the war busted their dreams. A few dug their way out of the dust and into the big time, but most did not.

"Over here, over here!" I yelled to Sunny, who joined a number of our friends, Dean, Earl, Shane, Enoch, Jerky, Ove, Corky, Chris, and me behind the home plate backstop. Enoch had his St. Louis Cardinals cap pulled tightly on his head.

"Corky, get in here so you can see!" Shane raised his voice as he grabbed the little lad by one arm and shoved him toward the screen.

"Cut out the crap—don't do that—I can get in there by myself!" Corky responded as he twisted from Shane's grasp. Corky was a spunky little guy.

"Okay, give it a rest. It don't make any difference to me. If that's the way you wanna be, it's okay!" Shane let go of Corky as he crowded closer to the backstop.

We all wanted to see, hear, and be close to the action. I pushed and nudged my way between a couple of people until I was able to reach the tightly woven gray screen.

By this time, Dad had found his good friend Preacher. They were talking, gesturing, and getting into the excitement as much as us kids. Preacher (Delbert was his baptized name) and his wife, Milley, along with their son Ove, who was one grade ahead of me in school, lived close to us on a small farm.

It was my understanding that Preacher was, although I never knew the denomination, an ordained minister. I don't believe he was ever the pastor of a church. In any event, he was always preaching to someone about something.

"The man's got a kind heart," I heard Dad mention more than once. "He's always trying to right the wrongs of this world."

Preacher was a sharp-looking man who displayed a Clark Gable mustache. He was very friendly and always ready with a good supply of jokes. Although he had seen better days, Preacher was the sort of guy to get things done. However, he was often more optimistic than realistic.

"He's sort of a gambler on things," I heard Dad say. "Not in the sense that he wagered, but that he dreamed big."

Dad told me many times that Preacher had a feeling for the game of baseball.

"He could shut his eyes and tell by the sound of the ball striking the bat whether it's a line drive, a fly ball or a grounder," Dad said. "He could tell what was happening just by the noise of the runner's spikes stirring up the infield. He could tell if it was a curve or a fastball by the sound of the *pop* of the ball striking the catcher's mitt."

———

Although this day was unusually warm (in the mid eighties), and the gnats and flies attacked in the humidity, I barely noticed. Like the rest of the kids, I was dressed in bib overalls with unbuttoned sides for ventilation. The colorful handkerchiefs we used to wipe the sweat from our dusty sun-ripened faces draped from the back of our hind pockets. Most of us wore caps; those that didn't sported flattop or heinie haircuts. We were used to being outside in days such as these while helping our parents put hay into the barn for winter feed.

"Ladies and gentlemen, your attention please," the announcer said over the microphone. "The ball game between the Kansas City Blue Birds and our local all-stars will start in a few minutes. The grandstand attractions and the first horse race will start in front of the grandstand at approximately 2:30. But first . . . would you all please rise . . . remove your hats . . . and bow your heads for a prayer for President Truman, our country, those in the soldiers' home up north, and in memory of our many sons and daughters who sacrificed their lives during this awful war that has just ended."

I glanced at Dad standing not far away. He removed the brown dress hat he always wore in public and held it down at his side in his left hand, making his balding head visible. The few gray hairs he had left blew in the breeze. He placed his other hand over his heart and stood with his head bowed and eyes closed. I looked around. Everyone was doing the same. Total strangers reached for the hand of the person standing next to them and held on tightly—the community was unifying and healing.

After Father Murphy recited The Lord's Prayer and issued a blessing on the players, Pastor Johnson read the message . . .

"Heavenly Father, we thank you today for freedom. We thank you for the lives of our sons, daughters, neighbors and friends that you have so sympathetically given back to us. Thank you for the opportunity to laugh and have fun again together as it was before this terrible war and as it should be."

I flashed an eye toward those standing close by and was struck by the many faces dampened by an occasional tear trickling down from eye to chin. The war also had its measure of internal casualties—the living dead. Mother pressed her lips together, took a deep breath, and exhaled slowly. For a brief period of time, one lady dropped to her knees weeping—her voice carrying in the silence—her brows drawing together in an anguished expression that spoke heartbreak. *Perhaps her son was one of the casualties.* A strong-appearing middle-aged man placed one arm around her shoulders, and another caught her hand as they slowly raised the lady and led her away to a secluded area behind the stands. Dad raised his head and stared at the sadness, eyes wide open, never blinking. People moved their heads, their vision following every step of the couple's lonely, private, journey—an ache swelled in my stomach.

I wish I could somehow help them.

Pausing, and obviously acknowledging what had just happened, the pastor set aside his prepared notes, and leaned forward, his sight transfixed on the activity that was taking place. He spoke earnestly . . .

"We do not understand, dear Father, why it is that in your sovereign wisdom you choose to take some and leave others, but we trust in your judgment and continue to ask for your mercy and care. Even so it must seem unbearable for those who have been affected personally. Our hearts go out to those especially, and to everyone who hurt today and every day."

He cleared his throat. "I believe we will someday be reunited with our loved ones who have departed this earth." He picked up his weathered Bible and held it high in the air to make his point. "His word says that we will—and I *believe* Him!"

"We pray this in Christ, our Savior's name…Amen."

—ᵥᵥᵥ—

After reciting the invocation, the two shepherds pivoted and stood rigid, side-by-side, their right hands in salute, as a member of the local American Legion Post Memorial Band played taps. I noticed a number of people wore "McCarthy for U.S. Senate" buttons.

There was total silence, except for a baby's cry, the far-off caw of a crow, and the occasional bark of an excited dog in the distance wondering about the loud sound from the microphone. A couple of yellow butterflies caught my eye as they circled above the backstop in a mating ritual, even the melody of the calliope slowed to a stop.

World War II still felt too close. While making a quick observation of the area, my eyes stopped abruptly. There, still hanging alongside an old clock attached to the concession stand was a calendar displaying the page, December 1941. "Nathan's Lumber Yard," it said. There were pictures of happy faces below the date, laughing, playing, working, and kids, lots of kids—all unsuspecting of what the future would bring.

I had known several of the young men who never made it home. It was not that long ago that a few of the local players had seen service. They looked older than their years. Written across their faces was what they had experienced. I swallowed hard, and tried to focus on happier times. The World Series between the Cardinals and the Red Sox had ended only a week before, marking the first time since 1941 that the Series was not depleted because of players in the war.

As I moved closer to the procession area, I observed a group of about thirty students from the Millersville High School Band, dressed in their striking orange and black uniforms, marching in precision to the front of the grandstand. A neighbor's two daughters, the Arneson family, were among them. After the instructor raised his right hand high in the air, they came to an abrupt halt. I raised a hand to shade my eyes as the bright sun reflected off their gold and silver-colored instruments.

Upon a signal from their instructor, they raised their instruments. A moment later the inspirational and unmistakable sound of the national anthem echoed through the air as the American flag, fluttering in the westerly breeze, was elevated to the top of a metal pole.

The Blue Bird's team stood riveted to their positions on the diamond and in the visitors' bench area. They held their heads high, their eyes locked straight at the flag as it waved at the top of the pole. Each player grasped his cap in his right hand and positioned it over his heart. A few had speckles of gray in their hair. *I wonder how old they are?* I glanced to the opposite side of the field and noticed our local players were doing the same.

"NOBODY FIRES AT THE FLAG AROUND HERE," I heard one spectator yell as soon as the final note carried into the distance. Most things heal in time, and with the worries of the war that occurred thousands of miles away past us, parents banded closer together in determination that these consequences would not control their lives.

The managers of the two teams gathered around home play for a coin flip to determine who would bat first. The all-stars won out.

"PLAY BALL!" yelled the umpire, who was also the high school agricultural teacher.

"Yaa," I hollered as I jumped with glee.

"Okay, this is what we've be waiting for," I heard a man standing behind me say with excitement in his voice. Smiles swept across the faces of everyone as they gestured to each other in agreement.

The crowd in the grandstand rose to their feet and roared their approval . . .

Chapter 3

WILLIE

A tall black man walked off the pitcher's mound to a distance of about twenty feet, removed his cap, darkened with use, and pulled a dark handkerchief out of the right back pocket of his trousers. After mopping his brow, the man fitted the cap firmly on his head, running his fingers across the brim to make sure it was in the position he wanted. I watched him intensely as he walked back to the mound with long sure strides and stepped to the rubber, deliberately toeing it with his right foot. As he peered down at the catcher, I could see the expression on his face quickly change from one of solitude to—serious determination!

Methodically, the Blue Birds' pitcher rolled the white baseball around with the fingers of his right hand and positioned his middle and forefinger across its seams. Raising both hands over his head, he swung his right arm around in a circular motion, sort of fanning the air, and side-armed the ball to the first batter for the Kickapoo Valley All-Stars.

Reacting to the pitch, the batter swung and tricked the ball down the third base line. The third baseman moved with ease across the dusty diamond, scooped up the bouncing ball, and in one continuous motion snapped it across the field to the outstretched arm of his teammate at first base.

"YOU'RE OUT!" the umpire yelled, with a sharp gesture of his right hand defining the finality of the moment.

The huge crowd surrounding the field yelled in unison, clapping and shouting their approval as chatter drifted from the first base foul line to the other portions of the field.

"How about that, Jake," Preacher said as he moved closer to Dad. He spit tobacco from one side of his mouth, and elevated his voice to match that of the crowd. "I'll be switched if that's not talent."

Dad just smiled, being careful not to remove his pipe, and nodded in agreement.

"Watch the way these players field, Bones," Preacher looked over his shoulder and said to me. "You boys can learn a lot by watching these guys."

Dad pulled his pipe out of his mouth and pounded out its soggy contents against the wooden bleacher.

"I suppose," he said, "but how'll they get a chance? There's no place to play, no one to instruct them, and no one to play against."

"That's funny, Jake," Preacher responded "You took the words right out of my mouth. We'll have to think about that." He moved closer to Dad. "It'd be fun to give them a chance at playing big ball someday. I didn't get a chance to play much when I was their age." His voice mellowed with emotion. "I always thought I could have been pretty good, but our coach didn't think so. I sure wish I could remember everything about what happened back then; maybe I blocked it. It seems like some sort of a distant dream to me now." For a few moments Preacher seemed to be not quite here, sort of a ghost, his eyes looked dull and far away . . .

Pulling a can of Velvet tobacco out his vest pocket, Dad tapped a fresh supply into his pipe with the forefinger of his right hand, struck a wooden match across a metal pole of the backstop, and lit the tobacco. Smoke floated to the east carried by a soft westerly breeze. *That aroma is delightful . . .*

—⚏—

Between innings, players from the black team mingled with the crowd, joking with the children and selling autographed pictures. Dad bought a picture, but we lost it the same day. "Oh, well, I guess I should've taken better care of it," he mumbled.

The game progressed to the crack of a bat striking a ball, the slapping sound of a fastball hitting the catcher's mitt, and the barking of the players issuing words of encouragement to batters. "Dig in Mike," or, "Way to go, Red, another one under his chin!" Tobacco spit flew through the air in every direction. Every so often a player would stroll past us for a drink of cool water. *Exciting!*

The game was tight until the last inning. More than once I suspected the Blue Birds were holding back by not trying to get on base or by letting the local stars hit the ball, allowing them to shine, at least for a time.

But suddenly things changed. In the top of the ninth the Blue Bird's team appeared to take on a more serious and a more work-like attitude. They decided to wrap things up and move on. A tall and thin man, who had been tossing a ball back and forth with another player along the side lines, approached the pitching mound.

"That's the guy I've read about," Preacher yelled with excitement in his voice to the rest of us. "They call him Closer. He pitches one inning and usually only throws nine pitches. Guess he throws it so hard the batter can't see it. This'll be exciting!"

Preacher was almost right. Closer threw eleven pitches, nine of which were strikes. Eight were called strikes.

Then, in the last half of the ninth, the manager of the Kansas City team interrupted play for a moment and signaled a large, square-shouldered man off the bench to pinch-hit. After picking out a long, brown bat from a group resting against the backstop, he stepped to the plate and smiled. As he moved into position—the bat seemed almost small in his hands.

There were a few casual words to the all-stars catcher and the umpire. From the laughter and returning smiles, I suspected more about the jokes that were exchanged then what I heard. *I wish I were close enough to hear all of the conversation.*

The man pawed the dirt with his back foot—digging in to propel his swing—like a bear preparing to attack. As he stood on the left-hand batter's side of the plate, his teammates rose in unison from their bench on the visitor's side of the field. They seemed to be expecting something dramatic to happen.

"It's gettin' late, Coop," the manager barked as he checked his watch. "The bus is waitin.' Got to get down to Dubuque, ya know."

The batter didn't swing at the first pitch, he just seemed to be judging the speed of the pitcher. Coop casually strolled out of the batter's box, took a few practice swings, and stepped back in. Though a pleasant smile remained on his face, he narrowed his gaze, and focused on the all-star pitcher. To simply say that he looked formidable didn't do him justice.

Then it happened . . .

The next pitch he hit farther than I had ever seen a ball travel before. With a thud-like *bang* that reflected back to the grandstand, it bounded off the metal roof of a stock barn down the right field line, through the branches of a big box-elder tree—and tumbled into a ditch on the far side of Highway 131.

Just like that, the game was over!

We all stood gasping while the large black man, his head down, trotted around the bases, pausing momentarily to shake the hand of each infielder of the all-stars as he went by. The Blue Birds players were careful not to over-celebrate by jumping and yelling. They strolled over to Coop as he crossed home plate and each one shook his hand, smiled, and walked back to the bench area.

Dad looked toward Preacher—speechless.

Preacher smiled, shook his head in amazement, and motioned toward Ove. "Let's go, Babe," a nickname he gave his son that evolved from his admiration of Babe Ruth. "We've got to find your Mother and see what she's doing.'"

Walking away, he paused for a moment, glanced back toward Dad, and said, "What we talked about,

Jake, was interesting, about starting something for the kids. We'll talk more about that!"

"Now you're talkin,' Dad responded. "I'd like to see them grow up someday to something better than pushin' a plow."

———※———

After the Blue Birds collected their gear, the players were very polite and respectful to the local team, patting them on the back and congratulating everyone, even the batboy and scorekeeper. Slowly they strolled across the field in small clusters and entered the huge bus parked nearby, another day's work (or play, depending on how you want to view it) completed.

"How you doin' young man?" One of the players said, pausing next to me on his way to the bus. "Bet you're gonna be on the All-Star team someday . . . am I right?"

Wow . . . he spoke to me!

He placed his rough hand on the top of my cap and looked directly into my eyes. It was difficult to tell how old he was, as there were no wrinkles or laugh lines, but I would guess his age to be in the mid-to-late 20s.

"I . . . well . . ." I stumbled over my tongue in my haste to speak. I'd never been his close to a black man before.

"Answer the man," Dad said as he lowered his head and spoke directly into my face.

"I sure hope so," I responded. "I sure hope I get the chance."

"You will, young man, you will."

The player strolled away with the same long graceful stride he displayed on the field.

Just before he reached the bus, I summoned up all my courage, and turning to the rest of the gang yelled, "FOLLOW ME." I ran as fast as I could to catch him, with Dean, Shane and Sunny in hot pursuit.

"Mister . . !"

With one foot still on the first step, he turned toward me.

"Did you ever play against the Yankees?" I asked.

"We not only played 'em, young man . . . we beat 'em . . . gave 'em a good spankin', too! Coop hit one on da roof in their big place. " A big smile crossed his face.

The windows were down in the bus, and I could hear some of the other players laughing and agreeing with his comments.

"Wish we could play all those big teams in their parks." He shook his head as he climbed another step. "The good white players don't worry bout us gettin' in the Majors. It's thos' weak guys who are scared we'd get their jobs. Someday we'll do it. Da only difference between them an' us is that they ride on da trains, we ride on da buss. Guess it all depends if da Big Boss wills it." He pointed to the sky. "All we want is ah chance." He lowered his head, shook it, and laughed as he entered the bus. "Just ah chance, and we'll show 'em!"

Though it was late in the day, not one player had requested a hot dog or a drink of water. I wondered if they would eat on the bus. As I walked with the guys back to the ball diamond, I found myself thinking about what he said, and about what a nice guy he was, and about his kindness.

He must be starving by now. It doesn't seem fair.

The sun was lowering in the western sky, the temperature dropping, and a few puffy clouds drifted from west to east as the large gray bus moved past the 4-H building and turned toward the exit of the fairgrounds. As it continued on its course, people stopped, stared, gestured and applauded. Spontaneous conversation broke out.

Eventually it moved past where Shane and I were standing a few yards from the main gate. Suddenly, the man I had been talking with poked his head out of a window located about two-thirds of the way back in the bus and shouted, "HEY, MISTER? WHAT'S YA NAME?"

"BONES," I shouted back. *Gosh, he called me mister, as if I were a grownup.*

"I'M WILLIE," He yelled as he waved his hand in a friendly gesture of farewell. "Good talkin' with you. All ya need is ah chance . . . keep tryin'. Someday ya'll get it," his voice fading in the distance as the bus moved away . . .

The gray vehicle lumbered through the gate and curved onto the highway in the direction from which it had come about twelve hours earlier. As the driver accelerated, a rumble of intense proportions exited its mufflers, and a blast from the bullhorn signaled farewell to the Kickapoo. "Blue Birds Baseball" it said on its side—what an experience!

—◊◊—

The field cleared directly, and as soon as it did, all the boys in the area, along with Chris raced to the infield. Chris was not the typical "girl next door." She was part of our gang.

Someone found a brownish, discarded ball and a tree branch that one of us modified into a bat, and using our bare hands for gloves, we quickly got the action underway.

In our fantasy game Enoch was the pitcher, Shane the catcher, Dean the shortstop, and I the first baseman.

In our imaginations, it was the Cardinals against the Cubs, Musial on one team and Nicholson the other. We were going to Wrigley Field in our minds, and about the only thing that limited our achievements was the vastness of our imaginations.

Someday, maybe someday, I'll be playing there . . .

Chapter 4

LOWMAN

As Dad, Sunny and I hurried toward the midway, in the distance came the joyous sound of calliope music from the merry-go-round and the Ferris wheel, alongside the clang of the steel guitar, fiddles and banjos of the country music bands that had arrived directly from Nashville. People stood transfixed, staring, as a tall slim man dressed completely in white and wearing a western hat whined in song about a broken heart. From somewhere came the thud of a large mallet hitting a projector. A ball flew to the top of a pole and struck a bell. The proud exclamations of men that exhibited their masculinity when they accomplished the feat was fun to watch.

"The comedy show begins in ten minutes," a barker yelled in front of a tent.

"Let's go see that," Mother nudged Dad. We scampered in.

"I'm planning on building a new house," the comedian said. "And I'm planning on living in my old house until the new one is built. Shouldn't cost us too much, because we're planning on using the lumber from our old house to build the new one."

Dad bent over with laughter.

There was the clatter of metal bottles collapsing as young boys threw baseballs in an attempt to win a prize, not that I wasted any time on such nonsense. I'd learned from experience it was rigged.

Where's that excitement coming from? I noticed that a lot of action surrounded a stand where, for ten cents, participants could shoot a BB from a gun at wooden Nazi paratroopers about the size of playing cards. They moved across a flat metal background object, and there were a lot of winners.

Of course, there was also the smell of popcorn, hamburgers with fried onions, cotton candy and fried bread. Dad pointed to a sign above a nearby food tent that read, "American Legion Post 308 - A Food Stand."

"We've gotta have a hot dog at the fair," he said with a big smile. "Isn't that right, Rhode?" Mother smiled, nodded, and gave Dad a big hug. *She's having fun too.*

The aroma of fried onions filled my nostrils. *I love that smell.* In a few minutes Dad returned from the counter with four hot dogs topped with onions, mustard and ketchup. As we chomped on the dogs, people were rushing toward the grandstand to get a good seat for the sulky races that were about to begin. One person bumped into me in his haste. I almost lost the dog I was eating.

Surrounding the ball field, and in front of the grandstand, stood a half-mile circular racetrack, where harness races were held. The arrival of the Standardbreds decked out in glittering harnesses and pulling lightweight sulkies was exciting! The *clack, clack, clack, clack* of their hoofs resonated in the stands as they trotted past on their practice rounds. Fresh from the tracks in Chicago, these mares and colts competed against the local competition in races that left us breathless. After the first race, I watched Dad as he slid several folded bills into the pocket of his overalls with a smile. "Pronto Hal won," he said with a nod to the gray in the winner's circle. "I made $3.75 off him."

Betting wasn't exactly legal but it paid our admission for the day.

The Kickapoo Valley was still a raw and rowdy frontier even after the end to the Depression in the early 1940's. Its aftereffects hung like a black cloud over the valley. Kids from large families wore hand-me-downs, and numerous patches were sown on faded, but clean, clothes before they eventually became material for more patching. Times were tough, and tough people were part of the times!

Along the midway of the fairground, various tents and attractions lined both sides of the road. Brightly colored and descriptive signs and fast-talking-pitch men advertised the shows. It cost twenty-five cents to see the freak show, the same to watch a crazed man kill and eat a raw chicken and there was a trans-sexed unborn baby in a large bottle filled with formaldehyde.

I lingered at the more exciting attractions. If some-one was up to it, he could wrestle a muzzled black bear, or the hairy-legged State Heavyweight Womens' Wrestling Champion, or have a bare-knuckle fight with the "Toughest Man in the Country."

"THERE'S LOWMAN!"

The shout drew my attention to a large, raw-boned, crude looking man. Whether Lowman was a first or last name I certainly couldn't tell. He had huge club-like hands, and a jaw protruded from the bottom of his head like the Rock of Gibraltar—and it was just as solid! When he snarled I could see gaps between some of his teeth; many were missing. His tanned skin resembled leather. Lowman had a reputation as a mean character that never shied away from a brawl. Few people knew him closely, but everyone feared him! Although I never saw the person, some said he had an older brother even bigger than he was who worked as a lumberjack around the Hurley area. Some of our friends admired Lowman. I wasn't sure what to think.

The only time I saw him before was one morning at the Sterling Cheese Factory. Lowman was helping to haul milk that day. He would grasp the handles of two eighty-pound milk cans with the thick fingers of each hand, and set them upon his shoulders as if they were empty boxes.

I'd certainly heard of him and his exploits. I understand a deputy from the Crawford County Sheriff's Department broke a wooden Billy club over his head one evening without facing him in the least. After which the deputy's face shifted pale with horror anticipating the counterattack that was surely to come. That particular episode occurred at the Circle D, a local dance hall some of our older friends attended on weekends. The sheriff, who was also a strong man, feared him and wanted no part of a confrontation. He dispatched a posse of five deputies to the location to finally bind and arrest Lowman for disturbing the peace. As was reported, four of the five required medical attention after the brawl was over.

Lowman was the Dempsey of the Kickapoo!

It was also widely acknowledged that Lowman worked part time as an "enforcer" for a man who sold moonshine and that he collected overdue accounts in any way necessary.

The word quickly spread through the crowd that Lowman planned to take up the invitation of the "Toughest Man in the Country." Around me bets started to circulate.

Although mean, when it came to fighting, Lowman was no fool. He knew there was no way he could beat the bear. Moreover, if he pinned the six-foot, broad-shouldered fat woman (which he most certainly would have been able to do), he knew people would look down upon him for taking advantage of the opposite sex.

But a fight with a man advertised as being the toughest around was another story—and Lowman seemed unable to resist.

The "Champion" stood on the platform in front of the large tent, in direct view of the crowd. Sunny and I scrambled up close so we could see. *There's a body odor about him,* I thought. A large, bald figure, about six-foot-seven, he must have weighed at least two hundred and eighty pounds. A scar protruded downward from the top of his head to his right eyebrow. Motioning the men from the audience to face him, he picked up a horseshoe, and as the muscles on his hairy body bulged, and with grit on his face, he bent it into the form of an S shape. "I'll take on any three of you cowards at the same time," he growled as he pointed to the audience with the forefinger of his right hand. As it played out, one of the people thc fierce appearing man pointed at—was Lowman!

Lowman received the invitation in a very hostile manner. He hurriedly rolled up the sleeves of his worn work shirt. Then he stood motionless for a couple of seconds, and glared at the provoker. I noticed redness forming across the back of his neck and a snarl building on his face.

I'm sure something's going to happen here, but the only thing I'm not sure of is what.

"I've seen him like that before," someone said from behind me, "when he was hungry and angry."

"LAY YOUR MONEY DOWN," the barker cried. "I'll give ya three to one."

"You don't say something like that to Lowman," I heard one person say to another standing nearby. "He'd do it for nothing."

Quicker than what Preacher would refer to as a "New York second," Lowman reacted.

"HEY—TOUGH MONKEY—I'm just gonna take you up on that slack jaw invitation" the barrel-chested Lowman yelled, his nostrils flaring, as he hopped up on the stage and started pulling his suspenders down from his strapping shoulders. His head spun and he shot the big man a cold look as he ducked through the tent entrance. The Champion may have been a little bigger, and he was questionably a bit stronger, but Lowman knew how to fight—and loved every bit of it!

Droves of people rushed to the booth where a frail, old, unshaven man, his stained dress hat cocked on the right side of his head, stood holding a roll of tickets. "Step this way." The dark coloring of his misshapen front teeth stood out as he spoke. "Don't push, there's time for everybody."

A younger man stood beside the tent entrance, keeping a sharp outlook for anyone who might not have purchased a ticket. *Doesn't look like he ever takes a bath.* Every inch of his exposed skin was covered in a film of dark grit.

But despite the barker's advice, people shoved their way inside at a frantic pace to see the war that was about to take place. Sunny and I glanced at each other. There was no money left for the fight. Earl, a neighbor on our ridge and my best friend, spied us. "Got any money?" I asked. Although Earl shook his head in a negative manner, his eyes were wide open. We both had the same idea. With a grin, we darted around to the back of the tent. Jerky, Dean and Shane were already there. To our delight, Shane found a much-patched hole that only needed a little encouragement to give us free view, right up until Dad found us.

"I don't want you goin' in there," Dad scolded as he dragged Sunny and me away.

We begged to watch Lowman fight this guy to a winner-take-all finish.

"Ahh, Dad, some of the other guys are going, why can't we?" I said.

"That guy's no good; he's the devil's own, and you've got chores to do." Dad's word was law, and we followed him away from the tent. "I still look for that guy's picture every time I go into a post office," Dad added.

———✦———

We found Mother with some of the other farm women sitting in the shade and having ice cream cones. She was engaged in jovial chat and laughter with Jerky's mother Martha. They didn't get a chance to get together that often, so they made the most of the opportunity. In the distance, I could hear the roar of the crowd inside the tent where the bare-knuckle fight was taking place. Every once in a while a sharp *"crack"* of a fist to a face would penetrate the distance and the crowd would respond even louder. *Gosh, I wish I was in there.*

"Well, looks like we've got to go. The men are here," Mother said to the other ladies as she rose off a bench and gathered her purse with the rest of her belongings. "Nice visiting with all of you."

The four of us strolled to our car parked almost a half-mile away, Sunny and I walked a little more slowly than Mother and Dad. We could still hear the noise from the brawl going on inside the fight tent. Apparently Lowman had his hands full for the first time in his life—but so did the Toughest Man in the Country.

"I'll bet one of them is starting to wear down by now," Dad said to us as we got closer to the car.

After milking, and as the sun sat in the horizon, I could hear a coyote howling on a distant hilltop.

I wonder who won ...

Chapter 5

MOLASIS AND MOONSHINE

A significant part of the culture of our area in the late 1940s was the brewing of moonshine, or what some people referred to as "corn squeezing," and the growing of tobacco. The backward hills and valleys of the Kickapoo were ideal for both. Aside from farmers and the villages, there also were isolated pockets of people who raised "specialty" products and lived along the river bottoms or in the back hills.

"I know some of these people may look and act strange," Dad said, "but in one way or another, they affect the lives of all of us."

"The River People," as we called them, lived off the river, selling catfish, bullheads, turtles, frogs, beaver, smoked carp, and raising small crops of tobacco. Tobacco was legal, that is assuming growers did not violate the government allotment—which they often did. Even so, the local authorities generally looked the other way.

"Most of these people have made friends with the law," Dad told us. "There's probably a few gifts passed on in exchange for favors."

The hill people, or those whom most people referred to as "Ridge Runners," were more elusive and shied away from the general community. These groups killed, trapped and sold wild game, collected honey, mushrooms, various "weeds" for smoking, and brewed moonshine for drinking. Unlike tobacco, moonshine and certain weeds were illegal.

A prosperous moonshine still, or a quality weed or tobacco crop, could pay for a dairy farm in two to three years. So debatably, these occupations helped prosper the community.

"That shine those folks brew, and that weed they harvest isn't honest," I heard Dad say more than once, "but to a lot of people in the back hills it's cash in the register, boy! There's a rumor, I don't know if it's true, that they help local folk who are down on their luck."

Most of these stills started during Prohibition and never shut down because the locals became accustomed to the unique taste, availability, potency, and perhaps most importantly—the fact that there were no government tax to pay. The authorities were now and then effective in preventing the distribution of the shine, but could do little to stop it permanently.

"It is what it is," Dad explained. "The local folks won't squeal on them."

Amazingly, many stills operated full-force right under the eye of the feds, disguised as sorghum mills. These people cooked two products, molasses and moonshine, side by side.

—w—

Sunny and I were playing with Rover, our black and white German shepherd and husky mix, one forenoon, when I saw the car pull into our driveway.

"Someone's here!" I called to Dad, who was working in the barn cleaning up after the morning milking.

I saw the cleanly dressed middle-aged man approach the barn after leaving his black polished sporty Chevrolet Coupe parked beside our windmill. A large, short-haired white dog with a dark spot over its right eye and a round flat jaw poked its head out of a back window. This upset Rover, who was determined to protect his territory. He lunged furiously against the chain that held him tethered to the barn, barking all the while and ready for combat. Arneson's coonhound had been howling all night. I don't think Rover had gotten much sleep.

"Jake around?" the stranger inquired with a friendly smile. The clothes he wore were in contrast to his facial appearance; as he was sprouting probably a four-day's growth and badly needed a shave. A very noticeable hawk feather protruded from one side of the brown dress hat he wore.

"Sunny, come over here," I elevated my voice while waving to my brother. "Wanna help this guy?"

Sunny was standing ankle-high in weeds in the garden. He leaned against the hoe he was using, reached down, and pulled an onion out of the patch. After peeling the outer skin off but leaving some topsoil still clinging, he ate it.

"No, it's your Dad I'm looking for," the man answered. "He around?"

"He's down in the barn."

The man strolled past us at a casual pace and glanced at Sunny while laughing, "Don't you ever wash that stuff before you eat it?"

Sunny kept chewing.

I had never seen the man before, but Dad seemed to know him.

"Leif," Dad smiled. "You old sinner, how you doing?" Dad was currying the horses and walked across the barn to meet him half way.

"Not bad, Jake, how 'bout yourself?"

Leif grabbed one of Dad's suspenders on his bib overalls and seemed to guide him off to the side, appearing not to want Sunny and me to hear what they were discussing. We acted as though we weren't paying attention but maneuvered as close to the conversation as possible without getting ourselves in trouble.

"I understand the feds are plannin' on payin' me a visit one of these days, and I'd like to divert them or better yet, drive 'em crazy. I was wondering if I could bury some of my shine in your manure pile out there." He pointed to the large heap of cow waste stacked about two hundred feet back of our dairy barn. "They'll never look for it there," he said with a laugh. "On second thought, maybe I'll just leave a small batch around someplace for 'em to find and sample. Some of that fresh shine, you know, if it's not ripened enough, it can make ah man see bad things. Sort of hallucinate, or whatever."

Both men casually strolled to the back of the barn, their heads down and their hands gesturing as they walked. I couldn't hear what Dad replied, but shortly thereafter the conversation stopped, they shook hands, and the man left the barn in the same manner he had entered.

"Pretty sharp car you got there," Dad yelled to Leif, "what did it set you back?"

"Around fourteen hundred," Leif replied. "The ladies seem to like it."

As he approached the fancy automobile, Rover, snarling and lunging against his chain, made it known he never cared for him or his invasive companion.

"Quite ah dog you've got there. He had me snortin' for a while. I like his personality. Wanna sell 'em?"

"Nah," I chuckled, "He's my best friend. You can pet him if he likes you."

I unhooked Rover but held him tightly by the chain. Rover bulled his way past the man and to the left rear portion of the automobile. In an attempt to show his displeasure, he promptly lifted a hind leg and pro-ceeded to spray a tire.

"Do you know where he hides most of his shine?" Dad asked us as the man drove away.

"Where?"

"Under fence posts," Dad replied. "He told me there was a fruit jar of shine hidden under every fence post on his farm. Good thing that sly old fox wasn't with Rommel in South Africa," Dad commented as he shook his head in amazement. "He'd have out-maneuvered Patton."

—⚊—

Leif Foley was a Ridge Runner. He owned a farm in the back hills that overlooked the Kickapoo River. Leif took the property over from a tribe of Indians who claimed squatter's rights before he made them an offer they couldn't refuse. A few stayed on in old shacks and helped him in a number of ways. Knowing he needed cooperation from the government to keep his operation private, he put on a wild game feast each year and donated the proceeds to the local baseball teams. Most people believed he migrated to the Kickapoo because it reminded him of his homeland in Tennessee. More than likely, it was to further the family trade. I heard things may have been getting a bit too hot for his clan in those parts. At any rate, Leif was a wise and crusted buzzard. He'd have to be in order to avoid the government for two generations. I never knew if he married, but he had a reputation of courting numerous barflies, none of which complained about sharing him. One afternoon after school I heard one mention his name to three other women at Fat Friley's Restaurant.

"I'm a dyed-haired woman past forty, and I know I'm not the cutest trick in shoe leather, but he makes me feel like I am. I like that," chirped the admirer as she patted her brow lightly with her handkerchief.

"As rumor has it," Dad said, "Leif makes a good product, and sells it at a fair price. In addition to that, his clan has been a fixture in our culture for years."

News traveled fast around this part of the country; there are few secrets among the local folk. One afternoon

Dad came home from town with quite the story to tell. I was at the kitchen table going over my homework and put my pencil down to listen. Dad poured himself a cup of coffee, dumped in three teaspoons of sugar, a little cream that made the color light brown, and sat down.

After taking a sip he proceeded to tell us what had happened the night before . . .

"It took place in the evening." Dad began with enthusiasm in his voice. "The Ridge Runner clan and most everybody else knew the fix was in, all except the feds and the sheriff and his deputies. In the dark of night," Dad continued, "five deputies from the Crawford County Sheriff's Department were creeping through dense brush and briar bushes, tryin' to reach a spring that flows under large rocks in the Johnstown area. I understand for more than twenty years, the feds had scoured the back woods of that area searching for the "Mother Lode" of stills they thought Leif and his family were operating.

"Funny thing," I interrupted Dad's story, "I heard Leif is the brains of the operation and his relatives the mules. Most of them walk with a wobble, sort of like a penguin. The doctors claim it's from hard work. Guess their hips had given out."

Dad continued with his story . . .

"Of course, everyone claimed to know the still's whereabouts but each time the law got close, they ran into another smoke screen, the location had been mysteriously abandoned. There's been high talk around town that Leif most likely has someone on the inside who is paid part of the action to be an informant," Dad said. He struck a match and lit his pipe. "There's never been as much as a thimble of proof to the rumor, though."

"Whatever the case," Dad said, "Leif was as evasive as a Kickapoo coon with a pack of hounds on his trail. But this time most people thought it might be different. Because the local press accompanied the law enforcement officers, they were that sure of success. To make it surer the deputies brought along Coronal and Bandit—two bloodhounds—both dogs with firm muzzles around their mouths.

"It was about twelve thirty in the morning when the deputies arrived at the location they were given," Dad went on. "They had walked and crawled for about three hours to get there. Although mist as thick as cotton had drifted through the hills, the terrain exactly matched the description of the area. As the story goes, when the party got closer, they could smell fumes from the still and the mash cooking.

"I guess the officer in the point position held a finger to his mouth," Dad said, "cautioning the four behind him to be quiet and to hold on to the dogs. But Bandit whined slightly and appeared nervous."

"What makes you so cocksure it's here?" a deputy whispered in a questioning tone. "I'm not sure I buy it anymore."

"Just shut up and follow me." The officer and his posse continued . . .

"Creeping slowly to avoid attention by anyone nearby," Dad was describing the scene, "they brushed aside poison oak, poison ivy, and crawled through cow manure freshly deposited by grazing cattle. More than one anthill was disturbed and bloodthirsty mosquitoes welcomed the intrusion into their area."

"After a lot of hardship," Dad remarked, "the group arrived at the scene of the crime and gasped in disbelief at what they were seeing."

"That dirty no good," a deputy said, directing his attention to the Captain. "'Leif had us conned all along. I thought it was going too easy. Just goes to prove you can't con a con."

"Tied to one of Leif's stills were a jackass and a goat, both drunk to the brim with shine," Dad said, "along with a note that the press chose not to publish. The jackass was wearing a brown dress hat on its head with holes cut out for its ears. There was a hawk feather attached on one side."

Dad laughed so hard when he told the story that tears ran down his cheeks.

For some reason Leif's wild game feast that year was celebrated better than ever.

Chapter 6

BRUNO'S RIGHT-HAND MEN

Although he considered himself to be self-employed, Leif did business with Matt Bruno, who was a racketeer of sorts. Bruno was the son of a Sicilian immigrant who found work in the De Soto area of Wisconsin, logging the Mississippi River, in the late 1800s and early 1900s. At thirty-nine, he had the look of a man well into his mid-fifties, with a graying head of thick curly hair.

"His skin was the color of coffee with a little cream," I heard Dad say to Mother. "He's kind of a man you don't pick up to easily."

Bruno operated a gambling machine business from his pub between Millersville and Rolling Ground. Regardless of the fact that it was never proven, locals thought the location was a front for his other activities. His henchmen distributed most of his machines to bars throughout the hills and backwoods, and although they didn't trust him, he was embraced by the Ridge Runners. After all—he moved their shine.

I found it easy to recognize Bruno because he always displayed a black western-style hat, dressed in cowboy boots, and wore a black leather jacket. There was a large silver display of a revolver on his belt buckle, and the gold-colored Cadillac he drove had steer horns mounted on the front of the hood. I understand Bruno's style resulted from his early work as a roughneck on a Texas oil rig and from his later hitch as a cowboy on the King Ranch in Texas. He always had a stable of attractive women around him.

Bruno was a very clever moonshiner who had various brushes with the feds over the years, but he was never caught. Although he lived in a backward and somewhat desolate area of the state, this man was no small potatoes when it came to underworld activities. Story has it that, on occasion he was able to call on "the big boys" in large cities, and even to the old country in Sicily.

"He knows exactly what to do, and just like a mosquito knows when its summer," Dad said, "exactly the time to do it. That's why he calls the shots."

Additionally, Bruno had interests in a local semiprofessional baseball team, and he gambled heavily on their success.

"Losing is about as exciting to Bruno as a run on the bank in Millersville," Dad said.

The team played against the best local and professional competition in the Midwest. There were a few unique teams in the area, and some of their players were ex-major leaguers. One player was with the Boston Red Socks for a time, and another was my friend Dean's brother, who played with the Detroit Tigers.

The rivalries between towns and teams were intense and drew large crowds. Traveling teams touring the country competed from time-to-time.

In addition to buying off the best local talent in the area, he imported players from the various universities and after the major and minor leagues professional seasons were over, paid some of these players (who were open to making an extra buck) good money for a few key games.

—⁂—

Bruno's Pub was having an exceptionally busy day, a steady stream of customers strolled in and out carrying brown bags of various sizes. Some were bold about it, but most tried to hide their purchases under a part of their clothing. I noticed they walked fast. It was a good thing for the community that business was prospering for Bruno, because he was a "colorful" person with many interests—including his professional baseball team. To finance the pay to imported players on his team, the sale of moonshine was a factor. Leif and a few other operators made the shine, and Bruno marketed it.

One of Bruno's right-hand men was Scooter Bailey, who was sort of a friend to my friend, Shane. Although Scooter was at least twenty years older than Shane, they hit it off.

"Never been the marryin' kind myself," I heard Scooter say more than once, "But I do like the ladies." For some reason most women addressed him as "cowboy." Scooter brought excitement with him, something Shane was looking for.

Scooter was a "bottom feeder," a name given by the "River People" to any member of their clan that strayed. He referred to his occupation as a "trader" of supplies to rural people, and he was a very controversial figure who lived "across the tracks" on the edge of town. From a religious standpoint, Scooter had eleven commandments, the first of which was, "Do unto them before they get a chance to do unto you." In Scooter's view, "the rich get richer, and the poor get taken to the cleaners." Scooter also ran moonshine for Bruno to some of the more backwoods bars in the hills that surrounded the Kickapoo River. More than once I'd borne witness to his liking his own product.

Shane mentioned to Dean, Jerky, and me one afternoon in Fat Friley's Restaurant something that had happened the week before at Scooter's house in Millersville. Bruno, Lowman and Scooter were sitting in his living room, going over the books, discussing business, and the fact that a "customer" was behind on his payments.

A large pile of cash lay on a nearby table alongside a pot of steaming coffee. Bruno poured a cup for the two men and one for himself. He added a little cream and sugar to his, stirred it with a teaspoon, and tossed the spoon on the table. It made a clacking noise as it tumbled to the center area.

"Wanna cup of this stuff?" Bruno asked Scooter. "It's strong enough for a spoon to stand in it."

Scooter held his hand over his cup, not saying a word . . .

Lowman pushed his cup forward. Bruno poured. As Lowman took a slobbering slurp of the hot stuff, a bit trickled down from his lower lip and dropped on his shirt. Although a brownish stain appeared, he paid no attention. Noticing he had also splashed on the table, Lowman swept a hand across its surface causing the wetness to fly toward a wall of the kitchen. Bruno glared in disgust as Lowman wiped his wet hand across his trousers.

"Okay," Bruno said, directing his full attention toward Lowman. "I want you to pay a visit to this guy's house while his wife is there." He sipped his coffee, intensified his voice, and pointed at Scooter. *"You ride shotgun for him."*

Lowman jumped to his feet. "What's in it for me?"

"Don't worry about it, you'll get yours," Bruno belted back. "You always do." Bruno slid his chair away from the table, leaned back, stretched his legs outward, and smiled. "On second thought, I guess you've already got what you deserve—that big ape at the fair sure cleaned your plow, didn't he?" Bruno chuckled. "Went through you like crap through a goose. You were a little over your head in that one!"

Lowman was really ticked now. "Don't you wish," he barreled. "I wanna know how much, and when!" Lowman crossed his arms—his eyes narrowing dangerously.

Bruno pulled his feet back, straightened himself, and reached to the stack of cash. He *snapped* out three one hundred dollar bills from the pile and slid the cash across the table to Lowman. "Get some sense back into your head, you're trying my patience."

"That's more like it," Lowman growled. "How much time shall we give 'em?"

Bruno leaned across the table the men were sitting beside and looked directly into the big man's eyes. "Just come back with the dough," Bruno said. His voice was full of money!

As Bruno rose, he struck a match to a stogie like the one he most always chewed, and walked toward a back door. He paused, and directed one hand to the knob . . .

"Don't push your luck, big man, never think you can throw your weight around with me. One of these days I'll call Toney's in Milwaukee and have someone pay you a visit." His voice was low, each word bitten off as if it tasted sour in his mouth to say it.

Lowman sneered. "Those ginnies don't frighten me."

"Well that's your misfortune; you're too dammed stupid to get frightened!" With that, Bruno walked out, slamming the door behind him with authority.

—⟩⟩⟩—

Nevertheless, Shane didn't have to tell us about Bruno and Lowman. Sunny, Earl and I happened to be eating a sandwich in Bruno's Pub one day and viewing a hotly contested euchre game, when Lowman came in . . .

"What are you doing here this time of day?" Bruno asked, turning toward Lowman. His dark eyes were hard despite his questioning tone.

"I've come to get that bonus money you promised me."

"Say what . . .?"

"You heard me, I've come for the bonus money."

"You'll get it tomorrow."

I glanced uneasily at Sunny. We both knew it was a con. Bruno had about as many scruples as an alley cat in heat and an urge to con that never slept. He'd try anyone, even Lowman.

"You'll pay me now, or you won't see tomorrow," responded Lowman in a threatening voice, sticking his protruding jaw in Bruno's face.

Two men at the euchre table rose from their chairs and scurried out the back door. Three others shuffled to a far-away corner of the room.

"Go to hell!"

"Been there!" Lowman bellowed—"Didn't care much for it either."

Bruno reached behind the counter and pulled out a shopworn cigar box. He opened the lid. A small revolver and a yellow envelope were clearly in view. The lone survivor at the euchre table threw his cards across the table, grabbed the cash that was lying in front of him, and ran for the front door, knocking over a coat rack in his haste. Sunny and I sat motionless. Making sure Lowman saw the gun, Bruno handed him the envelope, and paused for a moment, which seemed to go on forever. Placing his hand over the revolver, he looked straight into Lowman's eyes, and then removed his hand. Bruno closed the lid and deposited the box back in its place.

Lowman grabbed the envelope and left the store without saying a word, the door slamming with such force that a few pictures on the wall shifted position. The gush of air that moved through the area from the velocity sent chills down my spine. Sunny and I each took a deep breath, exhaled, and walked out with as much casualness as we could muster.

"Whew, that was close," Sunny was quick to say when we got outside. "Did you see the look on the face of Lowman when he saw that gun?"

"I'm not sure if it scared him or just made him madder." I shuddered.

Later that day we told Dad about the altercation.

"What were you doing in there in the first place?" Dad was upset.

I attempted innocence. "We had some time to kill. A friend drove us."

"You've got other things to do. Stay away from that kind—understand?"

I changed the subject. "Think we could get a ball and glove someday?" I asked Dad.

"We'll do that when we go to Millersville sometime."

"Great," I said, "Then we'd be able to play catch at school."

Sunny and I scurried off to round up the cows and spray the flies off them before milking.

"Whew," I spoke to myself as I wiped the sweat off the back of my neck with a handkerchief. Although it was hot outside our barn, because of the heat and perspiration of the cows, it was even hotter and more humid inside.

Can't wait to get this over with.

Chapter 7

SHANE

For some reason, our area was changing, and not for the better. With too much time on our hands other than farm work and baseball, some of the kids started to imitate the tough guys who looked flashy and had big cars.

Because of Scooter's connections, Shane was a bat-boy for Bruno's team and close to the action. Shane lived with his father and stepmother in Millersville and there were rumors that a certain amount of unrest existed. I think his stepmother may have been a bit tough on Shane. She was a strong disciplinarian, something Shane resisted.

"You're spending too much time with that no-good cowboy friend of yours," I heard her say to Shane at Sammy's Grocery one day. Shane and Scooter did a lot together. When Shane was not at school he'd sneak over to Scooter's house and play cards with some of the older men and listen to their stories about the wilder side of life.

Shane was the most adventurous of our group of kids, and as a result girls loved him. It wasn't that Shane was any better looking than the rest of us—but that he had an inviting and sort of mysterious personality.

"He's a tough one to figure out. Just when you think you know him, you find out you don't," Dean said. He closed his eyes and shook his head from side to side. Dean and Shane were "Kickapoo cousins," so to speak.

Shane told stories to the rest of us about the shine and about Lowman beating up on people to collect bets, and the time a rattlesnake mysteriously appeared under the bed covers of a customer who refused to pay.

"One of the cops said he was gray and all swollen up like a new brides biscuits," Shane said excitedly. "Let me tell you about what happened last night," Shane would often boast to the rest of us. "Lowman really cracked this guy's head!" What's more, he saw the money paid to these associates for their services.

───※───

One Monday morning a new kid showed up in our grade school in Sterling. Although a new kid in town always created a lot of interest, it didn't take long to figure out that Hank didn't have a "go along with the tide to get along" kind of nature.

"That guy's got a powerful mean streak in him," Sunny said to me one day.

Hank's family had moved into our area from a larger city on the east coast. He came from a large family of many brothers, one of which was doing hard time in a Wisconsin state prison for the crime of first-degree murder.

"Bad blood," Dad said.

One thing I found to be very noticeable about Hank was the way he dressed. He wore cowboy boots, faded blue jeans with the bottoms rolled up, and a white shirt, also with the sleeves rolled up. Hank did this to look cool, I assumed, but also to hide a pack of Lucky Strike cigarettes he tucked inside the rolled sleeve. Being young and naive, some of us young guns were starting to get interested in people like Hank, Bruno, Lowman, and the rest of the crowd.

"So you think you're tough, huh?" our teacher, Mrs. Young said to Hank as she was getting her Irish up during a class I was in. Hank was a bully. "You have no idea what tough is. You want to end up in the Crawford County Poor Farm down by Seneca when you grow up?" Mrs. Young used a stern and sharp voice. "You will if you don't get an education, boy."

No one wanted to end up in the Poor Farm. It was for people that were down on their luck, the homeless, or those who had social problems. The Farm housed around fifty people, and every able-bodied person helped with the daily chores, including the twice-a-day milking. A cemetery was a part of the land—and some who died while living there were buried in wooden boxes and unmarked graves.

—m—

As the winter winds began to blow and a magical spirit of the Christmas season filled the air, we would usually shop in Boscobel for a gift for Mother. It was always something she could put to good use, and she always appreciated it so much. Every year (after Dad had just broken in his old pipe) we always "surprised" him with a new one. On our way home Mother would hum to carols by Bing Crosby playing through our car radio. I remember the magic of believing and being comforted by the truth of what Christmas was really about, of sort of being in awe of something so profound and yet so real.

Dad brought us to school in the mornings, and we walked home in the afternoons. During the winter months, at the noon hour, I usually rode on the back of my friend, Buddy Thompson's sled along the road between the school and Sterling. We followed the lead of Hank and some of his captives. *I know I shouldn't be doing this.*

One day, a week or so before Christmas, I did not accompany Buddy because our family went shopping in Boscobel. While returning home we switched on the local radio station WRCO in Richland center to hear carols, however the local news was about to begin. Merchants were encouraged by an increase in Christmas shopping at their stores. Arrests for drunken driving for the week had also increased. There was advice from the Richland Center Medical Clinic regarding new methods to treat a winter cold. The farmer's market would reopen on the first weekend in May. The weather forecast was for clearing skies and temps in the single digits for tonight and in the mid-teens for tomorrow. A commercial for Tully's Fluid Drive Auto Sales chattered over the radio, when the announcer interrupted the advertisement with a news flash!

"The Crawford County Sheriff's Department has informed us that two grade school students were killed in a tragic auto accident just outside of Sterling, around noon today."

Dad's hands tightened on the wheel—he slowed the car almost to a stop—straining to hear every word from the broadcaster. Mother's mouth dropped. I stared at the radio, my heart pounding in my chest.

"Two young boys, students at Sterling Grade School, died around noon today when the sled they were riding was struck by a vehicle on Highway 171, east of Sterling. Both were pronounced dead at the scene. Names are being withheld at this time."

Oh my gosh, who could it be? I looked at Dad and noted his face was unusually pale. Tears moistened Mother's eyes.

Although I tried to reason with myself, going over all the possibilities, I could not get away from the most logical thought . . . *If it was Buddy, I would have normally been his passenger, and I would not be alive now.*

As soon as we drove into Millersville, Dad stopped at the Richardson's Filling Station, and we wasted no time in finding out. Dad and I jumped out of the car and ran into the building.

"Who were the boys that were killed?" Dad shouted to Richardson before getting all the way into the station.

"Bill and Vickie's oldest boy," Richardson replied. "I haven't heard who the other boy was." The expression on his face told it all.

"It was Bill and Vickie's oldest son, and another boy. He doesn't know the name yet." Dad was quick to inform Mother and Sunny as soon as we arrived back at our car.

Mother turned toward the back seat, grabbed Sunny and me in her arms, and hugged both of us as if in a death grip. Although I never told her I usually rode with Buddy on his sled during the noon hour each day during the winter, I think she somehow knew. I couldn't get past the fact that if we had not gone shopping that day, I would have been the passenger that was tragically killed.

The last time I saw him, he didn't have a care in the world. Now he's dead. My buddy took my place. It was all I could think about . . .

"Tiger saw it happen, but I was the first one there," Enoch told me at school the following week. "I'll never get over it."

When Preacher and the rest of the parents found out about this accident, and learned that their kids were following the lead of the wrong people, the problem became personal and closer to home.

"We've got to do something about this," I heard Preacher say to Dad.

Chapter 8

ENOCH

S ome of the older generation in our area referred to the winter of `46 -`47 as "colder than a well digger's butt and rougher than Lowman on alcohol." Sharply pointed icicles—as long as fence posts—hung from the eve spouts on our house and barn. There was coldness to my nose and numbness all the way down to my toes. My hands, inside my worn-out yellow work gloves, felt frozen most of the time. I often heard Dad say, "If we make it through February, we'll be okay."

Nevertheless, there's something about winter in the country that can't be matched in the city. As I strolled to our house after evening chores, a full orange moon glowed directly overhead, pleasantly lighting the snow-covered winter landscape without the brightness of the midday sun. A rabbit scampered, then stopped . . . rose up on its hind legs . . . its nostrils and ears twitching at smells and sounds, and when satisfied everything was clear hopped off to nibble on a branch. Little round dark turds remained where it paused.

As the late March temperatures became milder, people looked forward to warmer outdoor activities. This year we had an early spring. When warm weather arrived, brightly colored wildflowers began to appear in portions of the woods and fields where the snow had melted, and the sweet smell of lilac and crabapple blossoms filled the air. Life took on newness. The snow was going fast, and I could hear a rushing roar as the floodwaters broke through the holler below the barn. There was a big puddle of water just outside our front door. Robins, with their big orange breasts, hopped in the front of our house, searching for fresh and juicy worms to eat. Red-winged blackbirds warbled in bushes close to the fence lines. Morning doves snuggled beside each other on the power lines. In the evenings, coyotes howled in their mournful mating ceremony, not too far away by the sound of them.

Yes, spring was in the air, and to make it even more captivating, Dad had a plan for us. He had just returned from Ever's blacksmith shop in Sterling, where he had two sickles sharpened for the upcoming hay cutting season.

"Hop in the car, boys," Dad excitedly said after a breakfast Mother fixed of side pork, fried eggs, flap jacks, butter, sorghum, fresh farm milk, and hot coffee.

I looked up in surprise and hurried down the last bite.

"Where we going?"

"To Millersville, I'm gonna get something to keep you guys out of trouble."

Before we got to Jamison's Store Dad swung our Plymouth into Richardson's gas station.

"Filler up," Dad said to a man in greasy colored overalls.

"Want me to check the air in your right rear tire Jake?" the attendant asked Dad as he was fueling the car. "It looks a little low."

"Good idea," Dad replied through the open side window of our car.

After adding air to the tire, the attendant pulled a big cloth from the back of his trousers and wiped the front windows. "Want the oil checked?"

"It's okay," was Dad's reply.

Dad handed the attendant two dollars and got some change. The sign above the Mobil Gas "Flying Red Horse" pump read, "Leaded Gas 11 cents."

Jamison's store had a little bit of everything and not too much of anything. The door banged shut behind us and the bell nailed to it gave a sharp jangle to let everyone know we were there.

"What are you looking for?" I asked Dad.

"You'll see soon enough."

Dad strode past the grocery products stacked up front and past the cattle feed and the farm supplies that followed. Even the dry goods didn't slow him down. We went all the way back where miscellaneous items made their home. I looked past him and saw straw hats, rubber boots with buckles, skies without bindings, and some type of liniment that cured all ailments. Sunny and I exchanged glances and shrugged.

"Here's what we're after." With a grin, Dad reached for something that I couldn't see until I ducked around his shoulder.

There, deposited among piles of objects jammed together, were two baseballs, a fielder's glove, a catcher's mitt, and a stubby, shapeless, wooden bat.

"Take care of that stuff," Dad instructed us, as he handed a five-dollar bill to the lady at the counter. She handed him some change and deposited the ball and bat, along with the mitt and glove, in a big brown sack. "I don't want to see these things sitting in a box someplace while you're doing something worthless." We hopped in our car, Dad made a circle turn in the middle of the street, and we started out of town.

—⁂—

As short as the drive home was, it seemed to take forever. Before we had a chance to make our first pitch and catch, Dad called us for some instruction . . .

"You don't want to use that mitt and glove before you break it in. Rub some spit and lard in the center of it, like this . . . to form a pocket."

Dad rubbed the leather roughly, and it wasn't long before it darkened. I could tell the difference in the way it felt immediately, much softer and flexible. Dad talked about catching for the Sterling city team when he was young. He often displayed a twisted for-finger on his right hand.

"The result of taking too many foul tips," he said.

The ball often splashed in a fresh "cow pie" after a hit, and became sort of a greenish color. These cow droppings were not small. At any rate, this didn't stop us. We'd wipe the ball off on the grass and continue. As time passed, it became worn and heavy, and the seams would break and come loose, but it was the only one available so we mended it and continued.

Dad warned us, "You'll crack the bat if you don't hit correctly." We couldn't afford to buy a new one. So when the bat did break, he pounded a nail in the cracked part of the handle to tighten it and wrapped the area tightly with tape.

"The only way you're going to be any good," Dad scolded us regularly, "is by practicing." And that we did, day after day, during all kinds of weather.

—✺—

Every evening in mid-June, regardless of how hot it was or how humid, we sharpened our batting eye by using a stick to hit June bugs that swarmed around and underneath the yard light on our farm. Unlike the delicate lightning bugs that *sparkled* in the high grass and brush for a number of weeks, these thick hard-shelled bugs appeared for only a few days. It was happy hour at the bar for them, and their numbers must have totaled in the millions. Although ugly, they were harmless enough, unlike the bloodthirsty mosquito guzzlers looking for someone to feed on, or the annoying whining smaller bugs that danced around my eyes. As far as Sunny and I were concerned, they were in the wrong place at the wrong time. We usually used a lath (a flat piece of thin wood about a quarter of an inch thick and an inch wide) to whack them. When we'd hit a bug squarely, it made a loud noise, something like dropping an egg, and splattered the air with whatever. We had to react quickly to strike them. Sort of like trying to hit a knuckle ball, I thought.

"When you can hit one in every three swings you make," Dad said in our kitchen after milking, "you'll be able to hit any pitch by any pitcher." He pulled his socks off and *slapped* them in the air dust flew toward me in a round brown blast, as I ducked out of the way.

On rare occasions, Sunny and I watched a game on television. Unfortunately, the only source of coverage was the taverns. During the World Series, Dad drove us to Mike's Bar in Millersville, where we joined most of our buddies and watched the game on a tiny, round black-and-white screen RCA TV set. The reception was so bad it looked like they were playing in a North Dakota snowstorm; the players were barely visible. We'd talk about playing like the professionals someday. After returning home, Sunny and I practiced what we had just seen—hour, after hour, after hour.

Luckily, we had an old Coronado radio, because about twenty-five percent of rural homes didn't have one. Static was on more numbers on the dial than stations. We listened with rapt attention to Harry Caray announce the St. Louis Cardinals games and to the Chicago Cubs broadcasts. I became spellbound by the atmosphere, and dreamt I was playing on the same fields before large crowds and making game-saving plays. At night, I'd rest in bed picturing the Chicago Cubs Wrigley Field. The vine-covered brick wall, the scoreboard looming high in the centerfield distance, and the clock perched atop.

When we weren't playing baseball, we were talking about it. We never thought about the fact that we may have been poor according to some standards (we had no television to watch sporting events and no daily newspaper).

Summer passed in a haze of baseball and it wasn't long before fall began to settle into the Kickapoo. Nights were cold and days nippy, too nippy for baseball. Sun set early in the west, and on nights when there was no moon—stars were like silver spikes that spread around the breadth of the high sky.

We didn't have a football, so Sunny and I would stuff a paper sack with leaves and pretend it was the real thing. There was no football in the high schools. Every Saturday forenoon in the fall, Sunny and I hooked a wagon behind King and Queen, our two big draft horses, and drove into the cornfield to husk corn.

"Hurry as fast as you can," I yelled to Sunny, my breath floating in the chilly temperature. "We wanna get back for the football game."

We'd listen as Harry Wismer or Bill Stern announced the Notre Dame college football games coached by Frank Leahy. This was a time when men were coming home from the war and entering college so the Irish had the pick of the crop for talent.

—〰—

Dad watched my growing interest in baseball and gave me money to buy a book, *How to Throw Curves*. I read the pages until it was nearly memorized, and it wasn't long before I could make the ball bend in every direction. My favorite was a pitch I invented that I called a "drop." I held the ball differently and released it so it rotated directly downward. It broke so sharply that it resembled a ball rolling off a table. At grade school, Enoch and I had fun experimenting with various grips.

When I was not playing catch with Sunny, anyone driving by our farm would usually see me practicing my control by throwing the ball against a target I had marked on the stone portion of our barn. I still wasn't the best at it, and I'd often miss the target and hit the wooden part of the barn, doing a great deal of damage. The banging sound made what was happening obvious, and there was no way I could hide it from Dad. I virtually destroyed our milk house with wild pitches that slammed into the clay blocks of the side walls. Every so often at the clatter of breaking boards, I'd duck my head and hide. Although boards were flying everywhere, Dad never once complained. In fact he said he admired me because a day did not go by that I could not be seen practicing. Dad stayed busy in the fields and didn't have much time to play with us. He'd always been an avid fan however, and expected us to do well.

—⁂—

On my birthday in May of 1948, Enoch's dad dropped him off at our farm for some fun. Dale, Jerky's dad, drove in shortly thereafter.

"Bones . . . are you out there?"

As soon as I heard him yell I knew who it was.

I was out in our woods with Earl, and Enoch ran along a logging road to meet me the minute he heard my response. It was cool out there, even on such a warm day as this. Rover was with us, and we didn't want to leave him. He had gotten into a scrape with a skunk sometime earlier, and was not the better for it. *Stinks like the dickens.* Now, he was barking rapidly at a bull snake crawling up a weather-beaten oak tree in search of a bird's nest. The mother and father starlings were angrily flying in circles, trying to drive the intruder away from their young. The three of us took turns shooting at the big snake with my Red Ryder BB gun. Earl was the best shot. Eventually we distracted it enough so the snake abandoned its ugly mission.

Earl lived on a farm about a mile away, and although he was one year younger than me—he was my best friend. We were at each other's house almost every day trying to retrieve some stray cat. Each farm had about twenty cats and they wandered back and forth almost daily. Earl was different from most of my other friends in that he wasn't at all interested in sports. Maybe that's why I found him interesting. He had sent in for a bodybuilding course by Charles Atlas, and after a few months of exercising he could squeeze a scale to the max with his hands. No one, not even older boys messed with him.

Enoch was eleven days older than me, and we always celebrated each other's birthdays. Although it was still too early to determine the athletic abilities of kids our age, no one could deny the fact that Enoch would turn into something special. He was strong, well-built—and could run faster and throw a ball harder than any other boy our age.

Like me, Enoch practiced pitching hour after hour. He threw balls against a target he had placed on a chicken coop on their farm. Some of their neighbors said they could hear the *crash* of a fastball striking the coop from a quarter-mile away. Enoch was named after his grandfather, who had died at an early age after being gored by a bull. The name comes from a hero of the Old Testament Bible. Enoch's father and mother were farmers and attended church regularly, like most people in our area. Although Enoch's father was always kind to me, I always thought his mother was possibly the nicest lady I ever met.

I can never remember Enoch ever deliberately doing anything wrong. He got good grades in school and stayed out of trouble. If someone thought he was sort of "high on himself," they were wrong. That was simply his confidence showing through. He also had common sense.

On our way back to the house we strolled past an orchard of wild apple trees, a few blossoms still clung to a branch or two, and we hopped across a deep crevice where a horse and buggy road existed before automobiles were invented.

Back at the house Enoch and I played catch as we shot glances at Dad and Dale deep in discussion on the porch.

"Whaddya think it's about?"

Enoch shook his head. "Not sure." He dug wax out of his ear with the little finger of his left hand. "Something to do with baseball I think."

"Baseball . . .? Like forming a team . . .?" I discontinued tossing the ball for a minute, paused, and stared at the three men, their hands gesturing in every direction.

Enoch shrugged. "Not sure, but I thought I heard the word mentioned. Hey, you gonna throw that thing or what?"

Sidetracked by our game, I completely forgot to ask Dad what their discussion was about. In fact, I forgot it entirely until the following spring.

—⁓—

From the mailbox, looking down the gravel road on O'Dell Ridge, I could see Preacher's small farm which adjoined ours. It was located below in a valley, mostly flat land, with few trees.

One morning Preacher paid us a visit.

"Hey Bones, where's your dad?" Preacher called to me as he climbed out of his wood-paneled station wagon he parked in our driveway.

"He's over at the house . . . right behind you . . . look around."

Both men were not dressed in their usual work clothes, an indication they were taking a good portion of the day off. They wore their newest bib overalls and dress hats. Preacher had a feather on one side of his. There was a slight mist in the air, so this was a good day for farmers to go to town for supplies and conversation with their neighbors. Sunny and I lingered nearby in hopes of hearing the exchange.

As far as I could tell, Preacher started the conversation . . .

"Jake . . . I've got this feeling, and I just can't seem to shake it. I've been thinking about some of the things we talked about at the fair last fall. What do you think about starting a baseball team for the kids to have something to do besides gettin' in trouble?"

Dad strolled over to a couple of old wooden chairs that stood against the green-colored metal garage close to our house. Preacher followed him. Dad pulled a chair aside for Preacher, and they both slowly sat down.

"Whaddya have in mind?"

"Well, let me explain."

"You and I both know what's been going on around the area," Preacher continued. "Ove and your boys like baseball, but, as you said at the fair, there's no place to play. I've been talking with some of the other men around the area, and they think the kids are starting to look up to Lowman and some of the other no-gooders. Maybe they need to do something more than farm work all the time."

"Yeah, I guess you're right. Working behind the hay loader, mowing hay, or thrashing in that darn dust is not the most fun," Dad said, as he leaned forward in the chair, his eyes serious. "I'm not disagreeing with you, Preacher—but where'd they play?"

"I've got some flat land down below your place that'd make a good spot. Might have a problem if it rains too much once in a while, but it seems to be about the only place around. I haven't talked to the missus about it yet, but I think she might agree, especially if it would keep Ove and his friends out of trouble." Preacher gave Dad a confident smile.

Dad leaned back and pulled his pipe and a can of Velvet tobacco from one of his upper pockets of his bib overalls. He poured in a fresh filler of tobacco, scratched a match across his pant leg, and puffed away with a thoughtful expression until the pipe was lit. Whitish gray smoke drifted with the breeze . . .

"I'm thinking about having a meeting with some of the other parents at PJ's in Sterling next Monday evening to talk more about it, after milking is over."

I held my breath until Dad slowly nodded. "I think that'd be a good idea."

Preacher nodded cheerfully, and then with a sheepish grin across his face added, "The church has a special Lutefisk supper this weekend for the Larson's fiftieth wedding anniversary. I'll get the feeling from some of the people there."

"How can you eat that stuff?" Dad joked as he pulled his pipe out of his mouth and laughed loudly. "That's rotten fish, isn't it?"

"They make it out of cod," Preacher replied with a grin.

"Stinks like heck, you put lye on it so that it'll rot faster, don't you?"

"Well, actually it's something I wouldn't want to eat too often. It sort of cleans the plumbing out if you eat too much of it, know what I mean?"

Dad chuckled and shook his head. "Yes I do, I definitely do. I'll just stick to my lard sandwiches for that purpose."

"Whatever."

Chapter 9

PJ

If a stranger happened to stop into PJ's store Monday evening, they would have been surprised with the many shoppers, or at least the activity. Dad, Sunny and I were not the only ones who attended. Most of my school chums were there with their parents. There were about thirty adults, maybe more, who shortened their work for the meeting.

Burnside, our local dentist, was also in attendance along with his best friend, or foe, depending on your reasoning, Donovan, our undertaker. Sunny and I feared both. Burnside (who sprouted a big belly) because he was anything but a painless dentist and seldom used Novocain, and Donovan (who always wore red suspenders) for the spooky obvious. Although they were best of friends, and often could be seen in a hotly contested game of checkers during the noon hour at

Fat Friley's, they had a running debate as to who would get the other inside their establishment first. Both were avid baseball fans.

My brother and I didn't say much, but then we could hardly hear each other because of the noise. Dad mixed with his friends in laughter and conversation.

I guess there was a certain amount of anticipation among most of us. It's difficult to get the approval of everyone about anything, even a ball team for a bunch of kids.

Preacher was a good pitchman, and he started the discussion . . .

"I'm glad to see so many people here," he said with a tone of excitement. "Most discussions couldn't draw flies, but look at this group. I guess we all know why we're here," Preacher continued. "Our kids need something more to do during the summer than copy that bunch of hoodlums at Bruno's. Ove tells me some of the kids are drinking shine, and a couple of them have dropped out of school. And then there's that sled accident—Lord knows, what'll be next?"

There was a vocal rumble and heads nodded in general agreement.

"They need something to look forward to besides working behind the hay loader and pulling tits twice a day," Dad got in the discussion. "Some of the morals around here are starting to go downhill. They need some fun, like a baseball team to play on. Maybe we could get a league started, or something along those lines. Whatdaya think?"

"Good point," Clyde said. "These kids are going to be in high school in a few years, and if they're going to amount to anything in baseball they'd better get some experience beforehand."

Everyone nodded in agreement.

"I understand starting this year," Clyde continued, "there will be a state championship trophy where all high school teams can go through some sort of elimination games. Eventually they'll end up with a state champion—now wouldn't that be exciting if a little school like Millersville could get to the state and play against the big boys?"

I looked over at Clyde with a great deal of respect and admiration. With the exception of Preacher, he appeared to be the most knowledgeable about the sport. I remembered Ove telling me that he had seen a number of Major League games.

Donovan opened his mouth to voice his opinion but Burnside beat him to it. "Well, that's going to be hard to do with that coach we've got," Burnside said from one side of the room. "He's been coaching at Millersville for a few years now, not too successfully either, at least from a baseball standpoint."

"That's right," Donavan said. "I don't follow their basketball teams, but their baseball teams haven't been doing well the last few years. Dale told me the other day that Hooks, his oldest son, was on the team for awhile and that the coach doesn't know anything about baseball, just basketball."

"Is that right Dale?" Preacher asked.

"That's right," Dale replied. "They've never won their division since he's been here. Guess he only plays kids in baseball that play basketball."

Dad spoke up. "My boy Sunny's got chores to do during the winter. He can't be playing basketball during milking time."

"Neither can Hooks and Jerky," replied Dale. "How in heck does the man know if a kid can play unless he gives him a chance? That's all some of these kids need is a chance. I tried to talk with him about Hooks not playing basketball because of chore time and do you know what he said? He sort of stared past me into space and said something like, *'you do what you need to do at the time!'"*

"I guess he was in the Third Army with Patton during the war, and has his views about life from him," Pastor Gus commented. "He looks at everything from a military standpoint. Guess he thinks about the war a lot."

"I'll be switched if that's going to continue in our neck of the woods," Preacher said. He looked around the room intently as he spoke, meeting the eyes of each person there and hoping the rest of the group would follow his cue. "I've talked to PJ and he's willing to teach the kids a few pointers when he's got time."

"Well, we couldn't get a better person," Clyde said, grinning and clapping the shoulder of the man next to him. "I watched as he showed Enoch how to grip the baseball and throw it."

By the look on Dad's face I could tell he agreed.

Surprisingly, there was no opposition. A vote was called to start and recruit for a team and league, and every voice was raised in a unanimous "Aye."

———

No sooner had it been decided, than PJ walked in—sweat dripped from his face—his sweatshirt soaked with perspiration. He'd been running from the store to the grade school and back to stay in condition, and looked a bit surprised at the size of the crowd. As he greeted everyone, I gazed at him. *I would sure like to ask him a few questions about pitching and hitting.*

Although his first name was Peton, most people called him PJ, the J being an abbreviation for James, his middle name. His last name was long and difficult to pronounce and spell.

PJ was a tall slim man, with sort of a laid-back atti-tude toward life. Every day was Saturday to him. He returned to our region a few years back after playing professional baseball somewhere. I'd heard it said he could have achieved much more if he had the desire, and why he didn't no one knew.

PJ was someone we placed on a pedestal—and a baseball legend in our area. We idolized him after watching him pitch against the semipro traveling teams that toured the area after major league play had ended for the fall. I'd seen PJ practicing pitching in the store—his control was natural and amazing. For an instant you could see the athlete he must have been in his prime.

He walked behind the counter and reached for a towel to mop his face, neck and arms.

"That really makes me feel good, that you're doing this, and I'll tell you why," PJ said as he straightened up and looked at us. "Guess I've never really told any of you much about myself and my life." PJ usually didn't have a lot to say, but he was definitely in a mood today to make a point. He spoke rather softly at first. I stepped a little closer . . .

"The high school I attended didn't have a baseball team, we played softball." He glanced around the room as if assuring himself we were listening. The story came back to him like a plane ascending out of the clouds. His voice climbed a few notches.

"During the summer months I played baseball in the evenings with friends from other towns. When their high school teams played in the tournaments I just watched. They told me I was the best player on their summer team, and that they could have won the state championship with me, but it never happened and I never got the chance."

He paused a moment, his listeners rapt in attention, waiting him out. For a moment I could feel his disappointment as keenly as if it were my own.

"I used to lay awake at night dreaming, as I am sure some of you kids have. I fantasized about playing in the state high school and Legion tournaments, beating the bigger schools, and playing against the best players in the state. I visualized playing pro ball, and even someday making it to the majors. Of course I didn't know much about what that really meant back then, like being in the large cities and such." His face slack, his eyes low, his voice trailing off dreamingly . . .

"After I graduated from high school, I entered the Army and was stationed in the Philippines. Our unit had a baseball team that was filled with a number of major league players, Phil Rizzuto for one. It was there that I learned how to pitch. I wasn't long until I could spit as well as they could. After leaving the service I was offered a contract with the Philadelphia A's and some other clubs, but that big city life didn't interest me anymore. Maybe the war took it away from me."

PJ strolled from behind the counter, "You've got a chance to have a good high school team here, if you stick together and work at it," his voice rising with emotion. "I know you've got a long ways to go, but I'll help when I can. If any of you kids have a question about some part of the game, stop up here. I'll show you what I know. Even pro players need guidance once in awhile. Mornings are bad, but if you'd come in the afternoon or evenings, we could work at it a little longer and not need to rush."

"We'll do it then," Preacher said, "we'll get this thing going." He stood up, put his hat on, straightened the brim, and waved with his left hand as he scampered to a side door. "I got some hay down, gotta get it raked before bedtime—thanks for coming."

Everyone applauded.

Chapter 10

IN THE BEGINNING

"**B**y golly he's already at it."

It was about eight o'clock the next morning, and Dad and I were taking the milking to the cheese factory in Sterling. Admittedly, I hadn't been paying attention, so when Dad swung our car around in the middle of the road, my head *thumped* the doorframe hard enough for me to see stars, I rubbed it.

"What's going on?"

"I didn't think he'd start it yet—and besides, he's got hay down."

The words weren't directed at me. That much I could tell. Although I followed Dad's gaze as the car bounded through the deep ruts at the bottom of Preacher's driveway, as far as I could see things looked about the same as they always had. My gaze traveled over the rolling farmland lying between the trees with all the browns of fresh-tilled earth. I couldn't make heads nor tails out of what was interrupting a fairly urgent drive into town.

Preacher could be seen as a stick figure in blue denim, identifiable by the trademark red bandanna trailing out of his back pocket that looked something like a mule's tail flapping in the wind. He was bent over pounding a stake in the middle of the cow pasture (or what would have been his pasture had he had not dug it up) nearest the barn.

Dad barely had the car stopped before we were out and walking with quick strides toward Milley, who stood on the porch, one hand shaded to peer at her husband in the distance. Her face showed no trace of the tension that left her hand white knuckled and knotted in the fabric of her flour sack dress. She was country plain, but a handsome woman, who maybe wore a bit too much rouge for her age. Milley greeted Dad with a strange sort of smile, half-fearful, half-proud.

"He went and done it," Dad declared by way of greeting. "He took me by surprise."

"You know Delbert." Milley shrugged and this time the smile was more genuine. Once he gets an idea in his head...."

"That's his best field. It'll never be the same."

Her lips tightened. "Yes, I said that to him too, however, he had his heart set on it. Right there, across from the barn. Good and level, perfect for playing ball on he said."

Much like many of the families in the Kickapoo, Preacher and Milley, over time, had come to need and depend upon each other, not just for the day-to-day tasks and chores, but also for something much more deeply. Being together over many years had developed their lives into a subtle tapestry that was woven from their individual identities into the "we" they'd become.

"You can't take a ball game to the bank." Dad said, shaking his head.

I was counting posts. So far, three were protruding straight up from the dirt marking off bases. Preacher straightened suddenly, packed a pinch of Copenhagen under his lip, and started walking in a strange stiff-legged gait to some spot between it and the furthest post.

"Must be measuring distance between bases," Dad commented.

"I'm getting better about it," Milley said. "After all, it's for the good of the boys."

"I never disagreed with any of that, Milley, you know that, it's the location that has me worried—it's going to cost you some *serious* income to do this."

Dad shook his head and seemed at a loss for more words. "Perhaps it's best. I sure admire him." Dad spoke with sincerity directly to Milley. "He has the courage of his convictions all right!"

We stood in silence, our eyes riveted on the distant figure. Preacher had his next post in place. He appeared to be struggling to hold it upright while holding the hammer at the same time. I shot a look at Dad. "Can I . . . ?"

"Go ahead, Bones. You may as well get involved now, right at the beginning."

I launched myself off the porch and hit the ground running.

It was only a few days earlier that we had held a meeting at PJ's concerning the formation of a team and building a ball field. Although the entire neighborhood agreed on the idea, apparently Preacher couldn't wait to get started.

"We'll see you tomorrow," I heard Dad yell to Preacher. "If everyone shows up we should get it done this weekend."

"If the government's got some of that bomb stuff they used over in Japan, I'd like to get a dose to blast some of these boulders and stumps in the outfield," Preacher joked and waved as Dad drove away.

I stayed on to help. *This is exciting.*

—⊶—

If you've ever seen or heard about an Amish barn-raising, you know what this was like. A number of neighbors gathered at Preacher's farm the next day and helped construct the baseball field. Chris's Dad drove his brightly colored red Farmall tractor onto the field, Preacher his green John Deere, Sunny and I came with Dad on our gray Ford, Dale on his orange Allis-Chalmers, and another neighbor on his red and orange Massey-Harris.

At an adjacent pasture next to Preacher's, I saw a neighbor driving his team of draft horses that were pulling a manure spreader. The fertilizer was flying high into the air, and gulls and pigeons were swirling around looking for some undigested corn kernels or oat seeds for brunch. Every once in awhile, a gentle breeze passed by carrying a tint of the aroma. *I kind of like it,* I thought, as I stood at the edge of the field and watched. The air was dry and for once there were no mosquitoes around to drill through the back of my tee shirt while my mind was on other things. Sunny and I split up so we could take part in everything that was going on.

Preacher shot out instructions to the rest of the crew. "We've got to get the infield mowed, scraped and leveled before it rains."

"Do you know when they're going to get here with the screen for the back-stop?" someone asked.

"Nathans called last evening and said their truck would be here about eleven," Preacher responded. "I'll be switched if they're late."

Sure enough, with only three minutes until eleven, their truck arrived. Stores providing supplies couldn't afford to be late in this part of the country; cattle and crops couldn't wait.

By this time, the construction was well under way. Everyone seemed to know exactly what to do, but then these were responsible people who were used to making decisions. Sunny, Ove, Jerky and I ran fast behind individuals depositing a tool here or a bucket of nails there. Chris helped out in the kitchen. Even Tiger, Dean and Shane rode their bikes from Sterling and Millersville to help. Preacher had them scooping cow pies. What had yesterday been some stakes in the ground marking out a specific area was transformed almost magically as the morning progressed. Everyone chipped in with the cost.

Before long, the men raised the backstop and constructed the bleachers. The infield was graded and the pitcher's mound built. About three hundred feet from home plate, a snow fence circled the outfield to mark the distance for a home run and to separate the playing field from the cattle in an adjoining pasture. A few big boulders had to be transported out of the area on a stone boat that Dale pulled in back of his Allis Chalmers—and the big tires on the back of the machine spun for a few seconds before they got traction. Dark smoke belched out of the exhaust pipe on the top. We chopped a number of bull and Canadian thistles, whose pink blossoms were budding, and cut a few prickly nettles. After a few minutes of deliberation and discussion, a large Elderberry bush was allowed to remain in right field to support the snow fence.

"I don't know what's working on me," Preacher said, "but I just got a feeling' she's gonna'do us a favor someday for saving her life."

Wild strawberries and purple violets remained for color and atmosphere. The outfield was rough from the footprints of the cattle. *This will make it difficult to field a grounder or run down a fly ball,* I thought.

While the men were busy about their tasks, the wives fixed lunches and enjoyed conversation with each other. As soon as I entered the kitchen to fetch thermos bottles filled with lemonade for the men, I overhead Milley and Mother involved in merry as well as serious conversation.

"When Jake told me you were giving up some of your best land for this, I was wondering if there wasn't a better location that would not cost you so much." Mother paused in assembling sandwiches and cast a worried glance at Milley.

Milley's hands hung over a loaf of fresh bread as she shook her head. A proud smile crossed her face. "He wanted to do this, Rhoda, and after I thought it over—I just knew he was right."

"Well it'll only be for a few years," Mother said, as she stopped, and spoke directly to Milley with sincerity in her voice. "If you're ever short on things because of this, I'm sure you know that all you need to do is ask. We'll all be there to help." Mother *squeezed* Milley's arm as she spoke.

What a nice person, I thought.

Milley nodded her head, smiled, and hugged Mother tightly.

—⁂—

None of this could have evolved if it had not been for the farm wives and mothers who diligently put in many hours of activity. They loved and supported their kids and their husbands, and I know for a fact that Mother had happily sacrificed a new dress, or a purse, or a hat over the years so her family could have a better life.

"What did you gentlemen decide on a name for the team?" one of the wives asked as she approached a group of the men standing around the brand new pitcher's mound.

There was immediate laughter. "Guess we never thought about it," someone replied.

"Don't you think you should?" Martha asked. There was more laughter.

"How about the Misfits," Dale shouted jokingly.

"Oh no, no, that's not for this fine group of kids," Preacher said as he strolled toward the backstop with his head down in a thinking pose. "Which team is it that has those sharp uniforms we've often talked about . . . the Red Sox?" Preacher answered his own question.

"I like the Braves or the Orioles," Milley added. "They're pretty."

"What do you like, Bones?" Mother asked.

Before I had a chance to answer, Ove stepped in. "The Orioles really have sharp uniforms."

Sunny agreed.

"And there's an Orioles birds nest in a tree back of our house," Milley added. She was serious. The men hooted.

"Okay gang, let's do this the democratic way," Preacher finally said, "We'll vote on it."

"Everyone wanting the Orioles raise your hand," Preacher yelled as he raised his. I raised my hand and looked around to see how many others were voting, it was unanimous!

"I've got a question that I think should be a little important," Dad jumped in with his usual wisdom. "Who do we play against? It's no use in forming a team if there's no one to play against."

Everyone turned their attention toward Preacher, shook their heads and sort of grinned in agreement.

"I'll tell you what," Preacher quickly responded in a positive note. "We'll build this thing first—that's number one—and then we'll have something to show the neighbors. They'll come with a little coaxing, I just know it! They'll come with a little coaxing."

He looked at my brother and me and at the rest of the kids gathered around us . . .

"You kids know some of these boys from a few towns around here, give 'em ah howdy. I'll bet they'd like to do the same thing. Tell them to get some of their buddies and we'll get a league together." Preacher pointed to each of us in turn. He started with Ove. "Babe, you know Stan from church. He lives up at Fairview. Talk to him next Sunday.

"He's really a nice guy," Ove said. "I know he'll want to play."

"And Dean," Preacher said, "you know those lads on the hills back of the orchards that you talk about so much? I don't know their last names but I seem to remember you mentioning two brothers, Tim and Greg, and another lad by the name of Lance. Give 'em ah call."

"I know Tim and Lance better than I do Greg," Dean replied. "They're both my age. Rolling Ground has a city team and they play at Millersville next week against our team. Shane and I will talk to them then. There're always at the games."

With that, he placed one hand on his son's shoulder, took off his straw hat, and swatted it against a pant leg of his work overalls. A cloud of dust rose upward—evidence of a hard day's work on the field.

"I'll be switched," he said, "we'll pull this off!"

Chapter 11

JERKY

Within the next few weeks, and after a number of phone calls, letters, and meetings, a league formed that consisted of Fairview, Rolling Ground, Sherman and the Sterling Orioles. All were located within a fifteen-mile radius. The vision Dad and Preacher had two years earlier was about to turn into reality.

"I had a dream last night," I overheard Preacher say to Dad. "We'll play for a trophy of some sorts. "We'll call it the Kickapoo Kup."

"You crazy rascal," Dad said jokingly to Preacher. "That's perfect. Where do you get all these ideas? You been standing out in the heat too long?"

"Genes," Preacher replied, "Genes. I had a relative that went nuts."

"I don't think that's going to happen to you, old friend," Dad said. "You've got fox blood in you."

They both laughed and I saw a few happy tears travel down their cheeks.

Nevertheless, Preacher had a chore ahead of him. Recruiting in that area was no easy task. It was not extensive, by any means, involving mainly the Sterling and Millersville community. Mostly he recruited kids we knew from grade school. Then there was the equipment problem. Nobody had spiked baseball shoes. Tennis shoes were the norm. The parents of the players furnished bats and gloves for their sons and pooled funds to purchase balls and catching equipment.

The first day of practice was exciting for us kids but must have been a challenge for the coaching staff. Dad, Dale and Preacher stood behind home plate (which only days before had been home to a large patch of bull thistles) and observed the task before them. I'm sure I didn't hear everything that was said but I caught some of it.

"Well, fears like we've got the field but just look at that bunch of field mice," I heard Dad say as he pointed to us energetic young lads of questionable talent rolling around on the ground and playing roughneck.

Many of us didn't know how to grip a ball or throw it correctly, how to hold a bat or stand at the plate, or how to swing the bat with a level motion.

"Oh yeah—they're not much to brag about now—but they've never been taught anything either," Preacher replied as he stroked his unshaven face.

"PJ's the guy that could help us," Dale said with a tone of certainty in his voice. "He said he'd be happy to teach the kids a few tricks if they'd ask. We'll send a few of them up to his store once in awhile."

The three walked to the pitcher's mound and stopped. "Gather around us," Preacher directed. "Let's see if there's enough for a team here. Looks like nine to me. How about Chris? She's sort of a tomboy anyway. Is it okay with the rest of you guys if we ask her to play?"

"She's better than most of us anyway," Jerky commented. The mothers of the players present shrieked with glee at the prospect of a girl competing with the boys. They knew Jerky was right.

Preacher was a kind and fun coach for us kids, never cracking the whip—but he expected effort and he became clearly upset if goof-offs distracted practice.

"Spread out and start playing catch with each other," Preacher instructed with a bark to his voice.

There was no limbering up before the practice began, we had all of the limbering up we needed doing chores in the morning. Most of us hardly knew the basics, so Preacher started with the simplicity of the game.

"When you throw, reach back like you're going to grab an apple from one of those trees on the fruit farm, and then swing your arm forward like this. Step straight toward the person you're throwing the ball to."

He swung his right arm around in a motion. "Like that," he said. "When you're catching a ball, get your glove up in front of your face," he illustrated as he spoke, "and let the ball drop in your glove—don't grab for it—then clasp your bare hand over it so it doesn't slip out."

After the eager bunch of roughnecks worked at that task for a while, he positioned the gang around the infield.

"When a ball's hit or thrown to you on the ground, be sure to position yourself directly in front it, so if it bounces crazily you can block it with your body. Get down low, so it doesn't run under your glove or between your legs." Preacher illustrated everything.

The batting instruction came next. "Stand at the plate the way you feel most comfortable. Don't try to copy someone else. Hold your bat level, take a flat swing, and try to hit the ball on a line. Don't uppercut it. Follow the ball with your eyes from the time it leaves the pitchers hand till it hits your bat."

After practice, Preacher gathered the team around him in a tight circle by home plate. On his way in from the outfield, Sunny accidently stepped in a "cow pie" that was mistakenly left over from the field clean up. His right shoe had a greenish tint across one side. Each of the players rested on a knee anxiously waiting for what their coach had to say. Preacher looked into their expectant faces . . .

"I'd like to have Enoch here to do some pitching," he said. "But I know he'll be playing with the town team that his cousin coaches. So I want Smithy (Ove's cousin) and Bones to do the pitching. Hooks (we called Jim "Hooks" because of the way he grabbed balls thrown in the dirt), you'll start catching. Sunny, you're at first. Babe, you're on second. Dean is at short and Shane at third. Shane, you'll also be catching some of the time. Bones, you'll be playing right field when you're not pitching. Jerky, you're in left. Smithy will be in center when he's not pitching.

"Tiger, (which is what we called Rod Harrison) will play when the city team doesn't have a game. We might also be able to get a few players from the high school team once in a while. We'll fit Chris in, she'll be our utility player because of her all around ability. Any questions?"

We all rose with smiles on our faces and left the field.

—◦◦◦—

After milking the cows on Monday mornings, most of the neighbors hauled their milk to the cheese factory in Sterling. We drove an old Model A car that Dad converted into a pickup. The milk was contained in silver-colored metal cans that held approximately seventy-five pounds. Each farmer was designated a number to place on the cans to keep them separate from other patrons. Ours was a red number fifty-nine. A few other patrons wrote their numbers in black paint. After dropping off the milk, Dad would stop at PJ's Grocery to visit with the neighbors and rehash the Sunday game.

The store PJ operated was large for the small village of Sterling, and contained necessary provisions for the rural area. He sold overalls, work gloves, shoes, underwear, denim jackets, caps, hats and other wearing apparel. There were laundry and baking supplies, soap, canned fruits and vegetables, bacon, pickled pigs feet, pork liver, sacrum pickles, spices, flour, baking products, and such. There were flu pills and Nature's Remedy capsules for constipation, and JT, Spark Plug, and Day's Work chewing tobacco in square hard plugs. Dad would cut off a hunk with his jackknife and pack it in one side of his mouth, and he'd drink water without taking it out. If Sunny or I ever had a hankering for anything, PJ stocked it. From Black Jack or Cloves chewing gum, to Whistle pop, BB Bats taffy, New York ice cream or Cheerio ice cream sticks.

"I've got everything except Rocky Mountain oysters," I heard PJ say.

"What's that?" I asked Dad inquiringly.

"Pig nuts; makes me sick just to think about it," Dad responded with a weird look on his face.

As soon as we arrived at the store, Dad, Sunny and I made a beeline to the back where shoppers sat and "chewed the fat" around an old cast iron Round Oak stove. Parents and fans discussed a lot of things around that old heater.

Sure enough, Jerky was there, chewing on a stick of beef jerky like he always did and standing alongside Preacher and a number of other parents of the team players. Jerky came from a large family of Irish boys who lived only a few miles from our farm and on the same ridge road. Jerky had a wild, fun to be around, witty personality. He was the best marbles player around and seemed able to con most of us into a game and take our spare change. In stature, Jerky was about the same size as the rest of our gang, but possibly a trifle more combative and a natural athlete. He greeted me with a grin.

"So just what were you trying to do at practice when you threw that ball over Dean's head?" Jerky said. "Hit one of Preacher's cows?"

The telltale red crept up my cheeks, quick as a brushfire and about as noticeable. Ducking my head and scuffing my shoes against the floor, I stumbled over a box of oranges, sending them skittering every which way. Laughing, I tried as best to camouflage my embarrassment.

Jerky shook his head, walked toward me, grabbing my left arm. We angled over to the opposite corner where PJ stood talking to the men.

"If you've got a problem throwing, PJ can sort it," Jerky said quietly following my gaze. "Have him show you, he just showed me."

"Then he can show you again." I started to walk away, but Jerky grabbed my shirt tightly, not giving me the chance.

"No, I'll look like a fool," I said, but PJ had already spotted us.

"Bones, we were just talking about the team and how important pitching is." I groaned but Jerky shoved me past the neighbors and parents that were standing next to PJ.

"The first thing young guys usually have a problem with when pitching is balance," PJ said, taking my arm and moving me into position. "You're going to want to pivot, like this. And when you throw, bring your arm up a little straighter. Feel the difference? It takes assurance and poise to be a good pitcher," he continued. "Most never find their balance."

"I think PJ would have liked a little more involvement in the hands on part of coaching the team," Dad said to me on our way home from the store. "But he doesn't have the time and doesn't want to take any authority away from Preacher."

"I'm kind of shy about asking him questions," I said.

"Well, you shouldn't be," Dad responded. "I think he enjoys it."

"Great! I've got a lot of things to ask him." *That made my day.*

Chapter 12

DEAN AND STAN

I believe the most significant part of forming the Orioles, from a player's standpoint—was the fact that Dean would be a part of the group. Dean told me that his mother was a diehard sports fan, and that she named him after St. Louis Cardinals' baseball legend, "Dizzy" Dean.

Coming from a home without a father, Dean lived in Millersville with Amantha, his mother. His father passed away a few years after Dean entered grade school. Rumor had it that his death may have been a result of some virus he contracted while being a prisoner of war in the Philippines.

"I loved that man so much," I heard Amantha say to Mother one day at Jamison's Store, when the two were visiting in close conversation. She looked deeply into the far distance, beyond the valley . . . past the orchards, her eyes transfixed on nothingness . . . never blinking. Soon they became moist and red. "You never stop loving someone," she whispered as she left the store, "you just learn to live with it . . ."

However, even with such a difficult background, Dean didn't let anything get the best of him. He seemed to have his emotional feelings about what happened to his dad pretty well whipped.

"Do you remember what he looked like?" I asked Dean one day when we were walking along the main street in Millersville.

"Compared to me he looked big, that's about all I can remember."

—◦—

Dean was a likeable, very popular, good-looking boy with light brown wavy hair, and the best overall athlete of his age in our group. He absolutely loved to compete—and the tougher the competition, the better he performed. Dean took to playing shortstop like a hunter does to the opening day of deer hunting season. I often observed him standing alone at his position, observing the territory around him, calculating every move his victim might make. He was athletic and quick, which played into his position as shortstop. He had soft hands and a rifle arm. Dean could bobble a grounder three times and still throw the runner out at first by two feet. He was not only a good ballplayer, but there was something intangible about him—he had a color—and that's something you can't paint on with a brush.

Not unlike many other parents in that area and era who sacrificed much so her children could have the same opportunities as those with two parents, Amantha did laundry and cleaned houses during the day and had a sewing business from her home in the evenings. In addition to this, she always found time to practice athletics with her family.

Amantha taught her sons how to play baseball. She spent many hours playing catch and throwing balls to them for batting practice. Dean had two older brothers who benefited from the same training; one played for the Detroit Tigers in the late 40s.

—∞—

It was an exciting day for the team members when our parents pooled money and bought uniforms. The pants were gray, with red flaps on the hind pockets, and a red stripe that ran down the sides of the pant legs. We wore our red, white and blue socks high, and our caps and jerseys were blue and red, with the word "Orioles" printed across the front of the jersey. Amantha did the sewing of the team and players names on the uniforms without charge. We were proud to wear them, even though they were wool and became drenched with sweat on a hot summer day.

Amantha was also an important fixture in the unification of the general community. She helped out with almost all of the local events including the weekend dances at the Lewis Hall in Millersville.

We danced to big band music that was gradually giving way to single-artist recordings. Forty-fives by Bing Crosby, Frank Sinatra, Judy Garland, Gene Autry, the King Cole Trio, and the Glen Miller Orchestra, were some of our favorites. Of course the Grand Ole Opry from Nashville was on the radio every Saturday night.

But in the Kickapoo Valley, the *"pa, pa, pa"* polka bands were what really drew the crowds to the dance floors. Every Saturday evening a polka band equipped with a large silver base horn would play at the hall, which was located over the top of Jamison's Store in Millersville. Whoopee John and The Six Fat Dutchmen were two of the bands drawing the largest crowds. On some nights, as many as three hundred people turned out for fun, conversation, and jovial anticipation of the game on Sunday. At the dances, most of the fathers of the boys wore new denim bib overalls, some with stripes and some deep blue. Dress hats were common among the men—while some of the mothers wore dresses they made from colorful flour sacks. Mother used a Singer sewing machine that she paddled with her foot.

"Rhoda, did you make that pretty dress yourself," I heard Martha ask, as she touched the sleeve of Mother's dress.

"Yes I did . . . you like it?"

Martha studied it and nodded, her expression rapt. "Where'd you get the material?"

"Jamison's Store in Millersville, I get most of my material and patterns there."

This was an event that filled the people with as much merriment as an Irish wake and something to which the whole community looked forward. Although most of us kids didn't know much about dancing, a few brave souls tried. I was a bashful thirteen-year-old boy who was still more likely to be standing with the wallflowers along the sides of the dance floor than participating. Enoch didn't attend, but Dean was a good dancer (I suspect Amantha showed him how), and Shane could usually be found attempting to corral a gullible young maiden into taking a walk with him to some private place.

"I set 'em up by close dancing," Shane told me. "Then I know I've got 'em," he smiled with a confident grin, his eyes sparkling. "How about a stroll outside for a minute of fresh air?" he'd say. "Don't you think it's getting a little smoky in here? I'd like to get to know you better. You know, I don't see pretty girls like you very often."

These were only a few of the lines he used to capture his prey. I shook my head as I watched him work the room. *That's way out of my league,* I thought.

Most of the kids in our group did not have a steady girlfriend. Enoch and Stan were the only two involved in a serious relationship. I only saw Stan and Mary Ann together in town with their parents, but I know they were always together at the grade school they attended. Stan was a somewhat quiet farm boy who was a good athlete, but possibly not the caliber of a few of the other guys in our group. There was no doubt he had the ability, and that he wanted to win, but it wasn't the end of the world if we didn't. Nevertheless, you couldn't dislike Stan. He had his act in order and I admired him greatly because he always knew exactly what he wanted to do when he grew up, he absolutely loved farming.

Kiara and Enoch, however, seemed to be together from the first day they met—I don't believe he ever thought about another girl.

"As soon as I saw her," Enoch expressed to me one day, "I knew she was the one for me."

He and Kiara remained almost inseparable and somewhat distant from the rest of us. She was at every game Enoch played and by his side when team members and onlookers congratulated him after he played for his cousin's city team. Because Enoch was a popular athlete, a certain amount of pestering was to be expected. Although he would never admit it, I think it may have been something he enjoyed. Some of the time, however, I saw them just sitting side by side, quietly, not talking about anything at all. He enjoyed their privacy more than the usual activity surrounding school life.

Tim, who lived on a farm back of the orchards, was probably the best looking of our group and, possible because of that, was confident about his demeanor. Tim didn't have to canvass the crowd to find girls: the girls usually found him.

"If he'd ever kiss me on the cheek, I think I'd just die," I heard one admirer chirp to her girlfriend.

He was a well-built young man who would come to the dance in blue jeans and a white shirt, and wearing a class-ring attached to a gold colored chain around his neck. They both glistened when in the spotlight. He wasn't looking for attention. That was just the way he was. He, and his taller brother Greg, came from an Irish family—both were exceptional all-around athletes.

Jerky, on the other hand, had what some would refer to as two left feet. Jerky thought he could dance, but he most definitely could not, at least in the correct sense of the word. I felt embarrassed for him and sympathetic for his partner, or more appropriately, his opponent. He would trot straight forward, pushing her around and around the floor. They didn't seem to mind though—Jerky was fun to be with.

The adults did the Kickapoo Three Step, or what the hill people called the Kickapoo Kick. It didn't matter if the band was playing a waltz, a fox trot, a swing, or a polka, the Three Step or Kick was the rule. Dancers sort of hopped around on their first two steps, and then kicked their left foot outward on the third.

I'll never get used to that . . .

—◊—

I toed the rubber and took a deep breath, Preacher told me to do that.

"COME ON BONES," Sunny yelled from his position at first base.

"LET'S GO BONES," Hooks hollered from behind home plate.

From his low crouching position, Hooks held one finger down for a fastball. I glanced to my right to see if Dad and Mother were watching. It was the first game for the newly organized Orioles team, and we were playing on a diamond at Rolling Ground. I felt a proud and excited feeling sweep across my body.

"BALL," the umpire yelled as my first pitch sailed high and outside.

I caught the return throw from Hooks and tried to act cool like the pros. I rolled the ball around in my hands and pawed the dirt in front of the rubber with my right foot. *That's what the pitchers do on television in the World Series.* Following their cue, I bent forward from the waist and peered in for the next sign with a menacing *glare* in my eyes. Hooks held three fingers down. *A drop, that's my best pitch.*

"STRIKE," the ump yelled as he held up his right hand. Our fans stood up and clapped. *That's better, now I'm okay.*

"Strike two! Strike three!" The umpire sounded with authority.

I strutted around the mound with a cool gait to my step and sneaked a peek at Dad and Mother. *I'm a big deal now.* Dad ripped off a hunk of JT tobacco with his teeth, and his chewing intensified. Mother leaped to her feet, and the brown and yellow purse she brought with her tumbled on the ground next to her. Our infielders increased their chatter.

"Way to go Bones," Shane yelled from the third base area.

The next two batters went down on groundouts. After a half inning, the score was Sterling nothing and Rolling Ground nothing.

"Good going guys," Preacher said, patting us on our backs as we trotted past him to the bench.

The Orioles immediately set out to launch our attack.

Jerky led off, but he went down on strikes without taking the bat off his shoulder. Not in the least detoured, Dean hit a grounder through the shortstop's legs allowing him to reach first base. Shane swung at the first pitch he saw and hit a pop-up that the right fielder misjudged, the ball landing behind him. After picking up the object, he proceeded to throw it over the third basemen's head, who then threw it past their catcher. Both runners circled the bases. Our next two batters struck out without swinging at a pitch.

The biased Orioles fans shrieked in unbelief. Orioles two, home zero.

With a two-run cushion, I felt pumped with adrenalin. Two drops to the first batter got me ahead in the count. Trying to put him away with a heater, I overthrew my next throw, hitting the batter flush on the left side of his rump. Before taking first base, he hopped and hobbled around as though he were surely going to die. The following Rolling Ground batter hit a popup that unluckily landed in Jerky's glove, which was about the worst place it could have perched for us. The elusive object popped out and tumbled a few feet away before Jerky retrieved it. This catastrophe was more than my young spirit could possibly bare, my emotions immediately and completely fell apart—I walked the next five batters.

"Time," Preacher called to the umpire and walked out to the mound where I was standing like a pillar of salt. "Bones, you know how to play catch with Hooks?"

"Yes sir."

"Then just forget about the batter standing there and play catch like you would do back home . . . okay?"

"Yes sir," I nodded in agreement.

The next batter struck out on a ball over his head, the next fanned at one in the dirt, and a called strike straight down the middle of the plate retired the third.

"Way to go, Bones," Preacher said, seeming proud.

Between innings, the fans stood, clapped their hands together, danced, and sang "Roll out the Barrel," and "The Pennsylvania Polka." Ove's uncle played the harmonica, and everyone had a great time. Mother and Dad were enjoying slices of deep red watermelon.

In the home half of the fifth inning (these were five inning games), the Orioles held a six-to-five lead. Lance, Tim and Greg kept the opponents in the game with hits. Smithy had relieved me at the start of the inning, and I moved to right field. Rolling Ground had one out when little Corky strode to the plate. Carrying his weapon, a big brown bat that was larger than those used by anyone else on the team, he dug in for the battle. Corky was hard to pitch to because he was less than four feet tall, and crouched when he stood at the plate. He never swung the bat. I don't know if he could—he just stood there looking as menacing as possible.

After Corky walked on four straight pitches, he took second on a pass ball to the next batter. On the next pitch, the batter hit a fly to me in right. I positioned myself correctly and caught the ball, but in Corky's excitement to score the tying run for his team, he tagged up and after the catch attempted to advance all the way home from second base. I made a strike to Hooks and little Corky—although he tried to bowl Hooks over like a fullback, was out by a mile. *We won and I'm a hero!*

Chapter 13

THE LEARNING STAGE

That first year for the Sterling Orioles was some-thing special. We soon found out we were not as good as everyone expected. Preacher often referred to us as "a work in progress." It was clear most of us had hardly picked up a baseball because we couldn't play a lick. We made errors, struck out on called third strikes too often, dropped fly balls, and threw balls past each other during the games. Nevertheless, the team was improving and by the end of the year—we were show-ing signs of becoming a group of more capable athletes. The guys were tracking down fly balls and blocking hard grounders without the fear of most first-timers.

The Orioles played five games in `48. We beat Fairview twice and Rolling Ground once. Although Sherman beat us the first time by a large margin (nine to two), the second meeting between the two teams turned out to be much different.

As soon as I got to the Sterling ball field I knew something positive was about to happen.

"There's a big Monarch butterfly sitting on my bat," Shane yelled excitedly as he stood in front of the bats resting against the far corner of our bench. "That's good luck!"

Intimidation also played a part of the game. My first pitch to the Sherman leadoff man sailed halfway up the backstop screen, while prompting hoots from my teammates and uneasiness from the opposing batters.

"Watch out!" Hooks cautioned the opposing batters as they prepared their stance in the batters box. "This guy doesn't know where it's going."

After backing off the batter with a wild high and tight one, I usually came right back with a bender for a strike.

"That's not a bad thing to do," Preacher said between innings. "The kid at the plate will be scared of you and he'll bailout for fear of being hit with the pitch."

Whether it was through intimidation or whatever, Sherman only scored two runs through the first four innings. The Orioles were looking better than the first confrontation between the two teams. A four-bagger by Tiger (who made one of his few appearances) and a double by Hooks set up our first two scores. After his two-bagger, Hooks stole third and scored on a pass ball. Our only other run came on a single by Sunny, a ground out, and a single by Shane. The rest of the gang was swinging for the fences and coming up short most of the time.

"Stop trying to tee-off on that guy," Preacher scolded us between innings.

After Dean fanned, he tossed his bat aside disgustedly. "He's mine next time, Coach."

In the top of the fifth, Sherman took the lead on a walk, an infield hit, a bunt (allowing the runners to advance), and a clean single to right, scoring two runs. In the last chance fifth, Ove tomahawked the first pitch thrown to him and got an infield hit. "Way to go, Babe," Preacher shouted, clapping his hands.

While the next two batters were being retired, Ove advanced to second. Preacher called time and gathered his team around him.

"Gentlemen, we've proven we're as good a team as they are," he said. "If we just keep our wits about us, we can beat these guys!"

With Ove leading dangerously far off second base, Jerky got hold of the next pitch, a fastball straight down the middle, and hit a ball that deflected off the third base bag and bounced toward the shortstop.

"Stop, hold up Babe," Preacher yelled and held both of his hands high. But Ove, in the excitement of the moment, circled third without stopping and ran through the hold sign. The throw from the shortstop to the plate had him by a mile. Preacher didn't say a word. Although he must have been disappointed, he slapped each one of us on the back as we left the field.

"Played them tough this time," he shouted. "Four to three is a lot better than nine to two.

The Orioles tied for first place with Sherman, but lost to them in a playoff for the Kickapoo Kup. Sherman had a new pitcher for the game, a big kid, from around the Wauzeka area, who could throw harder than we were used to seeing. I don't know why he didn't play for them before, but he was a bear, a really tough competitor. He threw *white blurs* past most of us that smacked into their catcher's mitt before we were able to even flinch. All day we looked for someone to put the wind back into our sails, but against this guy, it was only so much wishful thinking. Aside from two singles by Dean, a triple by Shane, and singles by Sunny and Jerky, the new guy handcuffed us much of the time.

We didn't win every game that year, not by a long shot. But although there were embarrassing moments, most of us felt we were definitely getting better. The first Saturday forenoon after the playoff, the team got together for a brief discussion at Preacher's home and talked about the season. Most of us thought our team had made it over the hump and had arrived; however, when reality set in—we realized there was a lot more work to do before we could stake such a claim. Although everyone was disappointed, I heard, "We'll try again next year," repeated more than once. There was hope for the future, after all; everyone had a personal moment of glory sometime during the season, and that had to mean something.

"We'll set aside a day for grieving and then get back to work," Preacher said. "PJ's been asking about some of you kids. Between now and the start of the season next spring, stop up there and work out some of the things you've been having trouble with or would like to improve on. You couldn't go to a better coach. See you at the picnic."

—⁓—

From a sporting standpoint, we were all in a positive frame of mind. Citation won the Triple Crown of horse racing, and this rural community was as excited as if he were one of their own. But in the early fall of 1948, about the same time seeds were falling from maple trees like spinning propellers, sad news broke to baseball fans in the Kickapoo and across the world.

On August 16, Babe Ruth died at the young age of fifty-three, from cancer.

"I saw him play a game in Comiskey Park, in Chicago," Preacher told Dad and me one day after his death. "At that time, he was bigger than life itself."

This was also the year that Sunny, Ove, Jerky and Tiger entered Millersville High School as freshmen. The coach cancelled baseball for track, therefore the team was unable to compete for the North-South championship.

It was also election year, and candidates for president were decided during the Democratic and Republican conventions. On the radio I heard, "Mr. Chairman, the dairy state of Wisconsin casts all ten of its electoral votes for the next president of the United States . . ." Bands played, delegates marched and celebrated, and the gavel could be heard pounding for order. The presidential election in Wisconsin and in our nation went in an historic upset to Harry Truman over Thomas E. Dewey.

The Cleveland Indians beat the Boston Braves in the World Series, and the black Hall of Fame pitcher Satchel Page made baseball history by being the first Negro pitcher to pitch in a World Series game.

I'll bet that made Willie happy.

Two weeks after the end of the season, Preacher and Milley arranged a team picnic at the ball field.

The mothers of the players each brought something to eat. As a result of Preachers foresight and generosity, we also invited Stan, Tim, Greg and Lance from two of the other teams in the league. Their parents brought them.

"You'll all be playing together on the high school team someday," Preacher said, "so we might as well become united as soon as possible." Enoch and Tiger even showed up on their bikes.

"This is not a wake because the season is ending, it's a celebration," Preacher announced to us kids sitting as a group after eating. "This is the beginning of many winning years—and they're just around the corner for you kids."

Preacher called the players on the Orioles team forward one-by-one and presented each the team letter S, which was cut out of leather. "Your mothers can sew these on your favorite jacket," he said with a tone of pride in his voice. He had separate letters for the guest players.

Then he turned to the group collectively . . .

"This is just the minor leagues, the learning stage. We haven't won as many games as we would have liked, but we're getting better. We learn to win in life, and we learn to lose. How many times did Babe Ruth strike out? Many, but you never hear about that, do you? Max Schmelling knocked Joe Lewis down in a heavy weight championship fight before Joe knocked the kraut out.

"How many of our bombers did the Germans shoot down before we won the war? How many stones did your parents load onto a stone-boat and pull from their fields before they could plant a crop? You have to learn to lose before you can fully appreciate what winning is all about, and you're going to do your share of winning in the future, including the Kickapoo Kup, believe me!" There was a tone of certainty and destiny on his voice and mannerisms.

Preacher walked into the middle of the team . . .

"There'll be excitement—but there'll also be heart-break. You'll beat some big teams and win some big games—but you won't win all of them. You'll win because you have character, and when you lose, you'll lose with character. But we're going to have fun either way."

—⚉—

The morning was bright, and a few of us kids were sitting in PJ's store listening as he gave us some instruction.

"If you want to see how this game is played," PJ said, "come up to Grove tomorrow night after chores. Bruno wants us to practice. You can shag balls, throw batting practice, and warm up some of us players, would you like that? I can show you a few things here in the store, but seeing and being part of the play might be better."

Preacher jumped up with excitement and yelled, "How about that?"

"What time, PJ?" Dad asked with a slight frown, most likely worrying how we were going to get our chores done.

"Whenever you can make it, it'll probably go on to at least nine o'clock."

Wow. To play ball with those guys!

After milking the next night, Dad drove Sunny and me to the ball field. Virtually our whole team was there, along with their parents. I know they were looking forward with pride and excitement to see their kids on the same field with the stars of local baseball.

As soon as practice was over, some of us sat down alongside our parents in back of second base and chatted.

Strolling over to our group with PJ beside him was the catcher for the pro team, who was also the head baseball coach for a Midwest university. He stopped somewhere between the pitcher's mound and second base.

He was a well-built man who had charisma and respectability about him. Although it was difficult to explain, he was someone who could be very intimidating on occasions.

"PJ asked me to talk with you for a few minutes tonight, and you probably thought it would be about baseball, but that's not what I have in mind.

"I can tell, even at your young age, that a few of you are going to go places in this sport. The good Lord has blessed you with talent. But talent will only take you so far by itself. There are a lot of kids who want to play for me at the university who have talent, but little else. The ones I recruit have mental toughness. The pros have it between the ears." He pointed to his temples.

"What separates the good from the excellent are the intangibles. Talent you're born with, but such things as desire, a good attitude, willingness to learn, work hard, and taking orders, along with the ability to ignore the opposition when they say or do things that could get under your skin, these are the things you learn, and will need to make it someday."

He paused and looked hard at each of us . . .

"Obey your parents—you're here because they care about you and your welfare. Don't get in trouble. Things are happening, even here in the valley that are not good. Don't copy some of the guys who think they are tough or smarter than the rest of us, they're not. You'll never play for me at the university or succeed in pro ball with that attitude.

"There's a lot of young men trying to do what you do, and trying to do it better. Someday each one of you will get your chance to prove what you can do—so prepare yourselves now."

He walked closer to us and added very emphatically, "I'm going to leave you with the three most important words for any athlete who desires to succeed. Does anyone know what they are?"

Tiger eagerly raised a hand, and the coach nodded to him.

"Practice, practice, practice."

"That's right," the coach said. "Don't ever let anyone hold you back!"

Chapter 14

PRANKS AND THE GREAT BLIZZARD

As the fall sent her signals, brisk autumn air blew through the bare apple trees, their fruit picked clean except for the fallen few lying on the ground. Whitetail deer nibbled on the best of the lot, a Greening or maybe a McIntosh or a Red Delicious, if they were so lucky. Dad scraped thick frost off the seat of our Ford tractor before climbing on. Meanwhile, Sunny broke thin ice in the water tank so the cows would not be thirsty. I ventured to the closet in our living room and removed my mackinaw jacket for use against the northern chill.

Autumn in the Kickapoo also ushered in the excitement of Halloween and every crazy prank imaginable. Horseplay sometimes took on a show unmatched by Hollywood. Despite all of the help and best intentions of our parents and others in the community, we were, in fact, still kids, and kids will sometimes need to release their fantasies about having fun. The older we got, the more mischievous the pranks became.

Much of the spook to the moment, however, came from the tales handed down to us by family. Some of these tales, true or not, seemed so real that Sunny and I had nightmares. I visualized the villains in these dreams as being eight feet tall, eating raw rabbits, having rotted sharp jagged teeth, and patrolling the territory from the Mississippi to the Kickapoo. There were also the superstations . . .

"If it rains in an open grave," I heard Aunt Bertha say, "it means another death within six months!"

Nevertheless, among the Kickapoo kids, Shane was the instigator for most of the local shenanigans that were real. I knew something was in the works by the way he was acting. Lately he'd gotten all sneaky-like. Every once in awhile I'd glance at him and see him smiling and even talking to himself.

I finally got him alone. "What's goin' on Shane?"

He looked at me full of suppressed excitement and feigned innocence. "Whaddya mean?"

"I know you've got somethin' up your sleeve—out with it." I crossed my arms and stayed in his path, letting him know I wasn't going anywhere until I got an answer.

Shane had a habit of scratching his back in sort of a nervous gesture when he was planning some mischief. He was doing that now . . .

"A bunch of us guys in town have planned somethin' for Halloween night that'll be great if we can pull it off."

"You mean soaping windows?" I asked.

"That too."

"Okay . . . what else?"

"You know that pasture back of the grade school where Bacon has his cows? Well, we're gonna sneak one out that evening after milking. Dean, me, and as many other guys as we can get are gonna lead a cow into the school and leave her there all night."

"Wow!" I said, in awe of such a complex and well thought-out plan. We both laughed with excitement.

"They've been eatin' all that green grass and she'll crap all over the place." Shane jumped with glee, his eyes as big as quarters and with a broad smile on his face.

"Won't that be great? Want ah come along?"

"Oh no, no dice, I'm not that dumb. Besides, Mother wouldn't let me out with my bike that time of night anyway."

That Halloween evening, Dean, Shane, and some of the other guys did as Shane had planned. I wasn't there, but they told me about it the next day in great detail and with even greater enjoyment.

They gathered at Bacon's pasture after milking as planned. Shane took charge. Some of the kids complained that they were having second thoughts and didn't want to do this.

"It's stupid," Corky said. He was conned into tagging along. All, however, wanted to save face, and they couldn't turn Shane down.

"Hurry, get the gate open before Bacon hears us," Shane said to Jerky who heard about the scheme from one of his buddies.

After a few fumbled attempts in the dark, they finally got the gate open.

"Get the rope around her . . . easy now Bessie." The tame old brown-and-white Guernsey was easy to lead. One of the guys led her as Shane gave the orders and directions.

The trip to the school was harrowing to say the least. Transporting a cow through town without being noticed wasn't as easy as it sounded because the old gal mooed every now and then.

"I wish she'd give her mouth a rest," Dean said as quietly as possible. "She'll wake up the whole neighborhood."

Additionally, Bessie had a mind of her own, crapping on the street as she rumbled along and turning the street into a shade of green that would have done justice to Saint Patty's Day. The troops following her skipped to get out of the firing line.

"She won't have anything left for the school," Shane complained with a sense of concern in his voice. "Pull as much green grass as you can and leave it for her to eat when we get her inside."

Eventually they made it to their destination as planned. Shane whispered orders while keeping a wary eye out for a passerby.

"Get the door, Dean . . . that's right, lead her in this way. Stop bein' a chicken, you guys, give us a hand."

Bessie stayed there overnight and did exactly as Shane envisioned, depositing droppings on the floor in every room she entered. Shane glowed with enthusiasm as he told me about it.

"She dumped a great big one just as she came in the door. Guess she musthav' gotten excited or something."

From what I heard later, no one would own up to the escapade, so lucky for them no charges were filed and no one was disciplined. Mrs. Kelly, the school principal was less than amused by the prank.

"I know who was responsible for doing this," she said, glancing a mistrustful look in the direction of a group of sleepy-eyed boys sitting with their tails between their legs toward the back of the room.

Her knuckles were white as she gripped the yardstick and *slapped* it against a desk she was standing beside. Mrs. Kelly glared as she addressed the school assembly, arms crossed, and looking stern as any drill sergeant.

"Any more of this and I'll drop your grades!"

Shane knew he had to think fast. "Probably the Ridge Runners," Shane belted out with assuredness. "I was studying most of last night, Mrs. Kelly. Hope you don't think poorly about me."

"I don't want any lies about this, young man. I've got a good idea who's to blame. You're caught red-handed—admit it! Dean, I know you were one of them. Amantha will give you a good talking to." Then she turned her attention to the rest of the class. "Just look at the green manure on the tennis shoes of some of you; you ought to be ashamed of yourselves."

But that wasn't all that happened that same Halloween evening. Another group of older kids somehow elevated an outhouse to the roof of the local bank where a sign was placed stating, "Republican Party."

I heard one of the culprits was the son of someone who worked at the bank.

Pranks were only an opportunity to release mischievous energy. For the most part, these rural kids filled their time with schoolwork, farm work, and their one true love, baseball.

—⁓—

Now that the baseball season was ending for the Orioles, after church on Sunday we were free to spend time at Aunt Ella Smalley's house in Millersville. A few players on Bruno's team stayed there, especially the black players. Many of my teammates from the area were excited to talk with them when they had the chance. Tim and Lance biked down from the orchards. The players told us about the KKK, cross burnings, and segregated water fountains in the south. I think their stories somehow made us better people.

We also enjoyed just talking with Aunt Ella. She told stories about the past life in the Kickapoo, and about some of the baseball players who had roomed with her husband Mike and her home.

"Ma Smalley is the nicest person I know. She minds me of my grandma back home in Carolina," Lukas Brown said to a group of us at Aunt Ella's after a meal at Fat Friley's Restaurant. Their "Bomber's Blue Plate Special" consisted of sauerkraut . . . and something else. What exactly I'm not sure. I guess the title came as a result of the after effects it had on the eater, because a sign pointing to the rest room read, "Bomber in Back."

Lukas and some of his Afro American teammates knew or had played against Willie and the Kansas City Blue Birds. Although they were not nearly as good a group of players as the Blue Birds, they were able to show us a few pointers about batting, pitching, and the thinking process that went along with defense and base running.

Although Ella kept a modest house, neat and orderly, the task became more difficult after Mike was bedridden as a result of a stroke. He eventually passed away.

"Life is not always easy," Ella would say. She ought to know—after Mike passed away she was severely beaten in an attempted home robbery by a carnival worker.

"As long as I have a pulse there'll always be a purpose for living," she said.

A long, white, hand-embroidered cloth hung over the doorway of their living room with the lyric, "True love is not only seeing a sunrise, but sharing a sunset, and knowing whom to thank for life in-between." *Just looking at that sign makes my conscience sit up straight and realize how selfish I am at times.* Hanging on the wall back of an old piano were three pictures, side by side, of Pope Pius II, President Truman, and St.

Theresa, "The Little Flower." Wherever I moved in that room her eyes on that picture seemed to follow me. *Spooky!*

Although we did not realize it at the time, we learned a lot about life, toughness, and responsibility from Ella. As she accepted responsibility for Mike, so we became toughened and accepted responsibility for each other on the ball field.

—∽—

As the seasonal colors of the Kickapoo bluffs (which parallel anything New England has to offer) gradually gave way to the brisk breezes circulating down out of Canada, a few frozen snow flurries softly floated through the air and introduced the coming of winter to the area. At our farmhouse, Dad pulled his long johns on, which he did not plan to remove until the spring thaw. Mother removed a bottle of alcohol from a closet and placed it in a kitchen cupboard, alongside various liniments, salves and pills. A hot alcohol drink at night to fight the cough and help Dad sleep was her intent.

Somewhere between Thanksgiving and Christmas, the snow began to fall and it came down in record proportions. The large oak trees in our backyard swayed far over in the wind as the great norther' sighed heavily and hollered like the scream of a woman giving birth.

I heard Dad cuss it, somewhat jokingly, I guess, more than once. "Shut up, you ornery devil, or you'll get the best of us," he'd say. Although Dad prayed on his knees, he sometimes cursed like a stable boy.

The arctic attack caught hundreds of duck hunters by surprise on the Mississippi—and many drowned. I saw state and government workers working frantically, dragging the river bottom with hooks attached to chains in hopes of recovering bodies before the river froze. They only retrieved a few.

After almost two days of steady pounding—the storm stopped as suddenly as it had started. The after-effects in Millersville left drifts so high they reached the top of a wooden marker that listed the somewhat sun-faded names of local casualties from the first and second world wars.

—⁓—

I could hear the great county grader with a large plow attached to its front slowly forcing its way up the road toward our farm. Blasts of blue smoke rose from exhaust pipes jutting up from the top of the huge monster. The sound alone told the story. Men with shovels hurriedly broke the *drift-hardened* snow in front of the plow. Puffs of breath in the frigid air exited their mouths in white bursts as they strained with every load of their shovels. Every once in awhile, the plow had to stop—back up—and take another ram at the huge drift it was trying to move.

Ten-foot banks of snow formed on both sides of the road as the tractor—its tank-like metal tracks rotating under it drudgingly grinding itself forward, foot-by-foot!

As usual, Mother was ready to show hospitality to the workers. She had something ready as the men drew even with our place.

"Bones . . . Sunny . . . Take this pot of hot coffee and warm doughnuts out to the men when they get here."

Blizzards and huge snowstorms of the past two weeks had left three to four feet of snow on the ground, blocking side roads and preventing travel by any type of motor vehicle. Dad transported our milk to the factory in Sterling using a team of horses and a sleigh. It took hours for the horses to wade through the heavy snow-covered trail. King, the lead horse of the team, became lame on the way home.

"In all my years, I've never seen the likes of it," Dad said to Mother as he pulled his clothes on, layer upon layer, to go out. He gave a final jerk to his body and pushed his right arm through the sleeve of his denim jacket.

Mother was paying attention to what he was saying. With a faint worried look, she murmured, "I hope it don't all melt at one time."

Dad frowned and pulled the collar of his jacket around his face, muffling his voice somewhat. "If it does, Millersville will be in trouble." He gave a shivering movement to his frame that said to me, *I dread this. It's cold outside.*

Of course my young mind didn't grasp the severity of the situation. The only thing that came to me was how a flood would affect the upcoming baseball season.

"A lot of the snow from the hillsides will run off and flood our diamond, won't it?"

"Probably."

"Where'll we play then?"

"The schedule will have to be changed, I guess," Dad said, as he put on his boots and walked out into the winter weather . . .

I didn't sleep well during the night. Mostly tossing and turning. It had been an exciting day.

I sure hope the field don't flood.

Chapter 15

TIM AND LANCE

It was on a Thursday evening in early March of 1949 that it started raining. The temperature had been slowly rising throughout the day and now hovered around fifty-six degrees. Old timers referred to it as a "false spring." We could hear the rushing sound of water from the melting snow traveling north to south through the ditch that separated two hills in our woods. On other occasions such as this, Sunny and I would toss sticks in the upper end of the stream and follow them as they traveled in the flowing water past the rocks and fallen branches of trees that occupied the low areas. But this time it was different—this time it was evening and it was starting to rain harder by the minute. No thunder or lightning, just a steady rain that fell straight down.

"Golly, that's loud," Mother said as we looked out the kitchen window at the pounding avalanche before leaving for the barn.

As the storm continued, I could hear it thrashing against the tin roof of the barn when we were milking, and it seemed to be getting louder by the minute. I looked up and frowned from time to time as I sat on the milk stool. Every once in awhile a few stray drops would find their way through the battered roof and strike one of the cows back, startling her and causing her to jump.

I always enjoyed the sound of rain on a tin roof, but something about this was starting to get a little frightening.

Back in the house, after milking, we turned on the radio and dialed the local station WPRE, in Prairie du Chien. "Flash flood warning," the announcer said in an excited voice. "The Kickapoo is rising above flood stage in Millersville and Sherman. If you live in these areas, you are warned to take higher ground immediately!"

Mother rushed to the telephone attached to a wall in our living room. "I'm going to call the telephone office and see if I can reach Ella."

She picked up the earpiece, turned the crank, and spoke into the mouth piece. "This is Rhoda. Would you connect me with Ella?"

I listened for Mother's response intensively. Although the phone rang and rang and rang—there was no answer.

"What do you think we ought to do, Jake?" Mother said, stepping to the window. She lifted the curtain and peered out into the darkness and the continuous driving sound of the rain . . .

"Wait a few minutes and call again," Dad said. From the look on his brow, he appeared troubled.

Ella's small home was on low land close to the river, and when the water was high, hers was usually one of the first to experience flooding. Mother placed another call, this time to Ella's son, Mike Jr.

"Let me have the phone, Rhoda." Dad couldn't wait any longer to get some information.

Dad had an unusual way of talking on the telephone. If the other party was close by, he'd keep his voice low. But if the party was farther away, he'd elevate his voice. Anything over twenty miles away, he'd yell.

Mike Jr. told Dad they had evacuated his mother at first warning earlier in the evening.

"I'm glad she's safe," Dad said as he stopped pacing the floor in our farmhouse kitchen. He gave us each a reassuring smile, but I noticed a moment later he resumed his ceaseless back-and-forth tread.

"Sit down, Jake, and stop pacing," Mother said, walking toward Dad. "You're making us nervous. Here, chew on this for awhile." She handed him the biggest, reddest, and shiniest McIntosh apple I had ever seen. *Not one wormhole,* I thought.

"I've been saving this one for a special occasion," she said.

Dad peeled the red skin off with his pocket knife, the peel rolling in a circular motion nonstop until it fell to the floor. *He seems more relaxed now.*

"I'm going to throw my raincoat on and go out and feed Rover." I said to Mother. "He hasn't eaten all day except for those screening pad from the milking this morning."

As soon as I got back in the house Mother told me Dean had called and said the water was all around their house, but they were okay.

"Did you tell him the ball field down by Preacher would probably be too wet to play on?" I said. Mother never answered . . .

By noon of the next day, the water had risen over its banks throughout the Kickapoo Valley, flooding all the small towns, villages and lowlands that rested along its path. Water reached halfway up the sides of businesses in downtown Millersville, and word was some homes and shops were damaged beyond repair.

Scooter reported there were carp and sheeps-head swimming around in his basement. Rowboats transported people to the edges of town. There they got in cars and buses and shopped for groceries in towns on the higher areas away from the river. The Ridge Runners pitched in to help with the efforts. For some reason, the River People always recovered more quickly from the yearly flood than the rest of the community. They were better prepared, and they knew exactly what to do when the water subsided.

Of course, the ball field on Preacher's farm was flooded with water as a result of the washout from the surrounding hills. With no place to go, all we could do was wait for the water to evaporate. To our dismay, five weeks after the great flood, it was still too wet to play. The first two games of the spring schedule were cancelled, and made up later. Over the course of the winter months, Tombstone, Ferryville and Wauzeka were added to the league.

As for the Millersville High School baseball team, they were defeated in the regional tournament by La Farge. Tiger played basketball and was automatically included on the baseball roster, but Sunny, Ove and Jerky, who did not play basketball, were not asked to join the team. Needless to say—they were not happy about being excluded.

—∿—

Finally, for the Orioles, the long wait was over. I don't think I was the only player with a few knots in his belly. *Now I've got a chance to play baseball!*

Chris put on her uniform, tucked her ponytail under the blue cap she was wearing, reset it so the bill pointed directly forward, smeared a little dirt across her face, and waited for the call.

"Okay, guys," Preacher said when he gathered the team around him before practice. "This is what we've been waiting for all winter. We'll take batting practice first. Remember, this is just practice. Get the kinks out . . . get your licks in . . . have fun."

After warming up, Preacher called the team around him.

"Chris, you're in right."

I watched her burst from the sidelines and out to her position, keeping a watchful eye on the opposing team, but no one seemed to have figured out we had a girl playing. Even though her real first name was Chris, when Coach Preacher filled in the lineup card—he listed her as "Kris," a masculine name.

Let's face it, none of us wanted the opposition razzing us that we were a girls' team!

I walked out to the pitcher's mound and glanced to right field. Though Kris (Chris) could run fast, field well, throw hard, and even had a good eye at the plate, I wondered if she was going to keep up this year. We'd all grown some over the winter. She looked confident though, and truth be told there were other players in our starting lineup that I probably had more to worry about than her.

Everyone looked forward to today's date, the first game of the season. The opposition was Fairview. The grass was so green it looked like some first graders had colored it with crayons the night before.

From a farming standpoint, the crops were flourishing. Corn was more than knee high, and it was not even the fourth of July.

"Sure has been good growing weather," Preacher commented to Dad before the game started.

"Yeah, but a field of corn like that sure takes a lot out of the soil," Dad said. Like most farmers, he usually had something to complain about concerning the weather.

From a baseball perspective, the Orioles were ready to play. It was evident we had improved from the first year. We probably couldn't have gotten much worse. With a year under our belts to mature and develop our talents, we had gained a lot more confidence than we'd had at the beginning of the previous year. But how good we could get was still an open question. Additionally, a number of us kids had visited with PJ at his store and received some good guidance. More than one of us spent the winter practicing what he taught us inside a shed or in the hayloft of a barn.

"Come on Bones!" Chris shouted, breaking my reverie.

With her farm just north of ours, she would ride her quarter horse that she called "Tally-hoe," close to our place every day to drive their cattle back to the barn for evening milking. Chris loved horses more than anything. I'd often ride my bike to meet her. We'd talk and have fun in those moments. But out here, she was all business and very competitive.

After the first pitch, things began to settle down.

—ᗰ—

Although I couldn't throw hard, I had my moments. Because I didn't throw BBs, I used about every type of breaking pitch imaginable.

"All smoke and no fire," some of the players from the opposing bench yelled at me just before their man in the batter's box struck out swinging.

At other times, Shane, who was catching, yelled, *"Look out!"* causing the batter to bail out just before a curve bent across the strike zone. Nevertheless, and aside from my interest in pitching, I probably was a more natural hitter.

On this day, however, the team was too anxious at the plate. Sunny swung so hard in his first at-bat that he spun completely around in the batters box, his cap flying off his head. In the fourth inning, with the tying run on third, Jerky swung at a pitch he should have taken, and his pop fly landed in the glove of the left fielder; our fans groaned with disappointment.

By the seventh inning, the score had been seesawing back and forth. We were still down by one and my arm was tired. I took off my cap (fighting the mid-afternoon heat) and wiped sweat from my head as Coach Preacher called time and strolled to the mound. Shane followed. Preacher reached in a hind pocket of his overalls and pulled out a plug of J T chewing tobacco. After opening his multi-bladed French Army Knife, he whacked off a slice and stuffed it in one side of his mouth.

"Can I have a chaw, coach?" Shane asked. He wasn't sassing; it was an honest request. Preacher shot Shane a disapproving look without making an answer.

After a quick conversation, Preacher decided I would stay in.

Eventually we woke up, got our hitting clothes on, and pulled ahead. While the bases were busy with Jerky and Shane, Sunny caught a pitch flush on the head of his Adirondack bat that skimmed over the outfield grass and rolled past the confused fielder. Both runners scored. In the seventh inning we might have lost the game if it were not for Chris. With two out, the tying run on second and the winning run on first, the batter hit a short fly back of first base. Chris raced in, scooped up the ball, and threw home to get the runner. Suddenly there was reason for our fans to cheer.

As we walked off the field, I was having trouble slipping an arm through my warm-up jacket, when Dean trotted over to help me.

"Good game, Bones."

I thanked him, knowing he meant it. However, there were times when the nickname "Bones" didn't rest well with me. I winced, feeling the toilet paper (I wrapped around my shins and ankles to make them look bigger) slipping inside my baseball socks. Apparently, my attempts to avoid the nickname weren't working out all too well. Sunny grinned at me from where he was walking in from first base. He knew to what extent I'd gone to hide my skinny legs.

I wasn't surprised when Stan trotted over to say hello. He was like that, just a nice guy. We congratulated each other. Stan had a pair of hits in a losing cause. Within moments, the rest of the team surrounded me. After I drained the last out of my hugs, Shane and Hooks showed up together, still arguing good-naturedly over which one was the better catcher. I hid a grin and suspected it might have been a toss-up. Hooks was older than the rest of us and on the roster of the Millersville High School team, but Shane was a great all-around athlete and I think he might have excelled at the game, and the best player on our team, had it not been that he was distracted by the opposite sex.

My gaze found my brother, who, by the way, was sporting a strong case of pimples. In most respects Sunny and I were exact opposites. I was tall and skinny, Sunny was shorter and more firmly built. Sunny had an I Q that I understand was in the superior range. He naturally got good grades in school. As for me, school was a struggle. Most subjects didn't interest me. While I was insane about baseball, Sunny didn't have the same desire. He took the game seriously, but not for his own sake. Instead, he spent his time doing just what he was now, advancing my talents instead of his own. Being skinny, I always felt safe when my brother was around. Although he was of a quiet nature, he knew how to use his fists when he had to. I saw him bloody the nose of more than one agitator. I shook my head and turned to pay attention to what Ove was saying.

Ove, Preacher's son, played second base for us and was a good enough player, but he seemed not to have the interest as some of the rest on the team. Although I never heard him mention it, I know that must have disappointed his dad.

"I think he got his mother's genes," I heard Dad say more than once.

Preacher yelled with encouragement every time Ove came to bat.

"Come on Babe!" he'd cry. But Ove just didn't have the desire that his father had. He seemed to have more interest in girls and his appearance than in baseball. Most of the time Ove could be seen working and perfecting his "cow-lick" frontal hair cut.

I believe Preacher always looked at me as his second son. He sort of adopted me because he thought I had the determination that may have been missing in Ove. For the same reason, he must have felt comfortable calling me by the nickname of "Bones."

"So next Sunday is Rolling Ground?" Jerky asked, his eyes shining with excitement.

I nodded. We had home field advantage and would be up against Lance, Greg, and Tim. Good players but ones we knew. Not like today.

"It's gonna be good," I predicted with a grin.

We were on a roll, and the team cheered their agreement. After today—nothing could stop us!

—⚇—

Rolling Ground was everything we'd expected, with maybe a bit more to boot. Overnight some of Preacher's cows had broke through a fence and spent the major part of the evening dining and dumping on the ball field. The team spent most of their pre-game time scooping up cow pies.

Although the Orioles had been practicing during the winter, it was evident the Rolling Ground lads had been doing the same. Tim and his older brother Greg (who was an exceptional basketball player), had proven their mettle in the games last year, and Lance was at the top of his game. Lance came from a farm family of a number of older brothers who were exceptional baseball players. One may have played professionally but now was a part of Bruno's team. Just one look at Lance would tell you he was a full blooded Irishman. He had a great entertaining personality—and a strong throwing arm that would beckon that of a pitcher if it were not that he was such a good outfielder. He naturally used a "basket catch" like Willie Mays.

Rolling Ground also had one kid, a boy from a family back in the hills who could run like no one I'd seen before. Rumor had it he ran shine from the brewing location to the delivery point, where a waiting horse and rider carried it to a motorcycle man along a logging road.

I think a few of our problems on the field might have had something to do with Mother, Milley and Martha. They'd gone all out, organizing a feast to end all feasts prior to the game and we might have gotten our bellies a bit too full. The crowd dug into the homemade ham sandwiches, sweet corn, apple pie, bread, and ice cream with enthusiasm. I saw those two Irishmen from the opposition, Lance and Tim filling their plates also.

But it was Dean who bailed us out in the seventh. Greg, a tall, lanky, right-hander with a good fastball, was still on the mound trying to keep the Rolling Ground lead. His cause hadn't been helped by the Rolling Ground defense. When Dean stepped to the plate for the fourth time in the game, ducks were on the pond. Dean swung at the first pitch, a head high fastball, and missed wildly. A curve in the dirt brought the count even. Greg told me after the game what he was thinking...

"I knew if I could get another fastball past him, I could finish him off with a curve."

And so it was a fastball Greg threw, waist high and down the middle of the plate. Dean pulled it to left center, past the frantic running outfielders, and clearing the bases of the three runners. He'd gone four for four, and we won our second game of the season. The fans cheered gleefully, and the team slapped each other on the rump. Dean and I walked across the field and offered our condolences to Tim and Lance, nice guys that we were. Tim was rather subdued but Lance was his jovial self. *That guy sure has the right attitude.*

We were hot and on top of the world.

Chapter 16

TIGER

About a thirty-five minute drive south of Sterling, along the winding and muddy Kickapoo, stood our next opposition. Little more than a flyspeck on the map, this narrow area located between the Kickapoo and the Mississippi Rivers was where the past seemed to stand still.

Dad slowed our car to a halt and asked a man strolling along a road with a coonhound tagging behind him, "Where's the ball field around here?"

If there was a baseball game being played somewhere close by, Dad could smell it. The stroller gave us sketchy directions to a ball field hidden in back of some bushes along the Kickapoo River just north of town.

Only a few rods before the entry point to the small, unincorporated locality of Sherman (named after a Civil War general), a short and steep gravel side road turned to the right and dropped off into a valley adjacent to the Kickapoo River. You had to drive carefully because the bank was steep and there weren't any guardrails to prevent sudden disaster.

We pulled our car up to a group of bushes, most of which had been cleared to form parking spaces, stopped, and put on the parking brake. We'd arrived at the ball field.

—⁂—

Sherman was our toughest competition from the previous year. When we played them on their small diamond along the river bank, everyone from the neighborhood showed up to picnic and watch the game.

Their town consisted of a few houses, two gin joints, one with a dance hall overhead, and not much else. I highly doubted anyone would move to Sherman to live; its few residents were most likely born and bred there. The people of that area clung to their roots and kept to themselves. Rumor had it that it wasn't a good idea for outsiders to cause a ruckus in one of the bars in the evening, or any other time for that matter.

Sherman had a small, one-room jail with strong metal bars on the windows. The Crawford County Sheriffs Department sort of left them alone to sort out their own problems.

About the only recreation in the area was baseball, and the kids were playing it at a young age.

I couldn't recall how Sherman became part of our league. *Maybe it was as a result of hearing we had formed a league,* I thought. Nevertheless, the people did invite all the teams into their closed community with cheerful smiles and open arms. I felt comfortable playing there, and I liked it.

They could play baseball—really! They were good.

We'd "loaded up" for the encounter. It was Shane who noticed him first.

"Look, there's Tiger!" Shane yelled as Preacher drove into the parking lot with Ove and someone I couldn't quite see.

The two passengers hopped out and ran to the Orioles' side of the field before Preacher had a chance to turn off the engine. I stared and broke into a run to find out what was going on.

Tiger lived in Sterling with his parents and a younger sister. He was one year ahead of us in school and in the same grade with Sunny, Jerky, and Ove. We called him "Tiger" because of his aggressive style of play. He was built like a bull dog.

Tiger was a likeable lad and an outstanding all-around athlete. Because he was older than Shane, Dean, Enoch and me—he could arguably be considered the best player around. As soon as Tiger put on his uniform for any sport, no one could stop him. I saw him steal bases standing up, run out ground balls and pop-ups, back up other fielders, and always hit his cutoff man. He had range, quick hands, a sure throw, and could hit for average and distance.

"That kid's too good to be true," I heard Preacher say about Tiger after practice one day. Tiger played most of the time on the Millersville city team.

"What are you doin' here?" I yelled as soon as he was close enough to hear.

Tiger smiled. "Preacher asked me to play today because he was afraid you'd lose."

"Oh, give me a break," Shane said with a sniff. "Don't think too highly of yourself."

—ᴠᴠᴠ—

Preacher ran through infield practice before the game, shouting out instructions, batting grounders to each position, playing pepper, and hitting pop-ups to the fielders. He called it "situation" ball.

"Okay, what do you do if a teammate overthrows a base? That's right, back up the play. Do you remember what PJ said about throwing accurately, how you should pivot and step in the direction you're throwing the ball? It's the little things that count, don't get careless."

Preacher jotted down a lineup on a piece of yellow paper with red lines running across the page. He always used a pencil so he could erase names and change positions if necessary.

In the top of the first inning, Tiger pounded out a run-producing hit over the top of the pitcher's head and into center field. When he faced the Sherman pitcher in the third, we had a runner on third and two out. With a three and zero count, Preacher gave a take sign to Tiger. I could tell by his mannerisms that he was entertaining the thought. He stepped out of the box and looked again at Preacher, this time the green light was flashed.

"Come to me," the catcher barked encouragement to the man on the mound. "Bring it in."

A slight grin crossed Tiger's face just before he swung at an inside straight ball, but to his misfortune, his line drive arrived, chest high, in the third basemen's glove. He didn't have time to move a foot toward first base. Tiger kicked the dirt with his right foot, sending the brownish colored dust swirling into the air. He said something that didn't sound too good, and refusing to acknowledge Sunny's encouragement, tossed his bat tumbling end-over-end toward our bench area.

Before returning to the field, he strolled to a group of lilac bushes along the first base side of the field and lit a Camel cigarette. He only smoked Camels. Tiger usually tried to hide his smoking addiction, but this was different. *I guess he's trying to put his frustration out of his mind,* I thought.

—w—

Tiger agreed to give it a try at pitching for us. Although he had a good fast ball, he didn't use it that much, as he was sort of experimenting with other pitches. Dipping into his bag of tricks for support, Tiger came up with a knuckle ball that he must have thrown thirty-five percent of the time. The wind was blowing out from home plate toward center field, and the pitches he threw without rotation floated like butterflies as they zigzagged toward the plate.

"WOW, that last pitch darted up and down like a June bug!" I shouted to Tiger as we approached our bench after the final out of the inning.

The score became tied at two-and-two in the bottom of the sixth. Shane had a problem holding on to some knucklers that danced a little too much for him to handle cleanly. Two players reached first base because of the errors, one of which Shane righted himself by throwing the runner out attempting to steal third. This turned into an important highlight of the game because the following batter swung from his heels at a knuckle ball that didn't flutter, and belted it between two outfielders almost into the river.

The game wore on into extra innings when Tiger came to bat in the top of the ninth. Maybe the Sherman pitcher was getting a little too cocky as a result of his success for the day, or on the other hand, perhaps he was getting tired. Whatever the reason, he had frustrated us most of the day using a curve ball almost exclusively.

Positioning himself in the right-hand batters side of the plate, Tiger dug in. He was not tall, but stocky. His arms bulged as he stroked the bat across the plate, measuring the pitchers moment to release the ball. The hour was getting late. "Chore time," Dad called it. I gave a curious look toward the western sky. The sun, which looked like a big orange in front of my eyes, was slowly sinking over the Kickapoo River.

When the first pitch came to Tiger, a fastball high and tight, he could only get a handle on it, following the ball to the backstop. The pitcher then missed away with a curve. Tiger was all business, he never stepped out of the batters' box to relax or display nervous gestures.

The fans and the players had only one thought: *Let's get this over with.*

Tiger fouled off the next delivery, an off-speed pitch. Tiger couldn't hit slow stuff.

When the Sherman hurler delivered his next pitch, Tiger was looking for a curve—and got it! You could have heard the fans roar clear up to Sterling when he hit a hard drive past the shortstop into left field, putting the Orioles ahead.

The score didn't change the rest of the day, and the victors went home.

What Preacher, Dad, and the rest of the fans saw that Sunday was a group of kids beginning to find themselves, who could win against good competition.

"You're not exactly ready to tour the nation yet, like the Blue Birds," Preacher joked to us after the game, "but you're on the right road to the train station."

—⁂—

Whether we needed it or not, spiritual revival set up shop in Sterling for the next Wednesday, Thursday, and Friday evenings. Apparently a few people in the community thought we could use an extra dose of religion. A lot of my teammates went, some out of curiosity, some because they had nothing else to do in the evening, others because their parents brought them, and, who knows, possibly a few who felt a deep down conviction.

The Rev. Kermit Henderson was an evangelist who made his home and headquartered his ministry in Sterling. He and his wife and three children traveled the country preaching a "Jesus Saves" message through the inspiration of the Holy Spirit. Rev. Henderson was a "Holy Roller," but he didn't represent any particular denomination.

From our farm, we could hear his preaching resonating over the microphone from inside the camp meeting tent beside PJ's store. The windows on our house were open and the speaker's voice echoed through our kitchen. Rev. Henderson preached salvation, the evils of liquor, and the sins of the flesh and, sloth to anyone who would listen. I understand his preaching convicted a few people, although it didn't overly affect me. I really didn't understand much of what was said and neither did Sunny.

"What's he mean by all that stuff?" Sunny inquired of Dad and Mother as we were sitting around the kitchen table talking after the evening's milking.

"I don't know as much about the Bible as I should," Mother replied. "I guess he's sort of like a modern-day St. Jude. He changes everything he comes in contact with for the better. He's a good man . . . I hope he doesn't get discouraged. A lot of people couldn't operate a single day without people like him. Have you ever thought of that?"

The good reverend had an attention-getting and a powerful kind of voice that could parallel any of the great black gospel preachers from the Deep South.

"BEWARE!" shouted Henderson in his most convicting tone. I could imagine the evangelist's head quivering and his arms flailing in the air." YOUR SINS—WILL—FIND—YOU—OUT!"

"I hope those drunken half-breed brothers down the road from us get the message," Mother said with sincerity in her voice. She glanced at Sunny and me from where she stood peeling carrots for supper. "If anyone needs preaching, those bottom feeders do; all they know is barnyard religion. They've never seen the inside of a church."

These services were not without their interesting moments. As the evangelist was preaching on hellfire and brimstone from the top of a wagonload of hay, someone crawled under the wagon and set a match to the load. It wasn't long before smoke began to rise through the feet of the Reverend, and the visual effects, accompanying his message, was as startling as a Hollywood movie extravaganza. When fire started to encircle his feet, it got even better. Some believers started to scream, wave their hands high into the air, stomp around in circles, and speak in mumbled language. When they saw Hank crawl from underneath the burning wagon—and run like his britches were on fire—the crowd quieted and dispersed.

Rev. Henderson was a good person who wasn't content in sitting around and watching the grass grow.

He and his family did a lot for the village of Sterling and the surrounding area. During World War II he arranged for soup kitchens in some of the towns where work was scarce and he made special trips to the community to counsel the parents and wives of troops who were killed in action.

But after the camp meeting, life in the Kickapoo, with the exception of a few changed souls, continued as usual. Farmers worked their fields, mothers mended their children's socks and patched their clothes, laborers worked in the orchards, Bruno pushed moonshine—and us kids played baseball.

Chapter 17

CORKY

The summer months for most of the kids in the Kickapoo meant not only baseball—but also hard work on our parents' farm. Rounding up the cows, spraying and milking them, hauling hay into the barn, thrashing grain, hoeing in the garden, cutting thistles, the list goes on . . .

One exception, however, may have been Corky. I'm not sure if I ever knew what Corky's first name was. We always called him by his nickname. The name evolved from the colorful corks he used for fishing. Although he stayed much of the time with a family in Millersville, his blood relatives lived with the Ridge Runners in the back hills. One of his relatives ran a saloon called Corky's, and little Corky got his supply of corks from discarded moonshine bottles.

Corky was a boy with a physical disability from birth that left him much smaller than the rest of us. His misfortune, however, didn't prevent him from doing plenty of things. He was the same age and in the same grade as the rest of our gang. Corky never thought of himself as different—and neither did we. He wasn't a burden or a klutz to anybody. He was a very unique and interesting guy. Corky was one of our gang, our friend and an inspiration to all of us. Although Corky was the team scorekeeper, the players looked to him as being a part of the team, and no one dared razz him when any of us were around. Tim and Lance, two well-built athletes, were Corky's best friends and helped him with everything. They enjoyed it.

"I'd do anything for that guy," I heard Tim say to a group of us at Fat Friley's. If it wasn't for Corky, I wouldn't have the confidence that I do now when things go wrong. If anyone gives him trouble, they'll have to go through me first."

Corky's ability to catch catfish was surpassed by no one. In most cases he acted rather blasé about things, but not in the case of catching catfish. The River People invited Corky to fish with them in the backwaters of the Kickapoo, but he opted out. He might have colored his exploits up a little, but most of the time he was unequaled. I'm not sure if he ever told anyone, but we all surmised it had something to do with the bait he prepared. Corky, somehow, was able to gather the rottenest meat anywhere—and he had the determination to tolerate the *stink* and to handle it long enough to get it on the hook.

Each evening, just before dusk, one could see the bent figure of a boy walking and skipping along with an unusual gait toward one of the backward areas of the Kickapoo. In his right hand, he dragged a gunnysack filled with his special formula of bait. He called it "Ammo."

Corky had everything prepared for the attack. Even the grotesque chunks of meat had large and menacing hooks already implanted in them, ready to be tied to a throw line. Corky would swing the line around and sling it as far out into the swirling stream as his small body would allow. Then he would step back, and view his efforts with satisfaction.

Still standing on the shore, he would then tie the line to a strong stick and pound it into the bank with a nearby rock. The carefully manufactured catfish trap would lurk in the waters throughout the long night waiting for some unsuspecting and hungry monster to grab it.

It never failed. The next morning around five thirty, Corky would make the same journey to see if his efforts had been successful. Nine times out of ten they were, and you'd see him making a return trip with a string of catfish slung over his shoulder.

—⁓—

"I saw this big a fish down by the dam this morning," Corky said, holding his hands about two feet apart to illustrate his point to Dean, Shane and me when we were together in Millersville.

As soon as the fish started biting, everyone with even the least amount of spirit and adventure in his veins headed for his favorite spot along the banks of the Kickapoo. Dean, Shane and I were no different. Word circulated that walleye were active beside the dam, and while most of the folk headed for that area, we had our own secret place behind Shane's house. This was a place Corky had discovered. He led us along some old rusty railroad tracks that still existed from the height of the tobacco harvest days—and pointed out areas where hobo's camped during the depression as they traveled through the area in dreams of greener pastures.

"There's a ghost town north of here," Corky spoke excitedly as we walked along the path. "You can hardly see any part of it. I don't think many people know where it is except me." Corky was a fascinating story-teller; this was one of the reasons we loved him, and today he had a captive audience.

We now had the fishing area all to ourselves, with the exception of a few thousand mosquitoes lurking in the bushes waiting for some fresh meat. After a day of fishing, wading through brambles and skipping around poison ivy, we gathered our cane poles, the corks we used for bobbers, night crawlers, and other gear, along with a catfish, three bluegill, two large carp, six bull-heads, and strolled to Fat Friley's Restaurant.

Friley's had great chocolate sodas, and although they were the only game in town, their menu contained much more to satisfy the local appetite. The young guns, nevertheless, were there for the sodas.

"Know who that dude is?" Dean asked, nodding toward a man sitting by himself at the counter. When we shook our heads Dean continued his gaze, looking serious.

"That's our high school coach." We were sitting in a booth toward the back of the fountain area and had an unobstructed view of the man in question.

"Yeah, guess he's gonna cancel baseball for track, at least that's what I heard Scooter say," Shane was scowling in disgust as he spoke. "If I can make the team I'd rather play baseball . . . wouldn't you, Bones?"

"I understand he doesn't know anything about baseball, just basketball and track," Dean said after swallowing a sip of soda.

Although I couldn't put my finger on it, he appeared older looking and acting than his years. *Maybe because of the war,* I thought.

All of a sudden, the coach jumped, and in a startling manner that got everyone's attention, scurried past us toward the lavatory in the back of the room.

"Wonder what's with him?" I motioned toward his back as he flew by.

"Looks like he's getting ready for a track meet," Shane joked.

The three of us rose, paid our bills, and walked out. Fishing suddenly didn't seem quite so important. *Would he really cancel high school baseball?*

Chapter 18

TROUBLE IN TOMBSTONE

"Better get up," Mother yelled from the bottom of our second-floor stairs. "It's eight o'clock and you've got to eat. We've got to go to church before the game. Hurry up now."

"Be right there," Sunny responded. We'd overslept and the morning milking was already over. I don't know what Sunny was thinking, but the thought of playing Tombstone later today seemed overwhelming as I dressed and hurried down the stairs to breakfast.

Dad was already at the breakfast table, aggressively positioning his fried potatoes, eggs, and bacon on his plate, each in its designated place. There were slightly burnt homemade biscuits, lots of butter, and a full cup of hot coffee with cream and sugar.

I glanced over at him, thinking, *he could eat just about anything*. Some mornings he'd have a lard sandwich, or if we had pancakes for breakfast he'd sprinkle enough layers of sugar on them that it would make my teeth hurt just looking at it. Even when it came time for dinner his eating habits were a bit outside the usual. With chicken, for example, he always preferred the tail. "The part that goes over the fence last," he'd say, "And the neck—both ends of the bird." At the end of a meal, Dad always finished by pouring the balance of coffee that was left in his cup onto a saucer, and then *sluuurrrping* the rest of its contents until finished.

Dad reached for a biscuit and without hesitation asked me if I was ready for the game today. As I answered, I watched in wonder as he smeared butter and jelly on the biscuits and ate every single bite.

"Sorry I burned the biscuits, Jake," Mother said in an apologetic manner.

"That's okay . . . I kinda' like 'em that way."

"You like biscuits burned?" I asked him.

Dad grasped my small hand in his rough paw. "Your Mother has already put in a hard day of work this morning and she's tired—a few burnt biscuits never hurt anyone."

After Dad had everything arranged perfectly on his plate, he seemed to relax. He was reaching for his fork when Mother interrupted with a firm, "Let's pray!"

Dad nodded and bowed his head, Sunny and I respectfully followed suit.

We finished the prayer by crossing ourselves, "In the name of the Father, and of the Son, and of the Holy Spirit . . . Amen."

———∿———

After eating, Mother washed the dishes and packed the usual basket of food for the ball game. After a few outside chores, Dad came back inside and he and Mother hurriedly dressed. Dad always wore a suit and tie to church, that was the only place I ever saw him dress in such clothing. I'm sure it was out of respect. Before Mass, Mother lit a candle for Sunny and me and arranged the flowers before the grotto, hoping to bring us good fortune.

Tombstone was our next opponent. Located in a rural area in southwestern Wisconsin, it was about an hour drive from Sterling. There were no paved roads in or around this town, it was more than a piece off the beaten path.

"Isn't but one way to get there, by carrier pigeon," Preacher used to say. "I wonder what they expect a man to do, sprout a pair of wings?"

I remember Dale saying something similar. "Someone told me one time that the best way to get to Tombstone is to go straight to nowhere and turn right."

At one time Tombstone was home to the Dory railroad and a stock yard. Much damage was done to the town in a great flood during the early part of the town's history.

As we drove into town I could see a gas station with one pump, a grocery store, a tavern with a large Blatz beer sign hanging from a pole beside the outhouse, a small church with colorful stained glass windows, and a baseball field that would make most minor league teams proud. Their coach didn't need to prime the pump for the players to get excited to play; baseball was about the only entertainment around. They also had players from the Prairie du Chien High School team.

Although the people in Tombstone were hard working, friendly people, who took the sport of base-ball and their team seriously—this game was trouble from the start.

The first batter for our team, Jerky, swung at an eye-high pitch, hit a blooper down the left field line, and spiked their shortstop while sliding into second base. Jerky rose from the event, his teeth and eyes flashing, and offered no share of sympathy. He was not a happy camper to begin with—the day before he'd had a boil lanced on his butt, and it was still in the pro-cess of healing. This didn't ease his naturally combat-ive nature. The slide into second only made matters worse. Whether the spike was deliberate or not, I don't know. Nevertheless, I guess some of the Tombstone fans thought it was intentional, because when they saw their player limping and blood oozing through his sock, they started yelling—and it seemed as though everyone wanted a piece of the action.

I heard shouted threats at Preacher, and it wasn't long before I lost my concentration completely. Soon a fight broke out in the stands between some of the spectators—and a mob-like atmosphere started to develop. It was a good thing I wasn't the next one up to bat, because I doubt I could have hit the ball. As it was, Shane, who was the next batter, didn't get a chance to hit either, as he was *whacked* with the next pitch in the middle of his back between the shoulder blades. Shane, displaying his wild side, turned toward their catcher and was about to finish it if it were not for Dean rushing to the plate and pulling his friend away by the back of his jersey. Suddenly, fans from our side were the ones shouting.

Things weren't looking good on the field or in the stands.

In the last half of the inning Smithy started pitching, but things got out of hand almost immediately. To return the honor paid to Shane in the top of the first, Preacher flashed the "brush back" sign to Smithy. It wasn't Preacher's intent to land one on the noggin of the first kid that came to the plate, but to get it in on the fists, just to get his attention and the attention of the manager of the other team. However, Smithy got it a bit too tight—he struck the kid in the head with a fastball that sounded similar to my ball glove slapping against our bench. My stomach clenched, and I broke out in a cold sweat. We didn't have helmets like the football players wore. Before the injured player hit the ground, all heck broke loose.

"He didn't mean to do it," Sunny yelled from his position at first base. That's as close as anyone else on our team would offer as an apology. Shane held his ground and Jerky rushed in from his position in right field. In a few minutes, the EMS from Boscobel arrived, and the paramedics rushed in to see how badly the boy was hurt. Thankfully he didn't need to go to a hospital, because there was none in the area. However, his playing time for the day was over.

Preacher was not good at things confrontational or ordering people around, so what kept the trouble from spilling onto the field was the umpire for the game, Brad Harding. Brad was the catcher for the Millersville city team, the sheriff of Crawford County, and a man so strong he could lift the front end of a Ford tractor off the ground.

Brad called time, took off his mask, and strolled to the opposing team's bench. He pulled a handkerchief out of a back pocket and dried his brow. Whenever Brad got excited, he sweated profusely.

"Don't back talk to me mister or I'll have your head on a platter. I'll throw both you and your pitcher out of the game!" His voice carried clear out to the pitcher's mound where most of the team had congregated. I could hear the fire in his tone and see his mannerisms. Brad trotted out to the pitcher's mound where Smithy was standing with a tentative expression on his face.

"Don't worry kid," Brad said with a grim sort of smile. "When this thing's over, if any of them come after you, I'll take matters into my own hands and make sure you get out of here okay."

"Save that loud mouth catcher over there with the big red nose for me," Shane blared. "He's mine."

"Oh, no you don't!" Brad pointed his finger at Shane's nose, looked sternly into his eyes, and didn't say another word to him. He moved toward Preacher, who had also approached the mound.

"Listen, guys, I think it might be a good idea to let someone else pitch and put Smithy in the outfield for the rest of the game. Things could get out of hand here, very easily. This is a tight community, and I don't want them to try to get some type of revenge. Know what I mean?"

"I think that's a no-brainer," Preacher mumbled under his breath.

Smithy didn't say anything other than to hand the ball to Preacher. His face was a little pale as he trotted out to his position in the outfield. Preacher placed the ball in my glove.

"It's all yours, kid. Take no prisoners."

"I don't know if I'm up to this," I said to Preacher with a cautious look on my face. I swallowed hard, my face as pale as Smithy's.

The game was close and hard fought by both teams. In the last half of the seventh inning, Tombstone had the tying run on first with one out. Their next batter hit a sharp bounder to Dean at short, who stepped on second ahead of the sliding runner trying to take Dean out of the play, and threw to first just in the nick of time to complete the double play. Dean was lucky to escape without being spiked.

"You're out!" Brad yelled and signaled the end of the game.

Immediately, fans from both sides ran on to the field, and strong language resonated throughout the area. It wasn't long however, until the Tombstone police showed up, and shortly after, two deputies from the Grant County Sheriff's Department.

Walking to the car, we still kept a wary eye out for trouble . . .

"What happened out there was nobody's fault," Dad said. "They were just defending their team, the same as we would have done. These things shouldn't happen."

"Preacher's over there talking and shaking hands with the other coach." I replied. "Guess things are okay."

Despite the tired ache all the way down to my bones, I walked a bit straighter and finally felt like a real ball player.

—⚬—

The next game was at Ferryville, on a ball diamond located along the Mississippi River. A number of their players played on the Viroqua High School team. There was no advance warning for the exit off the main road to the park; it was down a steep slope that was little more than an alley.

Our car managed to maneuver to the parking area alongside the ball field. As soon as I hopped out, I noticed a cloudy like fog sweeping across the playing field.

"What's that?" I yelled to Jerky who was returning from some bushes after watering his horse.

"May flies . . . there's million's of 'em."

The game turned out to be a work in futility because it was May and the mayflies were swarming everywhere. Some of the local towns used snowplows to push them off the streets, they were that plentiful.

These bugs didn't hurt anyone. They were just a nuisance, to say the least.

"They won't bite," Jerky said. "There're just pains in the butt."

The flies had long transparent wings and when they fell in the river, the fish had a banquet. I swatted at them when I was playing right field. Peering up into a sea of bugs while trying to catch a high fly was no small task. And when I batted, it became very irritating with the distraction right in front of my face.

An exciting part of the game was when Chris hit for Dean, who unexpectedly had to go home early. She hit one solidly to center—driving in the winning run.

"That's the way to do it, Chris," one of the women yelled from the side of the field. The rest of the gals hooted and gave each other high fives and hugs.

Although we won, the flies were the real winners.

Chapter 19

ROMANCE

"ORIOLES PLAY PORT ARTHUR THIS WEEKEND AT STERLING FIELD!" This was a notice that was circulated to many of the businesses in the area. "Come out and support the Kickapoo Kids."

Local players were beginning to attract attention, and people searched details from the Crawford County Gazette. For as little as ten cents a week, ink from the printed page brought something to be excited about in this rural area of the state.

"Bring the family and enjoy a picnic at the beautiful ball park," the paper said. "And afterwards take in the ballgame. It will be well worth your time."

Due to the fact that Preacher had relatives who lived in Lancaster, he had connections with some of the leaders of the Junior American Legion team.

Therefore, he was able to schedule an exhibition or practice game with their team, and even on our home turf. These kids were a year older than most of us. Nevertheless, we welcomed the challenge to play a team from a bigger town.

Although our batting average for the first three innings was lower than the number of people in attendance, the Orioles gradually rose to the occasion. Regardless of the fact that we lost I guess things didn't turn out that badly. The game with the Legion team was nine innings, which was two more than our team was used to playing. Our attack produced one run in the fourth, sixth, and eighth innings on the Legion pitcher, who, by the way, was a junior in high school.

"You got a good bunch of guys," coach Ryan, of their Legion team said to Preacher as we were packing things together after the game—"a few years from now and they'll be kickin' some of the big boys' butts."

If there were Little League teams in Wisconsin during this time, we surely didn't know about them. Our world was the Kickapoo, and everything outside of that area was unknown territory. But that game against the older Legion team propelled us to a new level of confidence.

—◦◦◦—

The following Sunday we were scheduled to play Rolling Ground at our home field, which was still wet-to-damp in spots from two days of rain. The forenoon of the game—Dad, Preacher, Dale, and some of the other parents of the players spread hay and straw on the infield and set it afire in order to dry the area. The ground was like the lowlands next to the Kickapoo after the floodwaters had subsided. Preacher nervously paced the foul lines, glancing to the skies from time to time. He just wanted the game to begin. Fortunately, the sun came out after lunch, and between the earlier burning and the sun we were able to get the game in.

In the first inning their pitcher tried to throw a fastball past Sunny, who hit a line drive to right that bounded off the snow fence, driving in Jerky and Ove with the first two runs of the game. Sunny rolled around to third while the fielder was retrieving the ball. Shane did a good job catching. Three times a runner tried to steal second base, but he gunned them down. Lucky for us, each time Tim or Lance followed with hits that would have tightened the score. As Milley removed the number cards off the scoreboard after the game, the score read, Home six. Away one.

The guys and I cornered our coach after the game.

"Hey Preacher," I said. "When are you going to get us a game with a team from Viroqua, Prairie or Boscobel?"

Many of us had scrimmaged with the Millersville High School baseball players from time-to-time, and we had also played against high school players from other schools in the area, including some from larger schools. In most cases, we either held our own or were better players then them.

"You'll get your chance against those city guys," replied Preacher with a grin on his face. He probably had already been thinking along those lines.

"It's fun to play against teams like that," I said. "They all have new uniforms."

"They put their pants on one leg at a time—the same as we do," Shane replied.

"We could make that Millersville High School team today, I *know* it," Dean said with a decisive nod.

Shane agreed.

The parents could see a change in our attitudes.

"Those kids of ours are improving, can't you just see it?" I overheard Mother say to Milley and some of the other ladies watching the game.

—◦—

We were getting older and advancing into our teenage years of manhood. On Monday evenings, the young guys gathered at a parking space beside PJ's Grocery in Sterling to watch free outdoor movies. Other nights of the week we went to Seneca or Fairview for the same fun. From our farm I could hear the sound of the movie at Sterling, and Sunny and I were filled with excitement to get there and be involved in the fun. People turned out from the whole area, even if the movies were all westerns. It seemed that Gene Autry and Roy Rodgers appeared everywhere, riding their horses and singing and playing a guitar at the same time.

"Watch out from behind dem dar rocks!" Davy, an odd man who farmed about a mile outside of Sterling yelled as he jumped up in anticipation of an ambush of his hero.

Of course, some minor, and not-so-minor, romances developed on these hot summer nights. On this particular evening, by the time the cartoons started, the temperature clung to the low eighties. I didn't know much about the opposite sex, dating, and the like, although not for any lack of interest. All the guys in the know, however, were after the Elmendorf sisters, who had a reputation for sharing more than a bag of popcorn.

For some reason that evening, I got involved in unfamiliar territory.

Scott was a normal teenage boy, the same age as I, and one who didn't get in trouble. Because of this, his dad trusted him to drive his car at night.

Kurt was another story. He was in the same grade as Scott and I, but attended another school. Kurt had a wild side about him. He got in all manner of scrapes. I guess he would fit the description of a "greaser," because he slicked his black hair with Wild Root Cream Oil and combed it back in a ducktail like the wings of a duck. He wore a black leather jacket, tight blue jeans, motorcycle boots, and a loose shirt that he left partially unbuttoned with the collar turned up.

Aside from all this baggage there was something about the guy that I liked; I think he just needed a little more guidance. His family were poor folk. His dad took whatever jobs he could find and was currently working at the slaughter house in Prairie du Chien. Kurt worked as a hired hand during the summer months for some of the farmers in the area. He was a naturally gifted left-handed hitter who played for another town. This gave him some measure of respect in my eyes.

On this particular evening, after the movie, Kurt, Scott, and I hooked up with three of the famous Elmendorf sisters.

"Come on Bones," Scott said as he motioned me over with a sweep of his left arm, his index finger pointing straight at my chest so I had no doubt he was talking to me. "Hop in, we'll drive to Millersville and back with the girls."

I glanced at the waiting girls leaning against Scott's car and swallowed hard. The look in their eyes alone spoke of trouble, not to mention what would happen to me if Dad found out. Still, Scott was waiting on my answer, and he was a good guy. *Maybe there wouldn't be any harm in that short of a trip.*

"You'll drive me home then?"

"Yeah, we'll only be gone about a half hour or so."

As soon as I entered the old Model A car, I saw Kurt inside and knew I shouldn't be doing this. But by then it was already too late to change my mind.

"What are you doing?" Scott asked as Kurt opened the car door.

"Just ah minute," Kurt kind of slurred his words, "I gut's ta shake it off before we go."

Kurt climbed out of the back seat, and after urinating he wedged his way back in the car holding tightly to the door handle.

"Kathy, disss isss Bones," Kurt said by way of introduction, motioning to the pretty blonde with devilment in the depths of her blue eyes. She giggled and whispered something to her sisters.

Kathy was sitting there waiting for me like a spider lingering for a feast. Kathy was last year's queen of the Grant County Cow Chip Throwing and Tobacco Spitting Contest held annually in Tombstone. She attended a different high school than we did and lived with her "pappy," as she noted to us, among the River People.

Nevertheless, my heart jumped! Up close she was even prettier than I'd expected.

"Hi Bones," Kathy said as she extended her hand to greet me with a warm smile. "Come sit beside me." She snuggled to the middle of the back seat and patted the bottom of the cushion to her left.

The smell of perfume was in the air—and I was at once both mesmerized and scared to death. With me she had a captive audience. I couldn't think of a single thing to say. *Now what do I do?* I had already forgotten her name. But looking at her, I was positive I was in love, or something like that.

"Don't you just *looove* that song, Bones," Kathy tenderly whispered in my right ear, referring to the romantic ballad "My Happiness," which was softly flowing from the car radio. "Look at me," she said, turning my face toward her with a soft hand. "You know, Bones, you're sure a good-looking guy, bet you've broken a lot of girls hearts, haven't you?" She snuggled even closer. "A lot of girls have such bad taste when it comes to men, but I've got what I want."

Oh boy, I thought, *I lucked out*. Then I remembered the advice Shane gave me for when a romantic opportunity presented itself. "Even though they all want to be kissed, don't kiss 'em right away, bait 'em on a little. They'll want you all the more, that's the angle to use. Talk to 'em, tell 'em you know all about kissin' and that stuff, but when in doubt, go for it, what do you got to loose anyway?"

A few minutes down a winding back road, Scott turned his head to say something to Kurt in the back seat. In that instant he drove the car over a bank, sending us tumbling into a field. All of us were thrown out through the cloth top. I struggled to my feet, amazed to see no one had so much as a scratch on them. *It's like descending into a black hole,* I thought.

So ended my first romantic experience, rather ingloriously I might add.

Of course, this put an end to Scott's driving for a while, and I gained a lecture when I got home. I remained just as mystified about the opposite sex as I'd been before I'd even got into that car. All in all—it was probably easier to concentrate on baseball.

Chapter 20

DUEL AT SUNDOWN

F all was quickly approaching, and most of us farm boys began preparing for school. We all wanted to end our baseball schedule on a positive note.

Before the Orioles ended their season, Preacher kept his promise to pit us against more combative competition. We played against older Legion teams from Boscobel and Viroqua. Although Boscobel beat us by a close margin, we learned from the experience and set our sights on our next opponent, Viroqua.

By the time the Orioles line-up got around to their third at-bats, the stocky Viroqua pitcher was doing a good job of holding us to only two runs. The big right-hander worked every batter like Sal Maglie of the Dodgers, up and in, low and away. At the same time, his teammates were scoring three. Furthermore, luck didn't seem to be with us.

When our first batter, Jerky, stood in to take a rip, sure enough, he got a pitch in on the hands, a ball he could only catch on the thin handle part of his bat. He dribbled it down the third base line—but this time luck was with us. The third baseman was playing deep, and couldn't reach the ball in time to make the play at first. *Maybe things are changing.*

Our next hitter, Ove, took a high heater on his left elbow, tossed the bat away, and trotted to first.

I stepped to the plate for another shot, and I got a good one! After starting off with his usual up-and-in bullet, I looked for a curve out and over the platter. The Viroqua pitcher twirled in a sidearm curveball that sat for a split second on the outside corner, just long enough for me to cream it. *Crack!* The line drive instantly disappeared into the glove of the shortstop. What further evidence did anyone need? The evil eye was upon us—we were snake bit!

Shane bounced the first pitch he looked at back to the mound. The big guy scooped up the dribbler and, after looking Jerky back to second, threw Shane out at first. When Shane, in a moment temper, slung his bat against the backstop in apparent disgust, the umpire called time and cautioned Preacher. Dean, knowing Shane better than anyone, put his hand on Shane's shoulder and told him to relax, that it was only a game, but Jerky backed Shane up . . .

"You'll get the big dummy next time," Jerky countered, his combativeness obvious.

After Dean ducked out of the way from a high inside tight one, he waved at a curve that broke away, low and off the outside corner. The count leveled at one and one. Next, he took a BB up and inside, just under his chin. The count was two and one.

At that point, the Viroqua hurler took a risk. If he could sneak in another fastball while Dean was looking for the curve, then he'd have Dean two and two, with two chances after that to make him chase the curve. So the big kid threw a near-perfect fastball, just under the armpits, over the inside black of the corner. Just as he hoped, it froze Dean for an instant—but an instant wasn't long enough. Dean's Louisville Slugger smacked the ball right before it struck the Viroqua catcher's mitt. The ball shot on a line to the left center field gap, where the outfielders converged to cut it off, but they were too late. The ball kicked off the centerfielder's glove and rolled to the fence. Dean could trot to third base. Both runners scored.

That was all we needed for a four-to-three win.

—⁓—

PJ continued to be an inspiration to us, and when a playoff for the championship of the Western Wisconsin

Semi-professional Baseball League came up the entire community was boiling over with excitement. In an area dominated by farming, only the fall sale of a bumper tobacco crop exceeded the anticipation for this league championship game. It was also "I am an American Day."

PJ was scheduled to pitch for Soldiers Grove, the home team, against Clancy for La Crosse who also pitched for the Boston Red Sox. In one of his outings he outpitched Bob Feller of the Cleveland Indians in Fenway Park.

Clancy came from Boscobel, a town south of Millersville, but hired out to the highest bidder when the Major League season was over. This time it was to the La Crosse Indians.

It was little wonder baseball enthusiasts couldn't wait for the confrontation to take place. These two exceptional pitchers had ice water in their veins, and they had met through the years at different places with more or less of a standoff between them.

This duel took place on a neutral field in Viroqua, under the lights at night, after the rural community and the blue-collar crowd finished work for the day. Conditions for the game were not the best; some areas of the outfield lacked the proper lighting to prevent shadows from forming.

PJ was our hero, and our close-knit community was like family to him. We were there to root him on.

Parking anywhere close was almost impossible. Dad finally decided to take a chance and parked in the bank parking lot located about four hundred feet away from the field. A sign said "BANK PARKING ONLY. Violators will be towed away at their own expense." I looked at Dad more than a bit uncertainly as we walked away from the car.

As we approached the field, I looked around to see who was there. There were no bleachers. The banks around the field in the Viroqua ballpark provided the seating, and those were already lined shoulder-to-shoulder with thousands of onlookers. Kids in their teens flirted and danced back of the concession stand to polka music provided by a local band, and young boys played catch with their dads down the foul lines.

Both teams were loaded to the hilt with the best the local area could muster and with imported stars from college and professional teams. The Grove team even had three Afro-American players from a southern Negro baseball league who referred to what they were involved with as "White Folks Ball." La Crosse had some major league players that were temporarily in the service and stationed at the military base nearby at Camp Mc Coy. One was an Afro-American player from the New York Yankees who had hit a pitch from PJ over a church in a previous encounter.

The professionals went about business differently than most of the local players. During batting practice, each hitter started off with a bunt, followed by a hit to right, one to center, and one to left. Their final swing was wherever they preferred and they swung for the fences.

This, of course, was the atmosphere Bruno relished—side bets were everywhere. Bruno's henchmen could be seen working the crowd of onlookers. Hank was one of them. *I thought he would end up working for Bruno.* I noticed a few members of the local police slipping cash to Bruno's workers after what I surmised were hurried discussions regarding odds. Bets could be made on almost anything, from who would win, to the final score, to what would happen in the next inning.

"How much money you got, Bones?" Shane asked, hurrying to get enough funds together to make a wager.

I shuffled through my pockets and came up with coins totaling one dollar and sixty-seven cents. "Sunny, Ove, Tim, Lance, what you got?"

"Dean, help me with this," Shane said, holding out his hand to collect our money.

"What you doin,' Shane?" Dean asked, pulling his pockets inside out.

"We're putting our money on PJ."

In moments Shane had our collection in hand and took off through the crowd.

Bruno's crew was not the only group taking advantage of the setting. Members of Rev. Henderson's ministry were out in force—passing out tracts and witnessing to anyone who would give them an ear.

"Don't give your money to those no-good hypocrites," one shepherd barked. "A DOG WILL RETURN TO HIS OWN VOMIT!" He held a worn black Bible high in the air.

"What does he mean by that?" one of our group of kids said to another. Most of us shook our heads.

"That's true though," Tim piped up. "I've seen our coon hound do that a lot of times after he threw up from eating something dead down by the manure pile."

"Well . . . I'll tell you what. I wish I hadn't given my money to Shane now," I said as I leaned toward Sunny and Ove.

"Me too," Ove agreed.

"Don't trouble yourself with it," Sunny shrugged and went back to watching the players warming up on the field.

I noticed Bruno's gang didn't attempt to strong-arm Henderson's shepherds—I doubt it would have done any good if they had tried. Besides, I think all of his crew, Bruno included—were somehow afraid of the forcefully sincere evangelist.

Everyone knew what Clancy was expected to do against a lesser competition, but when PJ was "on" he was almost unhittable. He had a rising overhand fastball in the mid-to-upper nineties, a curve that could be accurately described as "falling off the table," and a personality that never seemed to acknowledge any kind of pressure.

Like fighters in a boxing ring—these two competitors went at each other with a vengeance, not willing to give in to defeat. Neither one knew how to lose well, and throughout their careers—they seldom did.

Unless a starting pitcher was doing poorly, teams seldom used relief pitchers, and this championship game was no different. In the top of the eleventh inning, the Indians pushed across a run as a result of an error, a stolen base, and a double down the right field line. By that time, I think PJ was getting a little tired. Clancy, possibly being more conditioned, set down the Grove team quite consistently.

In the home half of the eleventh, he made the first of two mistakes for the La Crosse team that cost him dearly; he walked the first hitter he faced on four straight balls. Bruno came off the bench like a wild man, waving his arms and yelling words of encouragement (that sounded more like orders) to PJ as the tall warrior casually strolled to the plate.

"Earn your pay, tall man!" he shouted, hands cupped around his mouth.

PJ didn't waste any time doing just that. Clancy's first pitch was a fastball, six inches off the inside corner of the plate. PJ turned on it and sent a missile into the atmosphere—clearing a grove of colorful oak leafed trees in left-center field and finally landing high up on the side of the hill next to a group of houses.

Although I was excited that PJ won, and that we didn't lose our money, I somehow didn't feel proud that I had placed the bet.

"Don't look at me as though I picked your pocket," Shane said. *That made me feel worse.*

—m—

After Dad, Sunny and I dropped off the milk at the cheese factory the next morning, we anxiously hurried to PJ's store to talk about the game. Although it was seven thirty, PJ was there as usual, stocking the shelves, ringing the cash register, and visiting with his friends and admirers.

"How do you feel this morning?" Dad asked PJ.

PJ had probably been asked that question a dozen times before the same morning, but his answer was quick and honest.

"What do you think?"

"You aren't taking this too well, are you?" Dad said, laughing as he patted PJ on the back.

"I'll get better as soon as these bones loosen up a little." He gave a weary grin. "Guess I'm not as young as I used to be. Old men can deceive themselves for a while, but when I look at myself in the mirror when shaving, I still think I've got a few games left in me before I take off my jock strap. One of these days some of those fastballs are going to start getting by me; I'll know it's time then."

He'd just pitched eleven innings, ten of which were scoreless, and he was still not willing to give up on himself.

Boy, that's the way I want to be, I thought as we drove home.

Chapter 21

MAKING THE TEAM

The fall of `49 issued in the beginning of high school in Millersville for Enoch, Shane, Dean, Tim, Lance, Stan and me. There had been rumors circulating for months that baseball was on shallow ground with our coach. The rumors played out to be much more than that—they became fact. Track was the sport the coach arranged for the athletes to be involved in during the fall, and basketball the following winter. The town kids participated in basketball but evening and winter chores prevented most of the rural boys from participating.

—⚬—

In the spring of `50 each day was like the one before. After study hour at 3 p.m., I made a beeline for the athletic locker room, looking for information regarding baseball tryouts. *There's nothing around anywhere,* I thought. Enoch, Dean, Shane and Tiger were suiting up each day and heading to the field. After the third day, I saw Tiger in the hall.

"How do I get on the team?" I asked my part-time Orioles teammate.

"Didn't he ask you?" Tiger replied.

"No!"

"Huh . . . that's strange . . . guessing he only invites the basketball team."

"No tryouts . . . ?"

"Guess not old buddy, talk to the dude if you get a chance—you guy's got a right to be ticked!"

Tiger was right. The same players that played basketball in the winter, Coach asked to play baseball in the spring.

On Friday of the following week, the school scheduled an intramural game between kids that wanted to participate. My Oriole teammates and I joined in. After watching me pitch, Coach asked that I join the varsity. The rest of Preacher's kids and the farm kids from the other teams in the Oriole's league were left stranded.

"I can't believe this," I heard Tim say to Lance.

"I'm sorry," Dean tried to comfort his buddy's emotions. "There's nothing I can do."

Another boy, Rob, was not available to participate in the make-up game that day. Rob was a chubby kid that the coach overlooked to play baseball because he, like me, did not go out for basketball. He was only about five-foot-seven inches tall (short for the sport), and possibly because of his lack of height, did not have an interest in playing basketball. But Rob loved baseball, and because of his love for the sport, and due to the fact that there was no other means available for him to be close to the game—he volunteered to be the team bat boy.

At baseball practice, Rob served as a warm-up catcher for the pitchers and a fly-chaser for the hitters. Although officially listed as being on the team, I didn't fare much better. Many days during recess Rob and I practiced pitching and catching on the outfield grass just outside the school agriculture building. It was very noticeable to me that he had unusual talent. Rob served as a great target—handled the catcher's mitt with ease—and had a rifle for an arm. He often told me his dream was to play professional baseball someday. I sympathized with him because we shared the same vision. We became close friends.

—⁊⁊⁊—

The Millersville High School baseball team was undefeated during our regular schedule and moved through to the district tournament. Victory there would lead to a sectional playoff to advance to the state tournament. The opposition was Prairie du Chien, a much larger opponent we were familiar playing against. Many of their players had played with the Tombstone team against the Orioles during the summer.

Everything was looking great, except for one thing . . .

"Where's Coach?" The cry went out among players and parents alike. It was the day of the big game and Coach was nowhere to be found.

How are we going to play without a coach?

The team waited . . . and waited . . . After a time Tiger took responsibility.

"I don't have any spikes," one of our players yelled.

"Coach was supposed to bring our gear," a player added with a gesture of his head in disgust.

"Borrow what you need from one of the teams that will play in the second qualifying game," Tiger ordered.

This game was one of our easier ones; we beat them ten to nothing. Millersville then rolled through two other school teams, Wauzeka and Seneca. I recognized many of their players that played against the Orioles during the summer months.

But our next opponent was La Farge—a team that had been our greatest obstacle in advancing to the state tournament.

When the game started, it quickly became evident that this would be a close one to the end. Although there was tight pitching on both sides, at the end of the day we were the victors.

—m—

The high school halls, classrooms, and even the study hall were ablaze with chatter and excitement over the tournament news. The school newspaper, Orange and Black, carried the stories. I glanced around the schoolyard as students gathered to discuss the possibilities of the first game. Of course, the seniors and starters on the team were the group most admired for their achievement. I was sort of riding on their coattails when it came to the popularity of the team. *I'd like to be in their place,* I thought.

La Crosse Logan was our opposition in the sectional tournament. As famous as the Green Bay Packers were to professional football, La Crosse was to high school baseball. A number of players graduated out of their program into the pros.

We didn't have to wait for Coach to show up for this game; he traveled with the team on the bus. A tornado warning for the western part of Wisconsin, however, delayed the game for three hours. Because of the late start and extremely overcast conditions, we played the game under the lights.

Some fans from the La Crosse area, didn't have the greatest respect for a bunch of Kickapoo kids. In fact, they were downright arrogant. When the group found out a bunch of farm boys from a hick town would be their first opponent, their laughter could be heard over one hundred miles away to the state tournament city of Menasha. From the start of the game they ridiculed us and attempted to strip us of our dignity.

"Apple pickers," a man dressed in a business suit mocked.

They even heaped ribbing against little Corky for his haircut. Corky was sitting on a corner of the bench in our dugout chewing on a hot dog. "Where'd you get your ears lowered?" someone hollered toward Corky.

A couple of days before the tournament, Corky had gone to Happy's Barber Shop in Grove, where he got scalped. Old man Happy couldn't see too well in his older days, and anyone that went to him for a cut got shaved from the middle of the head down to their ears.

"You're a communist, isn't that what your mama calls you?" Corky yelled back to the man. "Sen. McCarthy outta investigate ya."

The fans who represented Logan, however, were very respectful, as was the team. They were well disciplined. There was none of the trash talking out of them like we heard from some of the other kids from large schools. The load mouth was an embarrassment.

Mark Harper, our senior left-handed pitcher, hurled for us. Mark was an outstanding pitcher who, after three years of playing with mediocre teams, finally had an opportunity to showcase his talents. He illustrated a big overhand curve and did a great job of holding Logan to only one run. Dick Mickelson—a tall left-handed senior hitter in our lineup—who won our conference batting title, got two clutch hits. The little team from the Kickapoo won three to one.

This was the *first* time in the history of Millersville High School that their baseball team advanced to the state tournament.

When the team arrived home on the bus, we learned a tornado had struck about fifteen miles northwest of Millersville, causing a great deal of damage. There were reports that farm implements from Iowa were found in the upper limbs of big trees, apparently carried across the Mississippi River and dumped on the Wisconsin side.

"The skies opened up and there was an electrical storm like I've never seen before," Mother said as we were eating breakfast the next morning. "I'm telling you that lightning cracked the sky from top to bottom, and the ground just shook with those crashes of thunder. It could have been us. Count your blessings. We didn't get it as bad as some of the other poor folk up north."

—⚡—

Menasha was the site of the annual state tournament. The town of about fifteen thousand people was located in northeastern Wisconsin, about a two-hour drive north of Madison. Menasha was the home to a historic Chicago White Sox minor league ballpark. Paper mills, lakes, Holstein dairy cattle, and a combination of Dutch, Polish and German people populated the area.

Fort Atkinson, a much larger school east of Madison, was our opposition. They had a pitcher who signed a contract to play professional baseball with one of the major league teams. Because of this, the team received a great deal of press.

We lost!

"Snake eyes, we win!" The crowd from the opposing team chanted from the sixth inning on. "Kind of embarrassing," I mumbled to myself.

Millersville had a record of eight and one for the spring.

—⚡—

Although we were kids, without a so-called worry in the world, the Kickapoo Valley and our parents were unable to shelter us from the realities of life that were unrelated to baseball.

This was the age of the atom and the new thing for home construction was bomb shelters. But other than an atomic attack—America's worst fear was polio. Summer was the worst because people generally congregated together at fairs, swimming pools and social gatherings. This year, people were directed to stay away from such gatherings. Although most everyone heeded the caution, not everyone escaped.

Rose Marie, a daughter of the Arneson family, a neighbor of ours, and an older classmate, cheerleader, and one of two daughters who played in the school band died of polio that summer. Not that she died directly from the polio, it never directly killed anybody. The disease affected her lungs and the rest of the body. It came with muscle weakness accompanied by pain, and fever. There were no vaccinations for polio, so steamed wool blankets were used to help with the discomfort.

The funeral took place at St. Mary's Catholic Church in Millersville, and, regardless of the danger of contracting the disease, an overflow crowd attended, including Pastor Johnson from the Sterling Lutheran Church and our entire baseball team. We sat side by side in the third row behind her family. Our hearts were heavy. I think, perhaps Enoch took it somewhat harder than the rest of us because his younger sister had lost her life to a comparable disease a few years earlier.

Our community was going through some tough times. Only a few weeks earlier, word was received that the young son of another family and neighbor of ours, had finally died from injuries he sustained just before war with the Japanese ended in the Pacific. The young man had been institutionally bound for two years in a V.A. facility overseas. Like many of the other "living dead" soldiers of the war, this young man had succumbed to a lobotomy as a last resort to remove the madness of memory.

It seemed that Fr. Murphy spoke mostly to the young people in the audience, and particularly to our team, sense he knew us so well. I noticed his eyes dart occasionally to his best friend Pastor Johnson for, I suspect, an affirmative nod. My eyes watered and, although they tried to hide it, I noticed my teammates experiencing a similar experience.

"A young member of our community has been taken from us," Fr. Murphy spoke with emotion in his voice. "Not by the horror of war, as we experienced recently, or by a tragic accident, as happened by the Sterling school a few years ago, or by any fault of her own, or that of her family. These things we do not understand, but we somehow know that it must be part of His divine plan for her, and the lives she touched during the brief time we had to enjoy her.

Everyone in the church listened intently . . . hanging on every word that came out of the shepherd's mouth.

"Take comfort in what God's word says," the priest said as he opened his Bible to John14:2-3. "In my Father's house there are many mansions, if it were not so I would have told you. I go to prepare a place for you. And if I go and prepare a place for you, I will come again, and receive you unto myself; that where I am, there ye may be also."

He continued . . .

"I know some of you young people are asking— why? I cannot answer that. It somehow must be part of God's will. If Rose Marie received no care at all, and if it were God's will that she live—she would be alive today. On the other hand, if she received the best treatment known to medicine, and if it is God's will that she not recover—she will not. As Christians we must hold on to that truth and not question God's sovereignty. Some day we will know the answers to all of these mysteries. Every life is created by Him . . . and each has a purpose . . . and so it is with Rose Marie."

FR. Murphy closed his Bible, paused for a moment, and turned his attention to the adult members of the service . . .

"The passing of Rose Marie should remind each us of how fragile life is. But if we know the pilot, when we ride in that great airplane, as all of us will someday, we'll always drink wine."

Most of us aged a dozen months in the last few minutes of his message.

"We aughta say something," I spoke to Enoch in a low tone.

"I guess they need to be alone," Enoch replied, "for the hurt to heal." *He ought to know.*

Our community was numbed for a period of time, but recovered—we had to!

Although I didn't see much of the family of Rose Marie around town for awhile, I often thought about them.

Chapter 22

REALITY AND HOPE

I felt excited at the start of school in the fall of 1950 because track was dropped from the conference in favor of baseball. Our coach had no choice but to allow baseball again to be a part of our fall session.

Baseball was the popular sport throughout rural Wisconsin, and especially so in the Kickapoo valley. While kids from the inner cities were shooting hoops and playing makeup basketball games on outside cement courts, rural boys played baseball. There was not a lot of interest in professional football to divert our attention. The Green Bay Packers were not playing well, posting a losing record most every year.

By this time, we knew the important fundamentals needed to play the game at a high level. As a result of playing on the city team during the summer months, the seniors on the baseball team were a seasoned group of athletes. Additionally, the coach inherited a strong sophomore class that was well trained—and knew much more about the sport of baseball than their coach. This would be a unique circumstance where the student taught the teacher! All in all, the Millersville High School baseball team was in a position to go places and continue their winning ways of the year before.

I was shocked, nevertheless, when Coach sat down to plan for his team, he did *exactly* the same as he did in previous years. I was on the team—but the opportunity to participate in games was denied me because he thought the better athletes would go out for basketball. The advice he received from numerous men with much more experience, apparently fell on deaf ears. My Oriole teammates who did play expressed their feelings to me privately.

"I don't know what to say," Dean said, "I wish I could do something. We all feel the same way." More than once the words of Willie danced through my mind. *"All you need is ah chance."* I hate this, I thought. *It's not fair.*

However, I was not the only one. Although they were now allowed to practice with the starters, sort of like being used for cannon-fodder, the rest of Preacher's team never played either. Nor were some of the kids from teams we competed against.

"Ticks me off," Jerky said as he kicked a locker in the athletic dressing room.

The regulars on the team struggled through a five-and-one record for the fall.

—⁓—

In the spring of `51, the high school team went seven and nothing in the regular season schedule. I and the rest of the nonstarters were not allowed any playing time. *What can I do to please this guy?* I thought!

Possibly justice prevailed, however, because the winning streak didn't hold long. The team ran into a hornet's nest in the regional tournament and lost. In an ugly game, in which everything that could go wrong for us went wrong, we were defeated by Wauzeka, a team loaded with players the Orioles had played against in previous years.

Their pitcher was a junk-baller. He called it his "out pitch," a tantalizing slow curve. Our team made five errors. In one instance, two outfielders converged on a high fly yelling, "I got it! Mine! Mine!" The ball, however, dropped between them. On another occasion, when an opposing hitter tried to stretch a single into a double, one of our infielders threw the ball away. In addition to this, we left men on base that were in scoring position. Our team had runners on the corners in the sixth, but a lame grounder to third ended the threat. For one reason or another, the ball just seemed to bounce crazily for us all day.

"If that narrow-minded coach would have used some of the farm kids that played for and against the Orioles they would have won that thing," Preacher preached to Dad and a group of shopper at PJ's. "We can't allow this to go much further!"

Tension was growing!

—⚓—

The city baseball team in the summer of '51 needed some practice. One day their coach asked Dean to get some of his buddies together for a warm-up game at the fairgrounds diamond. Dean hastily made telephone calls to his Orioles and high school teammates and most of the players agreed to show up.

"You've got to pitch today," Dean barked to me as I entered the field. "Enoch can't make it, and Tiger's fishing."

Surprisingly, the score remained nip and tuck through the first four innings. Gaining confidence with each inning, our make-up team began to bear down, in fact we surged ahead going into the fifth.

The inning began with Sunny and Stan reaching base. When the pitcher for the city team tried to bust his fastball in and under Shane's hands, Shane wouldn't flinch. I watched as he stepped out of the batter's box, spit on his hands, and stepped back in. Meanwhile, the pitcher waited, removed his pitching glove, and massaged the ball with both hands. Most of our players leaned forward in their seat on our bench, anxious for the action to continue.

When the count ran to three and nothing, the pitcher knew he had to throw a strike, and Shane knew it also. The pitcher fired his heater out over the plate, and Shane slashed the ball on a line to right center, where it rolled up against the snow fence. The hit drove Stan and Sunny home. Shane, standing poker-faced on second base, brushed dust off his pants. We cheered and the city team stood stunned!

Sure enough, when the pitcher faced Shane at his next at bat in the seventh, he threw three straight balls. In desperation to hit, Shane reached for ball four and stroked a weak fly to left field for an out. The city team pitcher was good, and he handcuffed me much of the time. Luckily, I hit a grounder to short that the player couldn't field cleanly, allowing me to reach base. Ove hung in for a gritty at-bat that brought Sunny to the plate with Tim on deck.

Realizing this was turning into more than a mere practice for the city team, the pitcher began to bear down. He walked off the mound and pulled a handkerchief from his right rear pocket. After mopping his brow he stepped back to the rubber.

"Come on big guy," the catcher barked, gesturing with determination from his catching position.

As soon as Sunny walked, Tim hurried into the batters' box, positioned his feet, and held his bat motionless. Although he obviously didn't realize it, Tim stood at the plate like a right handed Babe Ruth. He held his feet together and sort of turned part of his back toward the pitcher before he swung, which propelled his swing. *He's not going to miss this chance,* I thought. *He plays his best when the chips are down.*

"Don't let that old man blow it by you," Lance yelled to his buddy from a kneeling position in the on-deck circle.

Tim didn't—on the first pitch, a low inside fastball, he golfed a bullet over third base and into the left-field corner. I watched intensely as he paused for a split second after rounding first. When he saw the outfielder didn't pick the ball up cleanly, he turned on the speed and dived safely, head-first into second. As he stood up I could see dark brown dirt across the front of his uniform. The red letter M over his heart was barely visible.

"WOW," I yelled to Tim. "That's kickin' butts!"

Lance was the next hitter. He fouled off five pitches before drawing a walk.

"Lemme borrow your bat," Dean said as he walked past me on his way to the plate. He picked up my thirty-three inch Adirondack, and swung it a couple of times. "Feels better than mine . . . care if I use it?"

"Just don't break it . . . Okay?"

Dean seemed to be in his own world and didn't respond. The first pitch was a fastball under his chin, and the second a sweeping curve low and outside. When the pitcher came back with another heater, Dean swung, but he caught it on the bat handle—breaking it like a compound fracture of a chin bone. The third baseman gloved the short pop-up and Dean was out.

"Sorry about that, Bones, you can use mine until you get a new one."

"Whaddaya do, hit it on the trade mark?" I replied.

The city team pitcher wasted no time with Jerky, who had switched from batting right handed to left. His first pitch was high and outside, too wide for anyone to reach. His second pitch was also well off the outside edge. But Jerky lunged at the ball—almost stepping across the plate—and sent it down the left field line, driving in two more runs. We all mobbed him with hugs, butt slapping, and hand shaking. Everyone knew he had talent, all he needed was the opportunity to expose it.

"Too bad Jerky has never had a chance to play on the high school team," Dean said to me as we walked off the field. "He's going to turn into something special as a left hand hitter."

I guess the players on the city team didn't know what was developing before their eyes, because we beat them eight to three.

From that time on, my confidence and the confidence of all of our players took on a new perspective. We now knew the extent of our abilities. Word soon got around the area that the team everyone had hoped for was developing right in our own backyard.

Chapter 23

GYPSIES

The phone rang in our living room, two longs and a short.

"Rhoda!" I could hear the caller yell in an excited voice. "The gypsies are coming into town. It won't be long until they'll be roaming the area—get everything locked up!"

Our area was used to the entertainment of a traveling carnival or a Chautauqua, but the gypsies were something different. It was late Friday afternoon, and a black flashy Buick Riviera pulling a house wagon, followed by a cattle truck and a moving van, was progressing relentlessly along the highway. Like a colony of ants searching for territory, gypsies (an ethnic group from Chicago who called themselves "travelers") were on the move along Highway 171between Sterling and Millersville.

The clan had gathered here before for funerals, weddings, and other family business, including paying a share of their questionable proceeds to their king (or sometimes a queen) for continued blessing.

No one trusted them, especially Mother. They lived together and had their own language, customs, rituals and courts which some outsiders consider superstitious. A gypsy court, called a "Kris," was made up of five men who settled disputes. Gypsies were all about loyalty, and blood came first. Everyone in the clan was referred to as a brother or sister, and those in another clan were referred to as cousins. Like some Ridge Runners from the Kickapoo, they didn't trust outsiders; it's always been that way.

To make a living they made flowers from crepe paper and sold them door-to-door. People had to be very careful not to let a gypsy in their home; they were masters of sleight of hand and picking a pocket. The clan was involved in horse and mule trading, basket making, rustic furniture building, home repair, barn painting, and retail theft!

It wasn't long before they claimed squatters' rights to camp in a park beside the Kickapoo River in Millersville. In a flash, and tents were set up and temporary shacks built.

The local business people in adjoining towns dropped what they were doing and hastily arranged for a meeting. Sterling officials met at Uncle Tom's barber-shop. At home—Dad loaded his sixteen-gage shotgun with double zero buckshot.

Every time the gypsies moved through our area, the men folk would run into them in the taverns in Millersville. Sometimes they would buy the locals drinks before the clan went off together to talk business. For some reason they set up shop for their entertainment behind PJ's store in Sterling.

"I've never heard of any of our girls or women folk going out with a gypsy," Mike Smally said.

The Saturday morn drifted into twilight, and the Kickapoo hill and valley people stirred for entertainment. Fortune-telling, shell games, magic, and inviting music filled the gypsy encampment. Mystical dancing women twisted in shows that extended throughout the evening. "Isn't that weed I smell?" Shane said to me. "These guys got their own kinda shine."

I saw Dean, Sunny, Jerky, Ove and Tiger hanging around the tent where the magic man performed, and Hank seemed to be interested in viewing the dancing women. *Where are the rest of the guys?* I knew Enoch wouldn't be here. *He was always with Kiara.*

Crowds formed, and I suspect more than a few onlookers returned home only to find their pockets picked clean to the bone. The shell game caught the attention of Earl, Lance, Tim, Shane, and me, as well as a lot of other suckers—one being Lowman. For some reason, Lowman couldn't get it through his thick skull that he was being conned. Try after try passed him by before he was down to pocket change. Lowman stood up from the chair he was sitting on and motioned toward someone he apparently knew, who was standing nearby.

"Lend me ah twenty," I could hear him growl. The man walked over to Lowman and whispered something into his ear. It seemed to take about fifteen seconds. Then the man stepped back—way back. The big man's face transformed from a scowl to one of *rage*.

"You piece of camel s," Lowman bellowed, the veins standing out on his neck. "You were workin' me all along. Now I'm gonna teach you somethin' you didn't learn in that sandbox you crawled out of."

Throwing his weight into it, Lowman kicked a bench out of the way that was in front of him and started for the shell man. Lance barked with a big jovial expression, "Feet get me going," and turned tail for the outer limits of the area, followed closely by Tim.

"Come on Bones," Tim yelled, looking out for the welfare of his friend. People scattered, including the Sterling keeper of the peace. *Maybe I should be doing the same thing.* Earl grabbed my arm and prevented me from leaving.

"It's usually better to give Lowman a wide berth," I heard the officer say to another man, "than to stir things. Just step back and watch what happens. Bruno can usually talk him out of anything too rough, anyway."

"Yeah, but he's not here," someone answered.

Apparently, the clan was used to these types of occurrences. The shell man jumped back quickly and grabbed a long curved blade about three feet long. He swung it around like a majorette in the Millersville High School band does with her baton. Such a fashion made one believe he was some sort of an expert in its use.

"I'll coot off youse ears, bigga mon!"

Lowman didn't flinch. He grabbed one leg of a nearby table and lifted it. With his other hand, he reached to the ground and picked up an empty wine bottle and, holding on to its neck, smashed the other end on a metal light pole. He held the jagged bottle high in his right hand.

"Okay, tough monkey," snorted Lowman. "If it's killin' you want—you're about to get it!"

No sooner had Lowman taken his next step than five gypsy brothers appeared almost out of nowhere. Each had a blade. Lowman froze, his eyes widened.

"These odds don't look good," Earl murmured to me. "I've got a bad feeling about this."

Everyone stood motionless. After what seemed to be an eternity, Lowman placed the table down to the ground, flung the bottle away, and sat down on his chair. He motioned to his acquaintance and whispered something in his ear. *I wonder what he's saying.* His associate scurried to a car that was parked nearby and raced away—wheels spinning and turning up gravel and dust. Lowman leaned back in his chair and placed both feet on the table in front of him. He appeared relaxed, as if he was waiting for someone to come or something he was sure would happen . . .

Sure enough, within a few minutes two cars swirled into the parking area. The men inside did not immediately get out, they appeared to be waiting for another person. About five more minutes had elapsed when Bruno swung in the lot in his gold Cadillac, past a sign marked DO NOT ENTER, and slammed on the brakes. I watched as the car skidded to a stop on the loose gravel. A large cloud of dust rose in the air and softly floated off in the distance, a stark contrast to the intensity of the action on the field. Lowman didn't move an inch. The clan froze—their faces changed in bewilderment.

As soon as Bruno leaped out of his car, I eyed the men in the other automobiles step out of theirs. With them was the King of the Gypsies. Bruno grasped the clan king by one arm and directed him toward Lowman—he looked like a man who had not slept in three weeks.

"You fool," Bruno yelled at Lowman with anger in his voice. He kicked the chair Lowman was sitting on.

"Can't keep out of trouble can you? They're playing tricks on your mind. Get tah hell outa here!"

"Buck," he said, motioning to one of the henchmen. "Take him over to my place and talk to him—nicely—okay? And watch yourself."

Bruno then swirled toward the clansmen. They looked at him with a curious expression.

"Gentlemen, we can do this two ways, and one is peacefully. As you can see, I've got your kingfish here; picked him up in Mikes Bar in Millersville. Doesn't appear to be too bad a chap, maybe a little strange to some of us Ridge Runners, but we're friends." Bruno always tried to get an edge.

"There's a game that little boys around here play called King of the Hill. I guess it's to determine who's the toughest. It starts out with someone like me making someone like you an offer, friendly like, at first. So here's my offer. It'd be a good idea for you to hand me that money you conned my man out of, it's not nice to take advantage of stupid people. You've got it right over there in that pretty colored genie jar." Bruno pointed to a multi-colored jar sitting to one side of a nearby table.

Nobody moved. Bruno paused for a few seconds, and then motioned to one of his men. I heard him say a few words in what I thought may have been Italian. The man walked to one of the cars and removed a double-barreled, sawed-off shotgun. The gun hung open and appeared unloaded. I could see two green colored gun shells in one of his hands. *They're weighing this over,* I thought.

As a result of Earl's boldness and self-confidence, he grabbed my arm and we crept closer . . . The idea was his, not mine.

On seeing the shotgun, and the shells, the king nodded to one of his brothers, who cautiously handed Bruno the jar.

"All I want is what you conned my man out of," Bruno said to the king, with a firm sort of strange kindness to his voice.

He reached in the jar, counted out the money, and handed the jar back to the clansman.

"I could care less about your damn money—I just want you to know that you're not the *king* around here!" The king and his brothers smiled, bowed, and seemed very pleased with the result.

"Can't insult that bunch of weirdoes," Earl mumbled in my ear. Before the evening was over he conned the clan out of a few dollars by squeezing a scale to its max. Even though they had it rigged, it made no difference. Earl had hands as strong as Lowman.

—⚓—

Preacher had us up bright and early the next day to play Sherman at Sterling field. I noticed a serious side to him that I had never seen before. We were all kind of somber, recognizing this would probably be the last regular season competitive game for the Orioles. It had become more difficult for other towns to form teams, and the Kickapoo kids were growing older and more involved in playing for city teams.

Any melancholy feelings we might have had soon drifted away when infield drills and batting practice began. Preacher put us through a whirlwind of activity, working on hitting the cutoff man, turning double plays, and bunting as well as hitting the ball to the opposite field. When the game started, we were sweaty and ready.

As I was standing on the pitcher's mound, I noticed a large vehicle moving slowly down the gravel road toward Preacher's farm. *Looks like the gypsy van.*

The van swung into the ball field and rolled to a stop behind the backstop. The king and his clan got out and set up shop. *They never stop.*

But this day was different. One member of their family had been married that morning in a ceremony beside the Kickapoo in Millersville. This was a day of celebration. They didn't sell anything; rather, they traded for goods they were short on and gave away their excess supplies. Mother traded some eggs for sewing cloth.

This day was also very special for the Orioles team—it was Preacher's birthday.

The game provided good competition, because most of Sherman's players were now on the Wauzeka high school team.

"Let's win this one for Preacher," Dean spoke to our team as we huddled in a circle before taking the field. As we broke the huddle, there was a look of determination on each face. We loved Preacher.

My hitting had improved over the course of the year. In the first inning, I caught a ball on the fat of my bat and drilled it straight back toward the family jewels of the Sherman pitcher. Pitchers didn't wear a protective cup like catchers did. The shot was partially deflected by the hurler's glove, and a good thing that it was, because he hobbled around for a few minutes, doubled over, and sank like a scuttled boat looking as pale as a sheet. *If I would have hit the ball a little higher,* I thought, *he would have been singing tenor.*

With the Orioles down by two runs in the last of the seventh, Sunny strode to the plate and lined a single to center. The next batter, Jerky, launched a high fly that bounced off the snow fence in right field, and dropped straight down, dying in the high unmown grass next to the fence.

Meanwhile Sunny scored easily and Jerky pulled up at second. Dean then lined one into center scoring

Jerky and tying the score. He circled the bag at first, hesitated, and returned to the base. Anxiously awaiting my turn at bat, I moved to a corner of the bench next to the on deck circle. With the winning run on, Ove hit a soft poke into the gap in right center that their fielder misplayed. Racing toward the ball with his Mickey Mantle glove unfurled before him like a fishing net, he misjudged how the ball would come down, and it smacked off the heel of the glove and rolled to the far reaches of the outfield eventually settling among the branches of an Elderberry bush. Dean roared around third—dirt flying from under his spikes.

"He slid so hard I think his body went six feet past the plate," Shane said. "But that's the way he always does it, hard and fast."

As Dean circled the bases, Ove raised his right hand in glee, and Preacher had a long awaited moment of pride.

"Wayta go, Babe . . . wayta go."

Happy birthday, Preacher, I thought.

Orioles five, Sherman four, the scoreboard read.

"Remember deciding to save that Elderberry bush when we were laying out the ball field?" Preacher said in a mysterious tone to Dad. "Remember me saying that I had this feeling that someday she would do us a favor for saving her life? Well . . . what do you think? Think that's possible for the old girl?"

"Preacher, you don't honestly believe that do you?" Dad said in a strange sort of reply with uncertainty in his tone.

"All I can say Jake, is you saw what I saw . . ."

Later that evening, Preacher called Dad and told him that six of his chickens were missing.

Chapter 24

CLOSING THE GATES

On a Sunday afternoon in the late summer of 1951, the Kickapoo Kids played our last game with the Sterling Orioles. The opposition wasn't Rolling Ground, Tombstone or Sherman. It was our parents and friends from the community. Even Father Murphy and Pastor Johnson came to play against the youth they had supported for the past four years.

The opposition was out for blood. They even went so far as to bribe PJ to pitch for them. Although PJ took it easy on us, sort of like throwing batting practice, we still couldn't mount much of an attack. Nevertheless, we made the game fun and interesting. No one kept score.

After the game, everyone joined together to picnic on the field or play croquet.

Before the town folk returned to their respective homes, and the farmers to their evening milking, Dad and Dale walked together to the pitcher's mound.

"Come on up here," Dale said, motioning to Preacher and Milley.

"About five years ago," he began, "Jake, Preacher and I talked about a crazy dream Preacher had to start a baseball team for our kids. Our dream was to give them something to do during the summer months in place of getting in trouble. I remember first talking with Jake about it, and finding out how he felt.

"I recall we both thought it would be very difficult to pull off, because there was so much work to do on our farms, but the person who never doubted, for one instant—was Preacher!"

There was great applause.

"As you all know," Dale continued, "Preacher and Milley gave up some of their most productive land so our kids could have a place to play competitive baseball. Today is payback time. Jake, I'll let you do the rest."

Dad had never spoken in front of a group of people to my knowledge. He reached in an upper pocket of his Lee's bib overalls and removed a brown envelope.

"Preacher and Milley, this is a check drawn on the Millersville Bank for your financial losses as a result of your land being out of production during these years." Dad smiled broadly as he handed the envelope to Preacher.

"Well, I'll be switched. I never expected anything like this," Preacher said as he moved toward Dale and Dad. A reddish flush swept across his face. "Did you know anything about this?" he inquired, turning his attention to Milley.

She'd lifted a hand to her mouth and was fighting away happy tears.

"Nothing . . . nothing at all," she said. "It's as much of a surprise to me as it is to you."

"We're obliged to all of you," Preacher said. "Thanks so much."

"There's one other thing that I know is more important to you than a check," Dad said, "and that's this!"

Dad reached into a box and lifted out a silver object that glistened in the sunlight.

"Here's the Kickapoo Kup that these kids earned for winning the league championship." Dad carefully handed the beautiful object to Preacher.

Preacher caught his breath, and jabbered a bunch of stuff to Milley in Norwegian. He then held the trophy and the envelope high in the air for all to see.

Everyone stood and applauded as Preacher and Milley walked back to the group seated on the grass.

Dad looked around, as if searching the crowd for someone, shrugged, and then continued . . .

"We have a small token of our appreciation we were planning on giving to PJ today, but I guess that'll have to wait until tomorrow morning, he's apparently gone home after facing such tough hitters as you guys." There was more laughter.

His eyes swept the crowd. "Anyone have anything more to say?"

Preacher stepped forward from the group he had been standing beside. There was excitement in his voice and on his expression.

"I know that Dean, Shane, Bones, Jerky, Hooks, Sunny and Babe have been playing together for a number of years, and sometimes Tiger and a few others. You're now in high school. For all these past years you've been playing in the minor leagues. You're now in the majors. I know Millersville made it to the state tournament recently—an achievement that is indescribable for a small community such as this. I know a few of you kids had something to do with it.

"I also know a lot of you do not agree with your present high school coach. I, and a number of others, share your feelings. But I also believe in miracles. Who knows, maybe something will change between now and next spring? Faith has a way of working itself out!"

Everybody applauded.

"Just to prove to you that I still have faith for the future," Preacher continued, "I've been doing some research on the subject. I understand that before long, there will be divisions in baseball in the state—five I believe. The way it is today, a small school like Millersville usually has to play against much larger schools in order to get to the state tournament. But that'll all change in the future. A division-five school, like Millersville, will play against other division-five schools—and not the big guys.

"But I think that's an insult to you guys." His voice rose as he spoke. "I know some of you haven't had the chance to play for the school team yet. Nevertheless—with faith—I believe you will in the future. I think most of you guys are as good as those who play for the larger schools—but you've only got two years left to prove it."

Everyone shouted and applauded.

"Now here's the mission," Preacher said, becoming extremely intense. He raised his right hand, his forefinger gesturing as if in a command.

"Listen . . . You are precisely at the right place and at the right time to make history."

He shifted his attention toward a group of us who were sitting together, his eyes glistened.

"You may not know this—but no school of your size has ever appeared in the state baseball tournament within a time frame of three-out-of-four years.

Why? Because schools our size usually get beaten by the bigger schools. It has never happened before, and when the division changes occur—it can never happen again!"

Preacher turned and strolled away . . .

"Nobody has ever seen me cry in public," he mumbled, "and I'm not going to break that record now. Guess I better get out of here before you do." The following day, the snow fence around the outfield was down, the gates closed, and Guernsey cattle again patrolled what was once the ball field of the Sterling Orioles.

"A little piece of him died yesterday," Milley told Mother over the telephone. "He looked sad all evening."

Chapter 25

CONFRONTATION

Autumn in the Kickapoo was surely painted by the brush of the Great Artist of the Heavens. Brightly colored wildflowers graced the landscape with their varying shapes, sizes and shades of yellow, red, blue, white and in almost any tint imaginable.

Monarchs and other colorful butterflies fluttered everywhere. Young birds had by this time left their mothers and were struggling to get the full force of their wings; soon they would be able to find food on their own.

The woods glowed with amber, maroon, gold, brown and dark shades of green. An invigorating, spicy smell from decaying fallen leaves circled the inside of our nostrils. Days were pleasant, the humidity was low, and nights were ideal for sleep after working late in the fields under the light of a glowing harvest moon.

As was usual around our house each year at the first sign of fall, Dad pulled on his fresh long johns for the approaching harsh Kickapoo winter. Robbins and red wing black birds must have taken his cue because they left the scene shortly afterwards.

I could see that the grass was white with frost as Sunny and I walked out of the house for our bus ride to school. The sun was coming up through the tree tops in the woods, and I felt a brief wash of warmth against the sharp chill of the morning. As the bus entered Millersville and continued past the dam, a walleye jumped on my left, making a spreading circle in the water that was yet to freeze. *That guy must be enjoying life,* I guessed.

To my right, however, a much different tale of the tape of life was evolving. Crews from the sheriff's department, with the assistance of Nicholson's towing truck, were snaking a pickup out of the rough and muddy Kickapoo. I stretched my neck to get a better view of the action. The truck was standing about forty feet from the bank. There were heavy chains attached to its winch, and the motor was grinding in an effort to pull the soaking vehicle to dry land. *I wonder if the guy's body is in there.*

At the start of my junior year in the fall of 1951, the community built a new baseball diamond adjoining the high school. The field had a short right field because the south end of our high school building was about three hundred feet from home plate. Balls often hit off its brick wall and rebounded back into the infield.

Enthusiasm in the neighborhood was high. From time to time, a few men from town would stop down to watch or participate in practice, and their excitement carried over to the team. The school had a new fight song also, the "Notre Dame Victory March."

—m—

I hustled to our athletic locker room one afternoon, as I always did around 4 p.m. during the baseball season. Everyone was busy changing into their baseball attire for practice, while chatting about the upcoming tournament. A white sheet of paper hung on the bulletin board next to the shower room, and I strolled over to read the message. "Players scheduled to travel on the bus for the tournament next Tuesday . . . " it said. I anxiously scanned the note for my name, and the name of my Oriole teammates, they were not there!

I can't handle this any longer.

As soon as I got home from school in the late afternoon, I made a beeline to Dad, who was doing some cleanup work behind our chicken coop.

"What's the matter, Bones?" Dad said when he saw me racing toward him and instantly knew something was wrong. I guess I was so angry that I was almost in tears.

"He has kicked me off the team."

Dad spit tobacco juice on a corner of the chicken coop. It slid off and blended into a mud puddle.

"Off the team . . . ? What are you talking about? Why?"

"I don't know, all I do know is that I'm not listed to travel with the rest of the team to the tournament."

Dad dropped his pitchfork and bucket where he was standing—didn't say another word—and headed straight toward our car parked in the driveway. He had a determined look on his face!

"Where are you going, Jake?" Mother yelled as she saw him scurrying.

"To Millersville to talk with someone. Be back in an hour, or so, if he's lucky!"

Mother caught her breath, and paused for a moment. "I hope you don't lose your temper, Jake. Don't go off half-cocked, now. No sense in getting huffy about it . . . Okay?"

—⟊—

In about an hour and a half, Dad returned—his blue denim work shirt soaking wet under his armpits from perspiration.

"I'm afraid that coach, whatever his name is, got a load," Mother whispered to me before supper.

I looked toward Dad, "What went on? Did you talk with him?"

"It probably won't do any good, son, but I got a load off my chest. He knows how I feel now. I took Preacher with me to kind of calm me down, but I think he got more excited than I did!"

"What did he say?" I was anxious.

"You do what you have to do at the time." Dad said. "That's all the man said."

"Huh?"

"I'm telling you," Dad replied. "That's all the man said. But I'll tell you one thing, Preacher sure gave him something to chew on."

"I'll tell you this much," Dad recounted how Preacher had let loose, 'I understand you were in that darn war, but you're not the only one that's ever been shot or injured, ya know. You'd look just as well without that chip on your shoulder. Don't give me that hard nose stuff. There's such a thing as being injured emotionally as well as physically. Coaches like you treat these kids as if you were a general in the army and they were privates. You can literally make or break a kid's attitude and self-confidence for life. For some reason a lot of you guys make that same mistake—and it's a hurtful thing to do to the young man—and a dumb thing to do from a coaching standpoint. Ask PJ, he'll tell you the same thing. You'll be ahead or behind by a dozen runs, and still keep the regulars in, I just don't understand the reasoning. You have no idea if some of my kids can play because you've never given them a chance."' Dad seemed intense as he related the lecture.

Millersville lost to La Farge High School in the North vs. South league championship game.

—⚍—

I stood outside our house in the evening and pondered my decision. The season had ended and I was depressed. I walked into our living room and sat down.

"I'm thinking of quitting the baseball team and not attending practices in the spring. He'll never play me anyway. I wish I went to Grove, Wauzeka or Seneca. I played against most of their players, they know me. They know I can play. Don't you see—if I went to those schools I could have been somebody instead of sitting on one corner of the bench."

Dad moved his chair closer to mine and leaned forward, he looked troubled.

"Well," Dad sighed, "we can't do anything about it now. Guess we'll have to wait and see what happens when spring comes. Don't quit though. Don't ever quit!

"I'm going to talk with Preacher and see if we can arrange a meeting to settle this once and for all," Dad said.

"It's all right, Bones," Mother said as she untied her apron. Then she paused and said something I will never forget...

"You know son, I sometimes wonder if you kids, and you in particular, appreciate what Preacher has done for you. There are certain kinds of people in this world who are born to help others when no one else will, that's Preacher.

"Better get some sleep—it's a new day tomorrow."

Outside, the wind blew and the trees swayed and leaned.

Winter was approaching...

Chapter 26

THE BOYCOTT

Times were changing, rock 'n roll was catching on and Marlin Brando was the new star of the screen. The most popular place for students to hang out was Fat Friley's Restaurant, with its soda fountain and a beautiful rainbow colored jukebox where we could play forty-fives by Johnnie Ray, Frankie Laine and Patti Page, to name only a few.

As the fall months passed and winter approached, the first sounds of dissent were heard in the school hallways.

"What's this guy trying to do?" Shane said to Tiger and another player on the school baseball team. There was a tone of anxiety and anger in Shane's voice that caught Jerky's and my attention and made us pause in our journey to our next class. Dean was in the area.

"I never thought he would actually go through with it," he said.

Other students stopped what they were doing and gathered around for a closer intake on the discussion. Without hearing the entire conversation, I knew what they were talking about. It hadn't taken long for word to get around that Coach intended to continue his intention to not play kids in baseball that did not participate in basketball. As each month passed and basketball season approached—the situation was becoming critical. If something wasn't done soon the team would be performing at far less capacity than they were capable. We all knew Coach was basketball oriented, and knew nothing about baseball, but this was turning into a big mistake for our community.

"We're not going to let this happen," Tiger said as he glanced toward Jerky, "It's only going to hurt the team."

I let out a sad sigh and strolled toward my next class, head down. I heard Dean take a deep breath also. *I know he feels the weight of our disappointment.*

It wasn't long before the town folks got word as to what Coach intended.

"Are you serious?" I heard a concerned parent say to Preacher one morning at PJ's store in Sterling.

Preacher stopped shopping for the day's supplies and joined the rest of us at the back of the store. "*You bet*

I am," Preacher said with intensity. "Dean was the first to tell me. Dale, you've heard about this haven't you?"

"I've known this for a long time," Dale said. "What do you think we can do?"

"Let's get a meeting together with some of the players and interested people in the area—there's power in unity," Dad responded.

"Who knows, maybe we can get him fired and bring someone else in here," another person from the back of the room added.

"We don't want to go too far," Dale said as he removed some canned goods from the shelves and brought them to the counter.

"I've been talking with some of our guys who were on the Orioles team, and some of the kids we played against. Some of us have an idea to propose," Preacher said. "Dean and the town kids think it's a good one. We'll meet at Fat Friley's this Saturday. Let's notify as many of the town people as we can, and as quick as we can. I think it's time for a little hard ball of our own!"

"I'm going to talk with Fr. Tom," Dad said. "Preacher, why don't you do the same with Pastor Gus? They'll know what to do and the proper manner to carry it off. People respect them. There're the ones to lead this thing."

—m—

Saturday morning of the following week when Dad, Sunny and I arrived, Friley's was overflowing with concerned parents and interested parties, including a number of the high school team. Most of the Millersville merchants were there. Fr. Tom and Pastor Gus arrived together.

"Where's Lloyd?" Preacher asked in a puzzled tone.

"Probably still out on his mail route," someone said. "You know that nudist farm off the Halls Branch road? Lloyd said a few times when he turns up the driveway to their mailbox, that he's seen a bunch of them lady nudies out in the garden ah hoein' corn, naked as jaybirds. Guess they wave to him when he takes a peek."

"Well, I guess that'd delay any red-blooded man, wouldn't it?" Preacher said with a big grin as he glanced toward Pastor Gus.

"Speak for yourself," Gus replied.

"Okay," Preacher responded, "I'll try to remember that."

Another attendee was Clyde, one of the more highly-respected men in our area. There was nothing Clyde would not do for his beloved hometown. He was both a cheerleader and a one-man chamber of commerce. We always talked louder around Clyde because he was hard of hearing, and consequently, he spoke much louder than the average person. His voice resonated throughout the store.

After pumping the hand up and down of everyone in the room, Preacher pulled a chair off to the side of the group, climbed aboard, and got right to the point.

"You all know what we are here for. I think it's about time we bare things straight. A group of the kids tells us that this coach intends to not play our lads on the baseball team who do not play basketball. Is that right, guys?" He looked at the four players who were sitting in front of him.

"That's right," one of the group spoke up. "We've only got two years left to go places and we need the best players to play."

"We all know a number of the kids who are on the team who are good ballplayers—but they've never gotten a chance to play one inning or bat one time; they're simply hired hands." Fr. Murphy was getting his Irish up. "I'm not talking about putting weak players in tight games just to give them a chance to play. I'm talking about lop-sided games where they're ahead or behind by a lot of runs." Fr. Tom stood to his feet and his voice rose in intensity as he voiced his opinion. "The guy never puts kids in that we all know are good players simply because they do not go out for his basketball team. They're nothing but cannon fodder to him—and it's heartbreaking to these lads!"

"That's a shame," Preacher replied as he lowered and shook his head sadly. "I take what he's doing personally. If he knew anything about baseball he'd know there are occasions like this that allow the players who have not been regulars to gain experience, and possibly even replace a starter if they prove themselves. My lads have been getting a raw deal and it's time to do something about it while there's still time."

"We've come to a crossroad on this," Pastor Gus said, stepping into the discussion. "What do you think we should do about it?" He scanned the audience with his eyes as he spoke.

"I think we ought to run the bum out of town while there's still time," Scooter jumped right in.

"Well, Scooter, you may have a point there but that may be a bit harsh," Preacher responded with a chuckle. The rest of the attendees laughed also.

Scooter was serious though.

"I know just the man for the job," he said. "He's not necessarily a thoroughbred but he knows how to pull a plow through a thistle patch."

"Now wait a minute," Fr. Tom quickly responded, looking around the room in earnest. "Scooter, I think this thing's hurtling toward the cliff too fast. Aren't you starting to itch before you get bit? That's not what this meetin's about." His glare hit Scooter square. "We're not looking for a way to harm anyone. We're looking for a way to play baseball this spring." Fr. Tom rarely raised his voice, but when he did, he plowed close to the corn.

"Tom's right," Pastor Gus responded. "We've got a family here, and we've got to make sure this doesn't turn out like Cain killing Abel. What do you think about it, Clyde?"

"Well," the old man said, reaching into the bib pocket of the striped Lee overalls he was wearing. He pulled out a pouch of smoking tobacco and ripped a sheet of cigarette paper from a packet.

"I guess I look at it this way. . . ."

Carefully, he poured a measure of tobacco onto the paper, rolled it, and ran his tongue across one side to moisten and hold the contents in place. He reached onto the counter where an open box of stick matches sat, grabbed one, struck it across the pants of his overalls, and lit up.

Everyone sat patiently waiting for his response to follow . . .

Clyde stretched back on his chair, placed his thumbs under the shoulder straps of his overalls, and paused for a moment . . .

"You never really know a man until you consider his point of view from his front porch," he said. "But from what I've heard here today, you've tried just about everything. Apparently, he's got a burr of some sort under his saddle. If he'd only meet you halfway, that would be different. But if you wear my glasses, he probably won't. So it seems to me if you don't like the product somebody is selling, you—stop going to his store. I think we could do the same thing with this Coach fella." His gaze traveled from man to man.

"If the players want the best baseball team on the field, and that coach doesn't want to listen to them, then the players should refuse to participate in basketball this winter. Sort of a boycott." A serious but mischievous sort of a smile swept across his face.

"That's the best advice I've heard all morning," Fr. Tom said, rubbing his palms together and meeting the eyes of each man in the room.

"But we've got to remember one thing," Pastor Gus said, stepping in. "When we start this thing, there's no turning back. Does everyone agree?"

"We all do!" yelled a man at the back of the room with authority in his voice.

"This book says it all," Pastor Gus raised his old, and used appearing Bible he always carried with him high in the air. "We are not to abide by unjust rules, whether they are by government—or man. We, as Christians have a duty to not obey so-called laws or rules that are against the Law of God and the natural laws of nature. Although this law existed thousands of years before the time of Christ, the father of the Christian denomination I represent brought it into more recent history. What we are proposing here today—is in complete agreement with this book!"

Talk of the meeting quickly spread throughout the school and especially among the players, and when the word got to Coach that the team planned a boycott, he soon posted a sign on the locker room bulletin board. It read:

"BASKETBALL PRACTICE AT 3:15 PM, MONDAY. CHANGES IN BASEBALL WILL OCCUR IN THE SPRING"

Coach had changed his mind.

"If you really want to get something done," Dad said to us that evening, "Tom and Gus are the men you can count on when the chips are down and there's nowhere else to turn. Everyone respects them and knows they will do what's right—regardless of the cost to them personally."

"That's what we need, people like them who have courage," Mother replied. "That's what our country could use right now!"

Chapter 27

DUKE

It was what old timers called "a false spring." The temperature forecast for this Saturday in late February, 1952 was expected to reach the low sixties. It was about 10:30 a.m., and after delivering the milk, Dad, Sunny and I stopped at PJ's to do some shopping. I glanced to my right where a jukebox stood in one corner. It marvelously glistened in every color of the rainbow. I knew Preacher had to be in the room because I could hear the melody of his favorite song, "Wheel of Fortune" playing loudly in the background. Wherever Preacher went, and wherever there a jukebox, "Wheel of Fortune" was always playing.

Soon we were joined by a stranger.

The young man was about twenty-six years of age, six feet, one hundred ninety pounds, and was wearing shorts and a light jacket. He came into PJ's store

with a nod for Dad and Preacher. Sunny and I were
a few feet away and he apparently did not see us.
He moved down the aisles with his head bent, pausing to take a hard look around the place. A woman,
likely his wife, trailed after him, fingering fabrics
and examining household items. Two small children
raced up and down the aisles despite frowns and soft
admonishment from their mother. I noticed Dad and
Preacher remove their hats as the lady walked past.
They always did that out of respect when a lady was
in a room.

"Can I help you?" PJ beckoned from behind the
counter where he was standing. His usual calm, debo-
nair self made the visitors comfortable.

Sunny and I moved toward the counter and sat
down on some sacks of corn seed.

"Looking for a few sodas for the gang," replied the
stranger with a weary smile.

"We've got 'em. What's your choice?"

The man considered for a moment . . . "How about
a couple of those bottles of Whistle, a strawberry, and
a ginger ale?"

PJ pulled four frosty bottles from back of the counter. The kids had them opened and were sipping and
enjoying the refreshments within a few seconds.

The man's glance took in the store as he accepted
his change.

"Just traveling through?" PJ asked, not about to lose out on a bit of news.

Not spending much time, the stranger nodded to his wife and the group headed toward the door, their rambunctious kids drinking their sodas as they walked. Just before leaving, the man glanced back toward PJ with a friendly sort of smile.

"Sort of . . . well . . . not really . . . kind of looking over the territory, I guess."

"Oh, that sounds interesting, for what purpose?" PJ's eyes widened just the littlest bit as he considered this.

After exchanging a few words with his wife, the man strolled back toward PJ.

"I'm the new coach at Millersville High School," he replied. "It came about all of a sudden. I just graduated a couple of weeks ago from St. Luke's Collage."

"Well, this all came about rather unexpected to everyone here, also," replied PJ with a slow drawl. "The coach we had here never showed any indication he was quitting."

"Yes, that's what I've been told. Too bad for him, I understand he didn't fit in."

"The problem was that he didn't know anything about baseball," PJ remarked, "and this whole area has always been a baseball hotbed. The kids play it, their fathers played it, and so did their grandfathers."

"Well, that makes us different," the coach replied. "I played baseball in college. I'm going to take a long look at everybody that wants to play and give them a chance. I understand the other guy didn't do that. There'll not be a lonely bench on my team."

"That's good to hear," PJ responded. "You're inheriting a very talented group of young men. Your slates clean here—but there's going to be a lot expected from them, and you."

"I've done some checking around," the coach replied. "I wouldn't accept a responsibility like this without doing a little Scotland Yard investigating. I understand you have had a great deal to do in the development of a lot of these kids."

"Maybe a little bit . . . here and there."

"You can tell some of your kids who didn't get a chance that bench time for them is over!" He spoke with sincerity and authority.

He glanced at Sunny and I. We didn't say a word.

"I might ask you for some of your wisdom now and then," the coach said to PJ.

PJ extended his hand to the stranger, "I'm PJ. You got a name?"

"Just call me Duke . . . we'll talk again."

"Then Duke it is," PJ replied, as he clasped his right hand with that of the coach.

"Oh . . . by the way," the coach eyed PJ up and down. "You play basketball? You're tall enough to hunt geese."

PJ laughed.

The man hurried out the door, and trotted toward their car where his family appeared to be impatiently waiting.

"Ever meet that guy before?" Dad said to PJ

"Never seen him before in all my life . . ."

"I've got a gut feeling we'll be seeing a lot of him," Dad said. "He's got class."

We watched through the window as the man got into his car with his family and drove away.

—ᴍᴍ—

I guess I was kind of shocked when I saw him in the home study hall that first day he arrived at school. I knew I had seen the man somewhere before but I just couldn't place it. *Where was it?*

When it came to me, I dropped my pencil on the yellow-lined sheet of paper I had been working with and turned toward Dean whose desk was beside mine. "That's the guy I told you about. That's the guy that was in PJ's. He's dressed in a suit and tie. That's why I didn't recognize him."

"So that's him." Dean responded with a slight frown while tapping his pencil on the desk in front of him. "You're right. He's dressed about as rich as churning cream. I wonder if he knows any more about baseball than the other guy."

—∞—

When our new coach sat down to plan his spring roster, he did not do the same as his predecessor. As a result of advice from numerous local people, six players who played with or in the same league as the Orioles were promoted to regulars, or rotated with regulars on the high school varsity team.

No sooner had we arrived on the practice field than Coach Duke directed us close to him beside the pitcher's mound. As we anxiously walked toward the coach, I noticed a tall man casually strolling toward our direction. *Is that PJ?* Most of us stopped, and stared as he approached. *Seems like a rebirth of the Orioles team,* I found myself thinking.

"PJ, could I ask you to step over here and say a few words to these young men?" our coach asked.

I could see PJ smile and continue. The speed of his movement may have increased a trifle.

The coach began . . .

"Let me start off by telling you something about myself and my thoughts. I'm not going to relive the politics of the past, or dig up the corpse. I've had a chance to visit with a few of your parents, a few of you men, and a few other meaningful people," he said.

"Now, first of all, I want you to know that I'm no idiot, I wouldn't accept a chance like this without first knowing what I was stepping into." He looked us straight in the eye. "I know you're a very talented group. I also know that my predecessor apparently didn't know a lot about baseball but, I can assure you of one thing—I do! And what I don't know—I'm willing to learn. That's the reason I asked PJ to step over here. This man," the coach said as he gestured toward PJ, "knows one heck of a lot more about baseball than I or you will ever know.

"We're going to do things differently from now on around here," he said. "We're going to build as a team and not as a group of separate individuals. The way to do that is by giving everyone an opportunity to play. That's the only way to prepare for the future. A coach who doesn't do that is either trying to run up the score for selfish motives—or is blatantly stupid!

"I'm open for advice, but I'll make the calls—clear?" His eyes spanned us. "There'll be no excuses or complaints around me. If you can do it, you'll get your chance. I can't do it anymore, that's why I teach. Playing is for those who can, teaching is for those who can't." Everyone laughed. "Maybe that's why the best coaches were not always the best players.

"I'm going to use any help that is available to see that you play to the top of your talents. That's why I asked PJ to help you with some fundamentals."

Enoch raised an eyebrow as I glanced toward him.

"I see magic in you guys," he said. "But you're not going to do this with magic, or mirrors, or whatever."

The coach motioned. "PJ, I'd appreciate it if you would come over here and say a few words."

—⁓—

PJ strolled across the diamond and stopped beside our new coach. He stood with arms crossed as he surveyed us. *What's he going to say?* I wondered.

"I've watched many of you play from the time you were young kids. You all know what you've been taught in the past. You know what to do. Now is your chance to put all the years of training behind you and compete with the big boys. It's now more about attitude than anything else. For that reason, some of you may not be doing as well as you're capable.

"You're lacking the character and dedication that's needed to become a champion!"

He scanned the team with his right hand, forefinger pointing, and he spoke with authority in his voice.

"You've got to play as a team, and not as individuals." His face reddened as he intensified his message. "I'm familiar with most of you as a result of playing for Preacher on the Orioles team. I know he talked to you about character, but sometimes we tend to forget some of these things and get sidetracked in disappointment or selfishness when things don't fall in line the way we'd like." *I'm sure thoughts of past experiences must be flooding through his mind.*

PJ looked at our coach. "You've got a number of exceptionally good players here. I know. The Braves and the Yankees have a number of individual stars also, but they shine because they play as a team. If you expect to beat the big boys, you're going to need to work as a unit, and want to win more than they do."

The rest of the afternoon PJ could be seen instructing during batters practice or working with other players on their throwing motion in order to get accuracy.

I'm sure glad he's here.

In the spring of '52, the Kids marched through five conference games by a combined score of twenty-four to seven. The two veteran pitchers on our team, Enoch and Tiger, took care of the pitching. Shane, Tiger, Greg and Enoch provided the clutch hitting. Interestingly, Sunny, Jerky, Hutch, Stan, Tim, Lance and Ove accounted for major contributions.

—m—

In preparation for the tournaments, Coach Duke scheduled a scrimmage simulated to parallel game conditions. Everyone took turns batting. Balls and strikes were called by Pastor Gus, who was standing behind the pitcher's mound. After a turn at bat, the player would move to a defensive position and another player would take his place at the plate. I was excited when the coach asked me to pitch.

"I'm not putting you in here for cannon fodder," the coach looked directly into my face as he spoke. "For some reason the other guy never gave you a chance. I want to see for myself what you can do—so go do it!"

Of the first twelve batters, I struck out nine. The other three didn't get the ball out of the infield.

"Just rear back and throw that thing," Gus hollered after a batter fanned.

"I've seen enough," Coach Duke yelled after forty-five minutes of practice. He motioned me off the field and called Tiger in to throw. I walked off bursting to the brims, my confidence restored. A few of the guys came up to me, smiled, and slapped me on the back.

"Bones," Tiger grabbed me by the shoulders, shook me, and then pulled his head back and looked me in my face with a big smile, "you struck me out."

At the start of practice the next day, Coach Duke strolled over to me where I was tossing a ball back and forth with Dean.

"I want you to loosen up every day with Shane," he said. "I'm going to start using you in these games—we'll go into a three man rotation."

Finally, I thought.

Chapter 28

"HE TURNED IN A THRILLER"

I n the district tournament against Readstown, on a neutral field at Soldiers Grove, Coach Duke gave me the opportunity for which I had been waiting, and I was brimming with confidence. I'd pitched against some of these guys before during the summer league with the Orioles and knew what to expect.

A black pitcher for the pro team that Bruno had a financial interest in warmed me up on the sidelines.

"Good pitch," he yelled and motioned to me when I threw my drop. "Hank couldn't hit that."

"Hank who?" I replied.

"He's just a kid about your age that I played ball with in our black man's league in Indy. He's in Eau Claire now playing for a pro team for the Braves. Hope he makes it."

When I approached the mound to start my warm-up pitches, Shane was waiting for me with the ball in his hand.

"You and I both know you can mow these guys down, Bones," Shane said as he handed me the ball. "Let's just play catch like we did with the Orioles."

As each inning went by my confidence swelled. I allowed two infield hits while striking out fifteen. *I always knew I could do this, just like Willie said, all I needed was a chance.*

"Let 'em hit the thing once in a while," Hutch yelled from his position at second base. "You've struck out almost everybody that's come up."

The Kids pounded Readstown twenty to one.

—⁓—

The next tournament game, the sectional, would decide who would go to the state. La Farge, our opponent, was an outstanding team—with two players who were sure to be offered pro and college contracts. Each year they had been our toughest conference competition. La Farge was a tough and competitive group of kids. They had a reputation of being that way. They came from a hardnosed Scottish and Welch blue collar community. Each year they had a good team, but some years they could be ranked among the top twenty teams in the state.

In the fourth inning, Enoch walked the first two La Farge batters, who scored when the next hitter doubled down the left-field line. La Farge had an aggressive style of play, taking advantage of every opportunity to score and score early. In an attempt to prevent the second run from scoring, Greg raced from his position in left and after making the catch, fired a dart-like throw to Shane at home. Shane tried to block the plate—but in the process he was spiked on his right arm. Our entire infield rushed in but Tiger was the first to reach him, even before Coach Duke.

"Everybody step back and give him some room," Tiger said.

But Dean wouldn't have any of it. Dean didn't say anything. He pulled the sleeve of his buddies shirt back carefully, and turned his arm over to observe the wound. Coach Duke entered the huddle with a medic who wrapped a bandage around the wound and told Shane not to use it for fear of the cut reopening.

"Can't do that," Shane snapped back with authority. "I've gotta throw." He returned to his position behind the plate.

"Sure you're okay?" Coach Duke yelled.

Enoch took a few steps off the mound in Shane's direction and asked the same question. There was sincerity in his voice. *He's got common sense.*

"Don't worry 'bout me," Shane rose temporarily, removed his mask—then snapped it back down over his face with force and resumed his position.

"Leave him alone," Tiger said, "He knows what he is doing."

"He won't listen to you anyway," Dean yelled across to Tiger.

As the game progressed, the La Farge coaches began to complain to the home plate umpire about some of the strikes that were called on their batters.

"He's really runnin' it up there in a hurry," I heard some of the La Farge players comment to each other. Obviously frustrated because they only had one hit, they swung at wild pitches and were becoming more desperate as each inning passed.

"Stop your bellyaching!" the home plate umpire bellowed as he removed his mask and took a few steps toward the La Farge bench. Although Dean had three hits in the game, and Greg (Tim's older brother) two, the Kickapoo nine could only muster one run until the seventh inning. Then Jerky finally got his chance to bat in a clutch situation—and he made the most of it! Our coach pulled one of the former regular outfielders, and gave Jerky the opportunity he so justifiably deserved. When Jerky drove in Shane and Tim with a double into left field—our advancement to state became secure.

"I knew you could do it all along," I heard Dean say to Jerky as he was being mobbed after his walk-off hit. *I agree. All he needed was a chance.*

Heading into the state tournament the team was eight and nothing and had won thirteen straight games.

—⟶ ⟵—

The weather was cool, windy, and cloudy when the Kickapoo Kids took the field in the state tournament in Menasha. Our opponent was La Crosse Central— one of the largest schools in our state against one of the smallest.

During warm-ups before the game, Coach Duke approached me . . .

"If we win this one, Bones, I've scheduled you to throw tomorrow in place of Tiger." I looked toward the coach in unbelief at what I thought I had just heard.

Is this real? I was pumped. *I sure hope we win. That's my chance!*

Central whipped through their pre-game warm-up with a blizzard of grounders, flies and cut-off plays. On the mound for the La Crosse team was a tall, lanky lefthander who was a farm club prospect of the

Washington Senators. He threw heat, a trifle more than we were used to. A stinger on a cold day was no fun.

The Kickapoo nine wore the collar most of the day. Not until most of the team was able to reach the plate for the third time, did we have the velocity of the pitcher's pitches measured. By that time, the powerful Central nine had pushed across five runs. A couple of vital errors on our part didn't hurt their cause either.

At the plate, La Crosse was smart, not swinging wildly at Enoch's hard stuff around the letters. They made him work for his strikes. As the game progressed Enoch settled down and our team held them scoreless for the last two innings. It was also evident the Kickapoo team was beginning to wake up at the plate. We were starting to lock in on their ace. Before that, Tiger was about the only hitter to dig in and not give him an inch.

Back in the first inning, Tiger hit a liner past the lefty's ear into center field. At his next time at bat, in the fourth, the pitcher's first pitch was at his head and Tiger ate dirt.

"He doesn't miss a trick, does he?" Hutch said to me while I was sitting beside him on the bench.

The next pitch from the La Crosse ace again backed Tiger off the plate—this time it was a barber shot under the chin. Now Tiger was starting to look a little uncomfortable. He shortened his grip on the bat.

"Throw strikes, dummy," a voice sounded from our side of the bleachers.

After two "purpose" pitches, the hurler came back with a hittable pitch. Tiger slashed his bat at the pitch, and finished in his follow-through, but the ball lofted into the air and settled in the left fielder's glove. The mini-rally was squelched before it got started, and so was the rest of the day for our club.

Although Central beat us eight to two, we had one more year to make history.

Leaving the field, I noticed the nauseating smell of the paper mill smoke stacks. *That's about the way I feel,* I thought.

—∞—

On a day in June of `52, Preacher approached the coach of the Richland Center Junior Legion baseball team concerning my playing on their team for the upcoming tournaments. They had the potential to be a good club but did not have pitching that could carry them to the state tournament. Their Legion team had never advanced to state before, and they had a great desire to do so.

"Gut instinct tells me all you need is the right chance to prove yourself," Preacher said, his remark echoing Willie's words from the past.

The coach was impressed with what Preacher said, and readily accepted his offer.

The Richland Center team won the first two games I pitched for them. In the first game, against a team of equal size, I only allowed one hit. The second was against a team from a large city in south-central Wisconsin. We then advanced to the sectional finals in Viroqua against the La Crosse Legion team. The La Crosse team was composed of players from Central—the team that beat Millersville in the previous state tournament—and two other city high schools.

Going into the top of the ninth inning, the Richland Center team came to bat trailing by two runs. As the inning progressed, ducks were on the pond. Two players had reached base, but there was also two out. Standing in the on-deck circle as the next batter stood in the batter's box, a number of thoughts went through my mind—I already had two doubles in the game.

Please God, just let me get up to bat once more . . .

Someone up there must have been listening because the batter before me opened my door of opportunity by receiving a walk—now was my chance!

I've been fantasizing about this very moment since I started playing baseball, I thought to myself, *and now it's actually happening, sort of like it's been predestined . . . just keep your head about you and try not to go bananas.*

The catcher for the La Crosse team telegraphed the pitch he wanted the pitcher to throw. I noticed he would hold his mitt directly behind the plate for a fastball, and off to the side for a curve.

As the pitcher looked in for the sign, touched the brim of his cap, and started his wind up, I glanced back. The catcher was holding his glove directly behind the plate, meaning a fastball. And—as if God had ordained it—the pitcher threw the perfect pitch. Perfect for me that is, knee high, over the middle. My eyes must have grown to saucer size. I never blinked. *Craack!* There wasn't any doubt about this liner, it shot over the right-fielder's head clearing the bases and putting us ahead.

When I reached the mound in the bottom of the ninth inning to start my warm-up throws, the infield umpire approached me.

"Are you Enoch?" he asked. "I see the M on your cap."

"No, I'm not," I replied. "Enoch is another player on our high school team."

"I'm Ernie Kingman, the baseball coach at Menasha St. Luke's. We won the state last spring. I saw your team. You had a good team. Enoch's a good pitcher, what position did you play?"

"I wasn't on the starting nine," I said, "but I was scheduled to pitch the second game if we would have won."

"What—a guy that can pick up a bat like you? I can't believe it!"

The umpire walked to his position between second base and the mound. I started my warm-up throws but he kept talking.

"When you get out of school you should tryout with our White Sox franchise up in the valley."

"I probably could," I replied. "I have a cousin who owns a big Ford dealership up there and is on their board of directors."

"Then go for it!"

A surge of adrenalin swept through my body and spirit. *Now I'm even more determined!*

In the bottom of the ninth, I managed to have enough courage to throw a drop ball on a three-and-two count, and the batter grounded into a force play to end the game. The Richland Center team advanced to the State Tournament—for the first time in their history!

"Bones sure hit today, didn't he?" I heard a good looking girl comment to her dad after the game.

I had three doubles, drove in five runs, and scored two.

The front page of the Crawford County Gazette picked up on my exploits and printed a report of the game. "He turned in a thriller before his hurling duties were through." the paper continued . . .

—⁓—

"Jake," Coach Duke greeted Dad as one was leaving and the other entering the bank in Millersville on the following week.

Dad told me he paused for a moment, a little surprised at the acknowledgement.

"I saw the write-up in the Gazette about Bones," Coach Duke said. "When I took the job here everyone told me to work your boy in the lineup. They were right. Last spring I moved him in the rotation with Enoch and Tiger. In fact, for the tournament I listed him in the middle of the rotation. Too bad we didn't get to that second game, I'd liked to have seen what he could do but—from the write-up in the Gazette—I guess I know now.

"One thing I didn't know," Coach Duke continued, "was that he could hit like that. Three doubles and five runs batted in. And against many of the guys that beat us in the spring. Apparently he can hit even better than he can pitch, and no one gave him the chance. I can't wait for fall practice to start."

Chapter 29

STARTING THE STREAK

It was a beautiful day when classes began in the fall of `52. I drove an old Model A Ford coupe to school that caught the attention of most of my classmates. Because Dad knew the deputy, I didn't need to take a driver's test to get my license.

On the field for the first day of baseball practice was a group of battle-hardened teenagers who were mature for their young age. Because of my summer exploits with the Legion team, my rankings among my teammates and our coach had escalated immensely.

"Guess you're sort of a big deal now," Lance joked to me through his usual big laugh. It was difficult to tell when Lance was joking or congratulating and I had stopped trying to figure it out. When the coach handed out uniforms, Lance grabbed my number eleven jersey from the previous year and left me with number nine from a graduated teammate. *He's just trying to trick with me, but I won't let him.* Coach Duke also passed out orange-and-black leather jackets with a large M over the heart. I guess our team had a little bit of an innocent swagger—not because we were cocky—but because we were quietly confident. We had played against the best, and were finally starting to realize how talented we were.

"Ever think about it, maybe we're just lucky?" I asked Lance when we were getting dressed in the locker room for our first day of practice.

Lance was looking in the mirror . . . turning his head side to side . . . carefully examining and searching for zits or an occasional whisker. Just then, Tim, Dean and Shane walked in.

"Bones thinks we're just lucky."

Shane stopped and focused his attention toward me.

"Bones, you say that?" Shane said, his eyes flashing suspicion. "Are you trying to tell me we're just lucky, is that all?"

"Now don't get your nose outa joint, I was thinking sorta out loud," I quickly responded. "I've heard a lot of pros say they would rather be lucky than good. Hit me if I'm wrong. I didn't mean we were only lucky for heaven's sake."

"Maybe we are kind of lucky," Tim said, jumping in. "But we're also as good as there is, don't you think?"

"You ever been lucky . . . I mean *really* lucky. Like winning something big . . . or just being . . . well . . . you know?" I said, gesturing with my hands and head as much as I could to get their attention and understanding. "Sure we're pretty good, but there's nothing wrong with being good and lucky too, right?"

"Bones got that right," Tim said, backing me up.

———×∞×———

When Kurt's family moved into the Millersville school district, Kurt asked Coach Duke if he could play for the team. Most of the players were familiar with his talents, but they were also familiar with his reputation. Kurt could play, we all knew that, but would he be an asset and stay out of trouble? Only time would tell.

Dean and I were casually playing catch along the third base foul line when Kurt trotted onto the playing field. I knew him better than Dean did.

"Kurt, come over here, I want to introduce you to someone." I swerved in Dean's direction to make the introduction.

"I've seen Dean play in one of the Sterling games last year," Kurt stated as he reached to receive Dean's hand. Dean nodded in reply and smiled cautiously.

"Kurt, come over this way." The voice was coming from the direction of home plate where Shane stood gesturing. With that, Kurt turned abruptly and trotted away without another word.

"What do you know about him?" Dean asked as he stood closer to me.

"The Orioles played against a team he was playing on. I don't believe you were there that day. It was on this field," I replied. "He's a left-hand batter. He can hit, I saw him hit a ball on the roof of the high school in right field."

"Hope he works out, he grates on me in a strange way. Don't know if he'll fit in." Dean looked concerned.

I couldn't deny there was a certain amount of wisdom in that observation. Dean tossed the ball to me, and we went about our warm ups.

—ᴍ—

In the first game of the fall season, the Kids traveled down river to Wauzeka. Wauzeka had a nice ball park, with a road that cut off right field making the distance to the snow fence only about three hundred feet. *I like playing here.* It was also made up of mostly players who had played for Sherman against the Orioles during the summer.

Before the game, I could see Coach Duke at home plate hitting fly balls to the outfielders and grounders to the infielders. PJ arrived while Enoch was warming up and I overheard him point out a few things . . .

"Keep your fastball high and inside, just under the armpits and your curve low and outside, just off the knees." PJ positioned his hands to illustrate. "You'll keep the batters pulling back and lunging forward.

Enoch didn't throw a lot of fastballs during the game. He stayed primarily to his knuckler. The wind was blowing out from home plate toward left field—and throwing into the wind made his knuckle ball dance all the more. Although Enoch mowed down fourteen in the game, it was three-to-two in favor of Wauzeka as we came up in the top half of the seventh.

Roger, our leadoff man singled, and after an out, Dean singled him to third. When Enoch bounced a ball to second base, Dean wiped out the shortstop with a hard slide. He dropped the throw allowing the tying run to score.

"That's playing aggressive ball," a fan yelled from behind the backstop.

On Shane's fly to right, Dean tagged and made third. The next batter, Tim, chopped a ball to the third baseman, who gunned it home, but Dean slid around the tag to make the score four to three. Tim advanced to second on the throw. After stealing third, Tim scored on my double to left. Lance singled me home.

"That's playing aggressive ball," the same fan yelled to Lance.

Lance had two hits in leading the Kids attack. We won six-to-three.

—⁓—

Seneca came calling the following week and I was excited because PJ warmed me up before the game.

"That drop of yours is a good pitch," he encouraged me. "How do you throw it?" I made a twisting motion with my hand. "Let me show you something," PJ said. "You need more movement on your fastball. When you throw it let the ball roll off the seam and the inside of your middle finger." He grabbed the ball from my glove and illustrated. "So it will rotate up and in toward a right handed batter. You'll get movement on it then. A ball moves according to the way it rotates."

PJ's presence made everyone settle down and perform with unity and confidence. I glanced into the stands, looking for Dad and Preacher. There they were, just as they had been through all of our Orioles games, sitting side by side. As I walked onto the field and approached the pitcher's mound, I could hear both of them yell encouragement—and I felt pumped. I *knew* I could handle these local teams because I had pitched against much tougher competition during Legion ball in the summer. *It's sure good to finally get the chance to be a starter.*

Corky, a one-man cheering section, kept up a continual round of chatter.

With two outs, and the game tied in the bottom of the seventh at two and two, Enoch hit a bouncer to short that resembled a Mexican jumping bean more than it did a baseball. The grounder was mishandled, and Enoch reached first. After Enoch stole second, the infield moved in closer for a play at third or first—but Shane drove in the winning run with a sharp single to center. He had three hits during the game.

"Did you see that? That's what I'm talking about," Scooter boastfully yelled for everyone to hear. "That's my man, ha, ha, ha."

I threw a two-hitter and struck out nine.

"Too bad, Bones, about those two cheap infield hits," Coach Duke said to me, as we walked off the field.

"Not bad for a rookie," Enoch yelled with a big grin.

The score ended with a three-two win for Millersville.

—⁂—

The following week our team traveled about five miles north to play at Soldiers Grove. Although their school had produced some excellent teams in the past, they were down this particular year.

Grove had a professional-looking ball park that was home field to the local semi-pro team directed by Bruno. Because of the Kickapoo River curving the outfield, the distance for a home run was very reachable.

In an exact opposite of Murphy's Law, this was a game where everything that could go right for Millersville did go right. From the Soldiers Grove side of the field, it was a catastrophe from the start. We played flawlessly in the field, and Lance put on a center field show with a couple of spectacular fielding gems and rifle-like throws. Everyone with a bat in his hands hit everything that came near the plate.

In the first inning, Dean singled. Then Enoch fought off a high, tight fastball and nudged a little pop fly out to right field. The second baseman raced back, the right fielder sprinted in and dove, but the ball hit inches from the right fielders glove and bounced away for a triple. We were off and running, and as I glanced into the stands I could see and hear our fans up and cheering.

Now it was Shane's turn—and with an effortless swing he launched a rising shot to deepest left center that cleared a group of elderberry bushes next to the bank of the Kickapoo River.

"That guy's as easy to hit as Cracker Jack is to chew," Dean yelled to me between innings.

Shane posted a perfect afternoon, going three-for-three, with three runs scored. Using his fastball most of the day—Enoch fanned fifteen and threw a no-hitter. Half of Enoch's strikeouts were called strikes, as a fastball tailed in at the last second and caught the outside corner.

"If I could throw a slider, I'd of struck 'em all out," Enoch said to me with a grin as we walked off the diamond.

We squeaked by twenty-three to one.

—— ⁓ ——

The last conference game of the fall was a return match between Millersville and our downriver rivals, Wauzeka. This time the game was played on our home soil, and we started out with a bang.

Although the Wauzeka pitcher set down our first two hitters with hard stuff inside, he knew he couldn't continue this with the middle of our lineup.

Dean, our number three hitter, knew it too.

"Come on Dean," someone shouted from the stands.

Dean guessed on a curve, nipping the outside corner of the plate, and slashed a line drive into right field, and jogged into second base. We were up in the dugout, shouting and waving towels.

Enoch continued the assault with a line single to left that sent Dean home. Shane hit another rope to left field and Enoch raced around second without hesitating. Our guys were on first and third. When Tim reached on an infield hit, allowing Enoch to score, we moved ahead two to nothing. I kept up the attack with another infield hit that filled the bases.

"Duck's on the pond," our coach yelled and clapped his hands.

Lance followed with a ground single into right field, scoring two runs. A walk and two errors allowed another run to score. We were up five to zip after one.

In the second inning, the opposing coach, fearful of another repeat of the prior inning, wouldn't let Dean face their starter again. He brought in their shortstop, a hard thrower, but a naïve one. Dean promptly greeted him with a shot that almost knocked the young man down, a line drive back to the mound. The pitcher could barely react in time to prevent getting badly injured. The ball hopped away, and by the time he reached it, Dean was standing on first, his cap in his left hand, his right paw mopping his brow with a bright red handkerchief.

That hit made a big difference in how the chucker responded to his foreign assignment. *He looks nervous.* I could see him talking to himself as he strolled off the mound and back on again.

"He's meat," I yelled to Enoch.

Enoch also noticed the nervousness of the pitcher and immediately took advantage of the opportunity. He hammered a shot to right that *caromed* off the brick wall of our high school so hard that it bounced back to the second baseman, holding him to a single and allowing Dean to move to third. Shane walked, and when Tim also walked, Dean scored.

Once again, the Wauzeka coach made a fear-filled move. He brought in a lad from left field to face me. I greeted his first with a single to left, scoring Enoch. The new recruit managed to get out of the rest of the inning, but he couldn't retire many of us afterwards.

The game ended in the top of the seventh when, after two outs, the last Wauzeka batter struck out on a drop that broke onto the dirt and got the laughter of my teammates—and the embarrassment of the batter.

"You really put something on the ball to that guy," Shane laughed and shook my hand. A sheepish, thrilled look crossed my face.

I allowed four hits. We won sixteen to two.

Chapter 30

ILLNESS

T his time of year along the hills of the Kickapoo, nature with all her color and glory displayed evidence of the Creator. I noticed a nip in the air. The hillsides were aflame with yellow, red, orange and purple leaves from the oak, maple, box elder and apple trees. Small horsetails of citrus streamed west of the field, and blackbirds flew in thick flocks preparing for their southern trip in advance of the approaching winter. Although the temperature was beginning to warm to the mid-sixties, earlier in the day I could see my breath fly in the chilly air.

Our baseball schedule was drawing to a close. Around four thirty, after school classes ended, we had baseball practice for the next hour and one-half. The whole community was buzzing with anticipation. Occasionally, PJ would show up, unannounced, and mix with the team. It was common to see town folk drop by to watch, and sometimes participate, making it like old times.

With Kurt added to the team, the bus trips became a little interesting. Kelly, Sue, Stacy, Linda, and the rest of the cheerleaders traveled with the team and usually sat up front and together as a group. But with Kurt there, the usual became the unusual. Kurt started a conversation with one of the girls, and soon the seating arrangements got out of hand. It wasn't long before Shane joined in. I'm not sure if it was because of attraction or convincing, but one of the girls decided to sit beside me on one trip, which "loosened my boots" a little. Because we were distracted, that practice quickly came to an end. Coach Duke was less than happy about it and made some swift changes. In order to keep our minds on the game we were to play, he ordered strict silence on the bus rides.

———⚏———

In the playoff with our old nemesis, La Farge, for the North vs. South league championship, the Millersville team arrived early at the neutral location in Soldiers Grove. Fans from both teams and interested spectators had already started to take up positions along the bank that circled the field from the third to the first base foul lines. Some brought folding chairs, while others spread blankets. The few wooden bleachers located directly behind the home plate backstop filled first. I noticed Dad and Preacher, both wearing their dress hats, already firmly implanted just right of home and about six rows up. They looked eager for the game to start. Within a few minutes, Dale joined them. Further to their left, Fr. Murphy and Pastor Johnson sat together eating hot dogs and popcorn. It appeared Pastor Johnson had spilled some droppings of ketchup on his pants because he was wiping his trousers in between bites of the hot dog he was holding.

Our players hit ball after ball into the far areas of the outfield as we powered our way through batting practice. The team finished with a round of meticulous infield drills. *We look sharp!*

Just before the first pitch, a gold Cadillac recklessly swirled off the blacktop road and into the dirt parking space by the announcer stand. Dust flew as the car came to an *abrupt* stop. Two men got out, one dressed in a gray sweatshirt and sporting a big black western hat, and the other in a red flannel shirt and faded brown dress slacks. *Bruno and Scooter,* I thought. Both looked a little hung over.

I noticed Coach Duke walking to the scorer's booth with a sheet of paper in his hand. After handing it to a person inside, he approached me outside our bench area.

"I'm going to start Enoch today," he said. "Not for any special reason other than the two of you are on a rotation bases, and it's his turn to pitch. I'm going to put you on third and Lance on first."

The first four innings turned into an exciting see-saw affair. In the top of the first, La Farge erupted for two runs, due to a combination of walks and hits. In the bottom of the second, the Kids returned the favor when Tim tripled and scored as I hit into a fielder's choice, third to first.

La Farge surged further ahead, with two more runs in the third and one in the fourth. However, behind our team's clutch hitting, the Kids came back in the bottom of the fourth.

"You don't wanna wake 'em up," I heard the La Farge coach caution his team between innings. "They've got some tough players on that team. Every time you knock 'em down they just keep gettin' back up.'"

However, that is exactly what they did.

Shane strolled from the on deck circle where he had been swinging two bats together, and tossed one away. He looked good at the plate. Shane had control of his bat, his balance, his swing, and the strike zone. He was an intimidator in the middle of the Kids powerful lineup—and had been pounding the ball at a four twenty three clip.

The first pitch to Shane hit him squarely in the middle of his back, a pitch he didn't particularly appreciate. It went straight at him; he could only turn around and take it. His eyes blazing, Shane said something to the La Farge catcher that necessitated the umpire to call time and caution the two players.

"Those guys don't know what it means to quit," I heard what sounded like their coach comment about our team from the opponent's side of the field. "They give one hundred percent all the time."

When Tim stepped to the plate, the left fielder shaded him toward the foul line, but he surprised everyone by slicing one down the right field line scoring Shane and taking third standing up.

"Better be careful with this guy," Shane yelled to the La Farge pitcher.

The La Farge pitcher was careful, perhaps too careful; he walked me on four straight outside curves.

After the gratitude to me, Lance hit a hard shot to third that the fielder blocked with his chest, grabbing and slinging the ball to second for a fielder's choice. Tim held at third.

"Lucky that didn't go through," Enoch yelled to Lance.

The third baseman backed up a bit, ready, or so he thought, when Stan stepped in. Stan didn't waste any time in keeping the pressure on. He hit another shot toward third that the baseman couldn't block this time. The ball glanced off his glove and twisted down the left field line, ending up against the yellow foul pole in the corner. Tim and Lance both scored and Stan stood on second. On a three-and-two count, Cletus signaled to center scoring Stan to tie the score.

In our half of the fifth, a walk to Enoch, a sacrifice by Shane, and a bobble on a grounder from Tim put runners on first and third, with me again at bat and all the money on the line. This time, however, it did not turn out so well. I hit the thing squarely off the fat part of my hickory, but directly at the third baseman.

"You got robbed," a fan yelled from the sidelines.

The tension held for a moment. Lance didn't try to overpower the ball that he hit. He reached for an outside curve and hit it solidly on a line to right field, which appeared to be a sure single to score Enoch. But the right fielder, in an attempt to rush his throw, over charged the ball and it got past him. Lance kept running all the way around third. The throw from the outfielder reached home at the same time Lance crashed into the La Farge catcher. The force of the jolt caused the catcher's mask to fly through the air as he dropped the ball—Lance was safe.

"You ought to play fullback for Notre Dame," Shane yelled as Lance strolled to our bench while dusting dirt off his uniform.

The rest of the contest was, for the most part, an afterthought. Aided by some outstanding defensive plays, and Enoch's pitching, the Kids held the opposition scoreless the rest of the way. Dean had three hits and Enoch added a round tripper to help his cause. We won eleven to five.

"Way to go Bones," Preacher yelled and waved as he and Dad walked off the field.

The team went undefeated, six and nothing—and another winning streak had started.

—⟶⟶⟵

A warm wind blew and rattled the chains of the flagpole in our schoolyard. Spring felt close. Graduation became more on our minds in the spring of 1953 than in the years before. Some of us knew what we planned to do after school, but my only interest was in playing professional baseball. Classes in school took on a different atmosphere; the relationship between teachers and students became more personal.

Baseball excitement was at fever pitch across the state. During the spring months, the Boston Braves moved their team to Milwaukee, and County Stadium was built to accommodate them.

On the negative side, I developed a severe case of strep throat—which resulted in my missing preseason conditioning and all the games preceding the tournaments. Nevertheless, while I was recovering, my teammates were taking over where we had left off the previous fall. Not being able to share pitching duties, Enoch was the one who had to perform all the action—and that he did!

Over the winter months the speed of Enoch's fastball increased drastically to the mid-nineties, and with movement. He turned the ball over when he released it so it would rotate upward and in toward a right-handed batter. Enoch had four no-hitters in his senior year—three of which were consecutive. In one game he threw all strikes through the first five innings, a total of forty-five in a row—striking out everyone he faced. Scouts came to games to observe his outstanding performances and the popularity of the team. Interestingly, Enoch didn't sit by himself on a secluded corner of the bench when he threw these no-hitters. He mixed with the other players, and the team wasn't hesitant about talking with him either.

PJ stopped at our diamond unannounced numerous times.

"On fly balls," he said, "always take a step back first. It's easier to come in on a ball than it's to go back. When you have two strikes, choke up on the bat. You have more bat control. Before the ball is hit think about where you want to throw." He kept constant control of the fundamentals.

For most of the time Enoch was unhittable. On one occasion, Shane forgot his catching mitt so someone rushed to a grocery store and got a slice of beefsteak to put into his fielder's glove so the ball did not hurt his hand when catching it. After the game—the steak was beaten to where it looked like ground beef from the force of the pitches.

Through the sensational pitching of Enoch and the timely hitting of Shane, Tim and Dean, the Kids easily won all their games leading into the conference elimination tournament.

Chapter 31

THE RIDE TOWARD
THE RECORD

Anticipating an end to the Korean War, excitement and romance filled the air during apple-blossom time in mid-May. The apple trees on the hills overlooking Millersville were in full bloom. As I drove our Model A Ford through the orchards (I never took a driver's test, the local deputy took Dads word that I could drive), I could see a blanket of beautiful white and pink blossoms stretching for miles. It was breathtaking. Aroma from the blossoms filled my nostrils. Some of my classmates frequented the orchards for hand holding and other gestures of love. *Hum, that's Julie with her boyfriend, riding in that red Buick convertible. I wonder what they're up to?*

The movie *From Here to Eternity* graced the silver screen and the theme for the Millersville prom was

"Moonlight and Roses." I displayed a huge red boil on one side of my nose, but a slab of salt pork taped on the night before solved that problem. I attended but was still too shy to date. The prom meant more than moonlight and roses to Shane and Kurt. Although they were not interested in dating (in the true sense of the word), the prom provided an opportunity for working the dance floor sidelines for an evening of romance.

The road toward the state began with a conference elimination game against Readstown. The game was played on a neutral field in Soldiers Grove. For me—it was the first game I played after returning from my spring illness. I did not start the game, but I was called in to pinch hit in the second inning.

"Bones ... you feeling okay ... ?" Coach Duke yelled.

"I'm ready, Coach."

"Then grab a bat, I want you to hit next."

Observing the pitcher from the bench during the first inning, I noticed he always started out with a fastball to each batter. *If he throws that thing down the middle, I'll pound it.* And that he did. Swinging on the first pitch as hard as I could, I smashed a single to left. Tim, who bloodied their noses with a triple just before me, trotted home.

"Line hit to left," Enoch yelled.

When I pinch hit again in the fourth, I again swung on the first pitch and lofted a double that fell just short of splashing into the Kickapoo River in right-center field. Lance and Stan both scored on that one. I stayed in to play first. *It feels good to get back in action.*

The two runs Enoch allowed through the first four innings were mostly as a result of a slap hitter at the top of their lineup, poor fielding on our part, and a brief spell of wildness by Enoch. Regardless of the score, it had reached five to two, the determined Readstown guys kept right on trying. Their pitcher even started throwing at the heads of some of our guys in an attempt to rattle our cages and keep the game within reach, but to no avail. We were too seasoned for all of that nonsense. When Shane started signaling Enoch to do the same they abruptly stopped their aggressiveness and accepted the reality of who they were messing with, after all, a ninety-five mile-per-hour heater on the temple could cause real damage or put the batter out of his misery forever.

In the sixth we finally busted it wide open, thanks to the two country cousins, Dean and Shane. After Tom (Jerky's younger brother), our leadoff man for the inning reached base on an infield error, Dean doubled him home with a smack that would have resulted in a triple if he hadn't stumbled after turning first base. Nevertheless, after Enoch walked, Shane hit one into the outer banks of the Kickapoo River, somewhere in purgatory, where no one could find it.

Enoch wanted strikeouts after that and he got 'em. The lads from Readstown dropped like dominos. In fact, no one got the ball in play. As I glanced across the infield from first base all I could see were our guys boringly kicking dirt and fidgeting with their gloves.

The final score was twelve to two.

—⁂—

I got my first pitching start of the spring in the regional tournament game against Desoto, a town located on the banks of the Mississippi River. The school's mascot name was the Indians. Desoto had a tradition of being a strong baseball community. In fact, they had a semi-pro team that was in the same league as La Crosse, Soldiers Grove, Viroqua and other towns. I was eager to get back in action. As Enoch had improved over the winter months, I was anxious to equal his success. However—my illness and lack of conditioning because of inactivity showed up almost immediately. I was not the pitcher that I was the previous fall. My control was off, and I struggled with velocity. *My arm feels weak,* I thought. The opposition answered my feelings with a run in the first, two in the second, and one in the third.

In the first inning our guys were mostly handcuffed, ground outs and pop ups. It looked like we were going to make a move in the second when our first two batters singled, and the next hitter walked, loading the bases with no outs. But the De Soto pitcher got our next two hitters to pop up, and our next batter struck out.

In the third, the reverse happened. After our first two batters bounced out, our next three loaded the bases through walks and infield hits, only to have our following hitter fly out to deep center.

Assessing that I may have been a little tense after my layoff, Shane called the team around him at the pitcher's mound.

"Listen up guys," he said. "We're not goin' to circle the wagons against this group of redskins. We're goin' to attack. This is our chance. We're better than these guys—let's take care of business!"

There was nothing more to be said. If I was a little anxious, Shane was the man to keep me focused. We clapped our hands together in agreement, any tightness I may have had melted like a snowman in July.

Down by four runs in the fourth, the Kids fought back. After we filled the bases with nobody out, Tim stepped to the plate, and dug in.

"If he lays it in there, be ready," Coach Duke cupped his hands over his mouth and yelled from the third base coaching box.

After falling behind on the first two pitches, the De Soto pitcher grooved one that Tim turned on and drove down the left field line scoring three runs. After

I walked—Lance's perfect squeeze bunt scored Tim with the tying marker.

"Way to go guys," I said, as they approached our bench. "I need all the help I can get today."

The final and winning marker for Millersville came in the fifth inning. Stan singled and moved to third when our next two hitters reached, one on an error and the other hit by a pitched ball. He was then driven home by Dean's single up the middle.

When the third batter for De Soto waved at one in the dirt in their half of the seventh inning, the game ended. Millersville five, De Soto four. Although I didn't pitch up to my standards, by any means, I guess I didn't do too badly considering the circumstances, I only allowed five hits.

Lance and Dean each had two hits in the game with one of Lance's being a long double.

—⚏—

Hopes were high and excitement was in the air as the team prepared for their sectional tournament game against Livingston. The game was held on a neutral field in Soldiers Grove. The game would decide who would advance to the state tournament.

For the first four innings, the game was a tight affair, a scoreless pitcher's duel between the Livingston pitcher and Enoch. In fact—neither hurler had allowed a hit!

At this point, time was called, and the game delayed for about fifteen minutes to allow a mother skunk and her three little ones to cross the outfield and waddle into the brush adjoining the Kickapoo River.

"Ha Lance!" Shane yelled to our left fielder. "If you get sprayed, don't think you're coming over here."

After Livingston took the lead in the top of the fifth by two runs, the seasoned Kickapoo team fought back in their half. I led off with a single to right—that broke the Livingston pitcher's no hitter. *I guessed right on that pitch.* Lance singled and moved to second when the Livingston pitcher hit Stan on a leg with a pitch.

"You okay kid?" Coach Duke yelled as Stan limped and then trotted to first.

With the bases full, the next two batters bounced out without a run scoring. Then fate, luck, or whatever, shifted our way. Roger, a hitter in a lower spot in our lineup hit a bouncer to the Livingston shortstop, who overthrew the bag at first. I scored and we were one run closer.

In the next inning, Dean swung on a curve that just spun and didn't break. The ball exploded off his bat so hard that the shortstop was defenseless to handle it cleanly. Although holding Dean to a single, our attack had just started. On the next pitch, he stole second with a headfirst dive. Apparently, the Livingston pitcher was either tiring or feeling the pressure, because he walked Enoch and Shane on eight straight pitches, again filling the bases.

I eagerly watched as Tim dug in at the plate; he glanced to Coach Duke who was on the edge of the third base coaching box sending signs. The coach touched his cap, his nose, an ear, and clapped his hands; the take sign was on. Tim nodded and returned his attention to the mound. The Livingston hurler promptly responded with two fastballs on the inside corner. His next delivery was an off-speed pitch that was low and outside. Tim misjudged the speed of the ball. In an attempt to recover his swing, he tipped the ball off the end of his bat. It dribbled slowly past the pitcher's mound, and by the time the shortstop reached the bouncer Tim was on first and Dean scored the tying run.

Behind the backstop, his nose pressed tightly to the screen, Corky called out to me as I approached the plate.

"There're all full for you . . ."

The infield moved in for a force out. I got what I expected, a waist-high fast ball on the inside corner, a perfect pitch to hit, and I smoked it, right into the third baseman's glove! He never moved an inch except backwards from the shot he caught.

I trotted back to our bench shaking my head in disgust and sat down on the corner closest to the action. When Lance's drive hooked sharply down the left field line, the Kickapoo fans rose to their feet—but it was just a long, meaningless strike. Foul by inches, but foul, nevertheless. Lance's legs crouched in anticipation of the next pitch, slowly waving his thick-handled bat in a swatting motion.

Three times he went through the same repetitive motion. He waved it back and forth, back and forth, rehearsing the next pitch in his mind. Preacher glanced at his watch; it was nearing about that time to start milking. Fr. Murphy was doing his beads in the stands, and his face had taken on an uneasy edge. His buddy, Gus, held tightly to his Bible, his eyes closed.

"Come on Lance," Tim yelled.

On the next pitch, Lance over-swung and hit a soft grounder down the third base line. The third baseman trying to be quick and casual at the same time, plucked the ball barehanded and threw wild to the plate—allowing Enoch to score with the winning run.

Millersville three. Livingston two.

The Kickapoo Kids, from the tiny Millersville High School, had just set a record. Competing against schools ten to twenty times our size—we advanced to the state tournament *three* times in *four* years!

—⚬⚬—

The next game would be a biggie. It was May 16th, and a special day of celebration for the principal of our school who was retiring after twenty-five years. Alumni from all across the country attended. Because of these unusual circumstances the game was played on our home field.

The opposition was a school team we needed to have revenge against, Wauzeka. They had eliminated us from progressing in tournament competition two years earlier. Because of the festive occasion, PJ was asked, and he accepted, the honor of being the home plate umpire for the big game on the big day.

The weather, however, had a mind of its own. The barometer was dropping, which usually meant a storm front moving in and a bad day for Preacher's arthritis. It was strange to see Dad sitting alone without his buddy in the bleachers. The afternoon was a *scorcher*. The marker on the oval-shaped thermometer hanging from the east side of the concession stand hovered around the low-to-mid nineties.

"Hot enough to make a preacher cuss," Coach Duke said as he approached our bench area before batting practice. He wiped his brow with a handkerchief.

"I'm going to start you today Bones," he said, "but if trouble arises I'm going right away to Enoch. You may not be strong enough yet. We'll see what happens."

After an inning-and-a-half, Wauzeka was ahead by two runs and things were not looking any better for our future. They had the sacks full with no outs. My wool uniform was soaked with sweat. It was also about that time that I began to feel dizzy, and lightheaded. The feeling came on rather gradually, sort of like a slow leak in a tire. *I have to stay calm; I don't want to make a public spectacle of myself.*

Shane called time and trotted out to the mound. "Bones, you tryin' to toy with these guys or something? Your fastball looks like a floater, I haven't seen one like that since I looked down the seat in our outhouse."

I failed to hear coach Duke calling me. He must have noticed I was unsure of myself, because he motioned to the home plate umpire, called time and strolled out to where I was standing next to the pitcher's mound.

"What's the matter, Bones?"

Without meaning to, I dropped the ball. It rolled off the mound and into the grass. I stared at it, trying not to give up on myself. I paused, swallowing hard, thinking I wasn't going to be able to tough this one out. "I don't have it Coach."

Coach Duke picked up the ball, waved Enoch to come in from his position at first base, and I strolled to the temporary seclusion Enoch had vacated. We slapped each other's butts in encouragement as we passed.

Enoch threw exactly nine pitches and we were out of the inning without any additional damage. *Whew, I'm starting to feel better already,* I said to myself as I trotted to our bench.

"No big deal," Shane yelled encouragement to the team as he pulled his catching gear off, sweat dripping from his forehead and nose. "We've got five innings left to get 'em."

—m—

The first score for the Millersville came in the third inning. With a runner on first base, Dean hit a line-drive home run that darted through an open door and rattled around the insides of our agriculture building. I could hear the sound of the ball striking the metal wall all the way to our bench along the third base line.

"That thing must have hit one of those empty metal drums," Stan said to Dean.

The game remained tied at two and two, going into the last of the seventh. We probably would have been ahead by a run if it were not for the Wauzeka left-fielder robbing Tim of a sure home run with a dazzling, over-the-shoulder catch in the sixth.

I led off the inning.

"Come on Bones," I could hear Preacher yell as I walked to the plate feeling totally recovered. I glanced in the direction of the call and saw Dad and Preacher, as usual, sitting in the bleachers in about the third row. *That guy just can't stay away even though he's sick,* I told myself.

There are instances when a batter can be so geared that he can "see" a ball better than other times—this was one of those occasions. When the first pitch came, I could see the red lettering on its white cover and the rotation the ball was spinning, and knew it was a curve. I jumped on it and hit a long walk-off home run that sailed over the left fielders head, across a street—and landed next to a house beside a parking lot. There was no doubt in my mind that it was gone as soon as it was hit, so I hesitated momentarily to relish the moment before starting my race around the bases. Their catcher rose and kicked the dirt while the hit was in midflight. High fives were everywhere when my sprint ended after I crossed home plate, and, although I did my best to act nonchalant about the whole thing—my seams were bursting with excitement!

Enoch saved my butt and had only allowed two hits the rest of the way while fanning fourteen. We won three to two.

"Bones has turned slugger," Lance yelled. He was smiling ear-to-ear.

Corky stood directly behind the backstop and got this look on his face where his eyes opened widely, his mouth expanding to the size of a cantaloupe and harboring words until they burst forth with enough energy to shout, *"Yaaa!"*

Dad told me later that the ball smashed the front windshield of a red Chevrolet pickup. The owner never complained.

"That's the longest ball ever hit at our new ball field," Coach Duke said smiling at Dad and me. Then he handed the retrieved ball to me for a souvenir. Dad looked proud—and I felt confident.

"A Frank Merriwell finish," Clyde commented to Dad and Preacher as they walked off the field.

"Heck of a hit," PJ said to Dad. "That's the longest one I've seen out here."

When Dad told me what PJ and Clyde said, it really made me feel good!

We were thirty-one and one over the last two years, and undefeated since losing to La Crosse Central at the state the year before. Next was the state tournament!

Chapter 32

A CHANCE FOR REVENGE

Prior to the state tournament, Kurt stopped attending practice and dropped off the team; his interests seemed to be elsewhere. He got into a fight at the pool hall and was seen drinking. Some of the local fans, however, were disappointed.

"He could have helped our attack," I heard Scooter say. "That kid was no angel, but he could hit. Too bad it didn't work out for him."

During the early part of the bus ride to the state tournament in Menasha, most of us never talked about what we were getting into. Our chatter was mostly about things other than baseball, like school, girls, classmates and fun things. But the closer we got to our town of destination, the team grew silent. We sat motionless, keeping deep in our own private thoughts as we looked out the windows . . .

The bus rolled through one-stoplight towns and the rural countryside. As I glanced out a window of our bus I could see farmers busy in the fields cultivating and planting crops. The view temporarily shifted my thoughts of the tournament to what Dad was doing at home. *I know he would want to be here.*

Although the players from larger schools did not intimidate us, I couldn't help but wonder what this unfamiliar group of players and teams were like. *Are they really any better than the other guys we have been playing against? Would we get a chance to play La Crosse Logan?*

Our team was a little different this year. We were resolved and sort of on a mission to prove something—and we feared no one. *I beat the pants off the La Crosse Logan and Central players that played on their Legion team last fall. This team can't be as good as they were.*

The press was aware of what our team had achieved and reporters were waiting for us when we arrived at Papermaker Hotel. We didn't know anybody. The team stuck together, as we always had. We were an item in a foreign land.

"The team that came from baseball nowhere to flirt with history," the sports section of the Appleton Post read—it made for a great story.

"Those kids from the small town along the Kickapoo River can do more than milk cows and pick apples.

They've beaten virtually everybody around. They play with the grace of a dancer, lunge for balls beyond their reach, leap for the stars, and always seem to throw out the runner by a step. They compete and no one knows how good they really are. But they're facing some teams in this tournament that may be a little beyond their reach."

Walking into restaurants wearing our hand-me-down orange and black school jackets, with a large M on the left front side was interesting.

"Are those guys in the tournament?" I heard Lance point out as he laughingly referred to a group of young men who appeared five years older than us. "I think they are deliberately attempting to grow beards to put fear in us—big shots!" Everyone laughed.

"I'll call 'em whiskers when they come to the plate," Shane barked loudly. "That ought to get under their big-city skin."

"Can't wait 'til tomorrow," Tim said. "I'm ready for a fight!"

Even Stan, who was usually quiet, looked anxious and confident.

Scouts from professional teams were arriving to scout a few of the players they had heard about, and they were especially eager to see Enoch pitch. The fact he had four no-hit games during the spring months was all the invitation they needed.

Shortly after we arrived at the Papermaker Hotel, our club received word that our opposition for our first game would be Colfax, the winner of the La Crosse sectional tournament.

Our team bunked together on the same floor of the hotel, two to a room. I bunked with Tom, our second baseman. I believe Enoch stayed in a room with his father who had driven up for the tournament. Wherever our team traveled, home or away, Enoch's dad was always there. Outside the hotel that evening we where serenaded by three of our fans who drove up for the tournament. They didn't believe in fine restaurants and big-city attire at a once-in-a lifetime chance like this. The trio had filled up at a truck stop somewhere along the way with roadkill and rum, and now, with the addition of some Kickapoo Moon in their bellies, they were bent on tying one on and carving up some excitement. Their celebrating was truly major-league. The trio sang (not unexpectedly out of key) outside our hotel window from the street below. They abused Wheel of Fortune most of all. Finally, in the wee hours of the night, someone from a floor above ours dumped a pot of liquid waste on them— ending their evening.

I don't believe many of us got much sleep, not because we were nervous (by now we had been in too many big games), but because we were anxious to prove a point, which was that we were as good as the bigger schools—and possibly even better. And that desire and talent were more important than the size of the school.

It's our final shot to win this thing!

—ᴍ—

In the clubhouse the next morning Coach Duke addressed the team.

"I know you guys were looking forward to playing one of those La Crosse teams, but these guys must be better. They kicked their butts in the tournament. If we beat them, it's the same as beating La Crosse."

After clearing his throat he continued . . .

"Listen up, I'll be quick!" Coach Duke was talking fast. His words raced his thoughts.

"Remember what PJ told you. Sports are not only about being able to run faster, throw harder, or about hitting a ball. Some players are better at this than others. But the players and teams that win do so because they are taught mental and character skills to defeat better physical skills of the opposition. Baseball is as much between the ears as between the bases. To beat teams like this, you must believe you can beat them.

"Most teams are intimidated by who they are, and they're beaten before the first pitch is thrown . . . the champions know that . . . they expect the crowd and the press will bring you to your knees. But remember this, it's the same distance from pitcher's rubber to home plate here as on the Millersville High School diamond.

"I understand the press is saying it will take a miracle to beat our opposition today, and that's a lie! In most cases, we make our own miracles." Coach Duke raised his right fist in the air and shook it. "Take this advice and strap it on tight. I've seen this type of thing myself more than once. You've got to *believe* you can kick their butts—and then you *will!*"

We almost broke the door down as we charged out of the clubhouse and into the afternoon sunlight. For the team, this was finally ground zero.

—☡—

"Remember what Duke said," Enoch's father yelled as we ran onto the playing field. "It's the same distance from pitcher's rubber to home plate here as on the Millersville High School diamond." *He's a wise man, I really admire him.*

A trio of older men, one dressed in a business suit without a tie, another in dress slacks and a white shirt, and the third wearing a Braves baseball jacket, sat directly behind home plate. I noticed one held some sort of a speed-rating device in his hand. The other two held clipboards on their laps; each had a pencil resting behind an ear.

It was evident from the reaction of the crowd that everyone was expecting an old-fashioned lynching, and it wasn't long before the hangman made his presence known. The scorekeeper had just announced the starting lineups, which resounded through a speaker located over top of the center-field scoreboard when a loud voice rose from the Colfax side of the bleachers.

"You hayseeds, why don't you go back to that cow town you call home, wipe the dung off your shoes, and start milking the cows?" a man yelled.

"They do have roads back in those hills and valleys, don't they?" joked another.

I flinched as soon as I recognized their voices; these were two of the men that had needled us at the La Crosse Logan game three years earlier. *What are they doing here?* Now the game became more personal.

I wished my eyes hadn't searched the bleachers to see who the big mouth was, wished I had waited until after the game. Maybe then I wouldn't have been as upset, and it wouldn't have got me thinking about anything except the game.

"Don't let that trash talk get under your skin." I remembered the advice of the university baseball coach from years earlier. His advice had a clarity to it that seemed more visionary than remembrance.

—⚹—

The mood in the stands, meanwhile, appeared to be intensifying.

I started to walk toward the interruption, but Lance put up his hand to stop me.

"Wait a minute," he said, grabbing my jersey with his left hand and halting me. "Let's stay here and listen to what the loud mouth has to say"

"I'll bet five hundred dollars against those hayseed farmers, who'll take it?" The voice became even more challenging and direct. The crowd around us went silent; more than one pair of eyes left the action on the field and focused on the sarcastic stranger in the Sunday suit.

Too well-dressed to have been from around here, I couldn't fathom what he was doing at this game, after all, who would come to watch baseball dressed for church?

"Who'll take it? Five hundred bucks," his shout broke over the crowd again, coupled with a boisterous laugh at his own joke, "I've always had a weakness for lost causes."

I looked down and saw that my uniform was sweat-stained and dirty—and that it didn't match half of the uniforms our team wore. Immediately, I saw in this stranger's eyes the point he was trying to make.

"When this thing's over I'm going to hang that S.O.B.," I heard Scooter snort. The scary part about that is, I believed he meant it! Some of the crowd seated in the area looked startled.

"He can't be with Colfax, they seem like a nice group of guys," I mumbled out loud to myself. "He's probably just intoxicated"

I guess a bystander heard me.

"Drunk is a better word, but I've seen him drunker. He's never been potty-trained. Guess he lives up around La Crosse someplace. For some reason he comes to all these games, wish he'd stay away," he said, shaking his head. "He's an embarrassment to the area."

After another boisterous comment by the same person, the sarcasm was broken by a direct response.

"I'll take that knee-jerk offer of yours," a familiar voice echoed from some distance away behind our bench.

Clyde stepped past me, his overalls worn but neat, a noticeable difference from that of the stranger as they stood next to each other. It had the appearance of rich versus poor, city against country. But little did the stranger know whom he was addressing. Clyde owned a few thousand acres of the most productive black dirt top soil in southwestern Wisconsin. I tensed—wondering if our mild-mannered neighbor was going to have it out with the loudmouth. Instead, he reached into the front pocket of his bib overalls and withdrew several folded-over bills.

With great deliberation he peeled them off, one after another, and laid them down side by side on the rail between him and the stranger.

"One . . . Two . . . Three . . . Four . . . Five hundred dollars," Clyde spoke the words directly to the booster as he placed each bill down with deliberate precision. I leaned in, I think everyone leaned in, seeing the one with two zeros in the corner of each bill.

The stranger took a step back, his eyes narrowed and then widened as he realized he had painted himself into a corner.

"I don't...I mean it's not like I carry that much..."

Clyde smiled really slowly, being sure to keep one hand on the bills to keep them from blowing away.

"People around our part of the country usually carry a little folding money with them in case an opportunity like this comes up with you rich, city guys. Don't make it a habit to blow our mouths off unless we can back it up with *cash*. But it'll suit me just fine to take a personal check from you, sir." He rolled and lit a cigarette as he talked.

The squeeze only got tighter . . .

The man looked around, trapped as a cornered coon. I could tell his feelings were beginning to fade.

With one hand, he pulled a handkerchief from his pocket and wiped sweat from his gleaming forehead.

"Well sir, that's big of you." He replaced the handkerchief, pulling out a checkbook with shaking hands. "Of course that's a great deal of money, I'd hate to see you lose."

"Right fine of you to be concerned, but I warrant I'll be okay. You're looking kind of pale, sir, like some of the thistles on my farm after we've sprayed 'em with that DDT stuff. Are you sure you're gonna to be okay?" His confident drawl brought a round of laughter from the onlookers.

"We better get back to the game, Bones," Lance said as he tapped my back with his hand.

—◆—

The quiet command from Lance brought me out of my daze. I'd forgotten the reason I was here. I'd never seen so much money in my life as I did when I saw those green bills fluttering under Clyde's hand on the rail. I nodded to Lance and tore back to the bench with the rest of my teammates.

"Whew, that's a lot of money even when you say it fast," Lance joked to me.

The kids from the Kickapoo regrouped quickly, though, and hardly seemed dazed by the incident. This band of battle-hardened seniors had been to the big show before and through almost everything imaginable together. One more diversionary obstacle was not going to detour our aim.

"Let's do it," Tim yelled encouragement to himself and his teammates.

"Just throw strikes. Keep the ball in play and throw your fastball high and tight like PJ said—they'll never be able to keep up with it," Enoch's father yelled words of advice to his son.

In the first inning Dean singled, Enoch singled, and Shane drew a walk to fill the bases. As their pitcher dropped down to whip in a side-arm curve, our next hitter, Tim was partially fooled. He reached across the outside corner of the plate and got just enough of the ball to hit a soft-liner into the gap in right-center field—driving in three runs.

Because of a spell of momentary wildness and clutch hitting, Colfax pushed across enough runs to take the lead after four innings. The Colfax pitcher was good, a recruit of a minor league team.

"Time to play hardball boys," Coach Duke yelled from the dugout.

In the fifth, Dean and Enoch again singled. While Tim was kneeling in the on-deck circle, Shane grounded to the second baseman, who looked at the runners to make sure they didn't try to advance and threw to first for the out.

Tim rose to his feet—his face expressionless. Preparing to hit by swinging two bats, he tossed one away and stepped into the batters' box. On a two-and-two count, swinging late on a fastball, he lined a shot off the right-center field fence scoring two more runs. After Tim advanced to third on my ground out, Lance drove him home with a deep fly to center.

From that time on, Enoch was on his blue-ribbon best. Nobody could hit him when he was right, and he was almost unhittable as the game progressed. Batter after batter returned to the dugout, shaking his head after trying to catch up with one of his ninety-five-mile-per-hour four-seam fastballs.

When Dean called the infielders to the mound at the start of the seventh inning, I knew he had a message for us.

"Three more outs," he declared with enthusiasm. "We only need three."

"This next guy that's coming up is a killer," I remarked with caution.

"None of those dudes are going to get past me," Shane said in a determined voice as he yanked his catcher's mask down over his face.

"You got enough gas left in your tank to finish this thing?" I asked Enoch.

"Don't sweat about it—just give me the ball," Enoch answered, as he pulled the brim of his Millersville cap down snuggly on his forehead, his voice taking on a quality that might pass for sarcasm.

"Okay, let's do it, and then get the heck out of here," I replied.

"High and tight, remember, high and tight," Enoch's father yelled from his seat in the stands back of home plate.

Enoch's first pitch was a little too high and a little too tight—it sailed over the batter's head and deflected off the backstop. Lance said later that he heard a scout holding a radar gun comment on the pitch to someone sitting beside him.

"Look at what that says," the scout said. "Ninety-six miles per hour." A murmur went through the crowd.

"That's a purpose pitch," someone cried—all the fans in the stands rose in unison to the intensity of the moment.

Shane lectured to each batter in a tone of sincerity as they stepped into the batter's box. "I wouldn't dig in if I were you," he said, "this guy can get wild once in a while and it's not safe."

It was evident by their body language that they heard every word Shane was saying—because we won, six to four, and everyone jumped with jubilation.

In the clubhouse, Coach Duke pointed to a calendar with a painting by Norman Rockwell on it.

"Take a good look at the calendar, it's an historic moment—something you can tell your great grandkids about fifty or sixty years from now. How a tiny group of kids from the sticks did the impossible—and set a state record doing it!"

Clyde donated his five hundred winning dollars to the team so we could get new uniforms.

Chapter 33

TENSION

O n the night before the semifinals, the team ate dinner at the hotel restaurant.

"Well . . . look who's here!" Dean said, heightening his voice for the announcement of a number of former players.

Tiger, Mark, and Dick shouldered their way past other hungry people and sat down at our table. It was fascinating being there and hearing them reminisce like old-timers. Tales of nostalgia permeated the area; I even heard the Sterling Orioles mentioned a few times.

Tiger was dressed casually, and looked strong and hardened from working at a creamery during the past winter. Mark and Dick looked much older. Mark in a sport jacket and slacks, and Dick (sporting his usual crew cut) wearing a sweatshirt belonging to the sheriff's department of some town. Of course, to hear them tell it, if the ball had bounced another way for their tournament teams, they would have won the whole shebang. Numerous heroic acts were stretched to the limit!

"Don't let this guy bother you," Shane joked to one of the waiters as he motioned to Corky. "He's having a bit of a culture shock, first time out of the Kickapoo, you know."

An athletic-looking man with graying hair and wearing a "Tigers/Cubs 1945 World Series" cap strolled across the room to our table and shook hands with Coach Duke and Dean. Reaching across the table, he grasped hands with Shane and smiled slyly.

"Tell Scooter I said hi, okay?"

"Who's that guy?" I mumbled to Tiger as I leaned close so others couldn't hear.

"That's Dean's brother, he used to play with the Tigers, you know."

Finally, it was time to eat, but before the waiters came with the food, Pastor Gus said a prayer to thank the Lord for the meal, and at the same time gave Him a little nudge in a personal direction:

"Father, we thank you for this food that we are about to eat, please bless it to our bodies. In addition, Lord, I mean no offense, but if it should be in your will, please allow these young men to kick some butts tomorrow. We ask this in Jesus' name. Amen."

Shortly before the meal ended, I asked Tim to loosen me up outside the hotel on the back lawn. I was scheduled to pitch the next day, and I usually threw a few practice pitches the night before a game. I didn't want to break my routine. It wasn't long, however—before I realized that I just didn't have anything left in my arm.

"Maybe you'll get it back before game time tomorrow," Tim said, trying to sound as positive as he could about my dilemma. "Maybe you'll have to go to mostly breaking stuff; you'll see when the time comes."

"We'd better get back to the hotel before the meeting is over," I said, motioning to Tim.

Back at the hotel dinner, Coach Duke addressed the team . . .

"You guys don't need any help from me. There's no desperation in this room, by any sense of the imagination. You started out a few years ago as a band of courageous underdogs with nothing to lose. With the help of PJ and Preacher you've come a long way since then. I see in the paper this afternoon that one writer refers to this team as 'The Kickapoo Kids.' But that term is no longer correct. You've graduated—you're men now—and I'm proud of *every* one of you."

Everyone rose and shook the coach's hand as we left the restaurant.

I don't feel good about tomorrow . . .

—⁀ɯ—

At 5:52 the next morning, the sun peeked over the eastern hillside adjacent to Preacher's farm, and Guernsey cattle that had been grazing on the old Orioles baseball field all night began their stroll toward the dairy barn for milking. Preacher's thoughts were not on morning chores, but far away. A cool breeze was drifting down out of Minnesota, blowing fluffy dandelion seed to the far stretches of what was once left field. Robins hopped about and listened for a wormy breakfast for their young. The field was returning to normal after seven years of roughhousing. A fresh crop of Canadian thistles prospered down the right-field foul line, burdock weeds had stolen second and third bases and a patch of bare dirt still claimed home plate. The pitcher's mound had lost most of its height.

In Menasha, at the scene of the state tournament, ground personnel were arriving to prepare the diamond for the final day of tournament competition. White chalk was laid along foul lines, the batters' box and the on-deck circle. The coach's box was marked and the infield diamond and pitcher's mound groomed.

Our team gathered for breakfast in the hotel coffee shop around seven am. The smell of coffee and bacon swirled through the air. As I walked by his table, Lance nodded at me while he glanced up from his platter of steak and eggs. I can't say that we were superstitious, but possibly out of habit, most of us ate and did the same things we always did before a game. I'd had a restless night. I was worried. Maybe troubled would be a better analogy. I knew deep down that I wasn't ready for this.

"I wish I was in the same shape as last year at this time," I said to Shane, who was sitting beside me in a booth. A waitress clanked a plate of scrambled eggs and sausages on the table in front of me.

"Don't worry about it," Shane replied as he looked toward me from the plate of pancakes he was attacking. "You'll do it with sheer determination, if nothing else." There was a tone of confidence in his voice. "Care if I have one of your sausages and some of that ketchup? I'm so hungry I could eat a bear with its hair on it."

I settled back in my seat.

The semifinal game was against Birnamwood, a town in northeastern Wisconsin. Their team had almost won the state basketball championship the past winter. Because of their basketball achievements, there was a great deal of press surrounding these men.

I immediately saw that a number of their player's had beards, which was a great contrast to most of us, who weren't even beginning to shave. Once we got started we saw this wasn't like other games we had played, games in which the opposition was just another team to roll over. This would not be a garden party—but a war! Nevertheless, we were not intimidated, after all, it was what we had been waiting for since the first game we played on Preacher's diamond in Sterling—and we were ready.

—◆—

The contrast between the two teams could not have been greater, notoriety against hope. The Birnamwood team had bright new uniforms. Ours were worn, and a few did not match.

As expected, Coach Duke asked me to pitch, but as soon as I reached for the rosin bag and *sucked* my first breath, the action got ugly. It immediately became evident that I wasn't in shape for this task, and my heart went out to the rest of the team. While my stomach churned, I unzipped my memory bag of past experiences. In a New York second—a thousand thoughts went through my mind. *I'm going to get myself dry-gulched if I'm not careful. If only I was in shape, I could have handled these guys.* Those thoughts, however, didn't change the reality of the moment. *I'll never forgive myself if I mess this thing up.* The fact that the wind was blowing out from home plate to right field at fifteen miles per hour didn't help matters either. At times, the American flag that hung on a pole down the right-field line almost stood stiff in the breeze.

With one out in the second inning, and Birnamwood ahead six to nothing, Coach Duke called time, and slowly walked to the mound. He squatted down like a catcher, then, leaned in close toward me, confidential like. He made a rule of never yelling at his players, no matter what. The rest of the infield surrounded us.

"How do you feel, Bones?"

"I don't have any life in my arm, yet."

"Think you can get it back?" Shane questioned.

"I don't know, man . . . I don't have zip to my pitches."

"Sorry Bones," Duke reached for the ball. I strolled toward first base, head down.

Duke looked toward the bench and waved for Freddy Mc Cumber, a chubby, round-faced rookie left-hander to come in. *Why he didn't bring in Enoch,* I questioned.

"We've sure got our work cut out for us now," I heard a spectator's voice echo from somewhere in the stands. *I wonder who said that . . .*

Surprisingly, the rookie didn't do too bad a job. Apparently Birnamwood was not used to left handed pitching. With a jerky windup and deceptive throwing motion, Freddy managed to keep the score reachable.

The Kickapoo Kids, however, refused to sink because they had hit an iceberg. The Birnamwood pitchers mixture of off-speed stuff and heat had kept us off balance in the first two innings, and we knew we had to work fast if we wanted to escape from being blown out.

—◆—

In the top of the third—a triple to the gap in right center by Enoch drove in two men who had walked. The next inning, a single by Lance chased across Tim and me. Stan reached first base on a line drive that should have been scored as a hit but was listed as an error. The Millersville crowd rose to their feet when Freddy greeted the reliever's next pitch—a high fastball—with a towering home run over the right field fence.

The first half of the fifth provided more excitement for the Kids. Our first batter walked on four straight pitches. At that point, the Birnamwood coach called time and motioned to the sidelines for a reliever to close the game out and get the save. The new guy had a big overhand curve, a pitch that was murderous to anxious late inning hitters who usually beat it into the ground.

Before stepping to the plate, Dean stared at Coach Duke, who was standing in the third base coaching area. He might have been looking for a take sign, but there was none. Dean touched the bill of his cap in reply, toed at the dirt with his right foot, and shrugged. Our coach would now have to play his trump card. It took courage to let Dean swing away without first testing the new pitcher's control. The fact that Dean already had a double and a single for the day must have entered his mind.

Coach Duke also knew Dean was a first-pitch hitter, and because of this he was willing to gamble that the Birnamwood pitcher would try to get ahead of Dean, that he would groove his next pitch in the middle of the strike zone.

The Birnamwood catcher called time and trotted out to their pitcher who was mopping his brow with a dark handkerchief. Trying to calm him down, I thought. When the catcher returned to the plate, Dean dug in. And just as expected, not wanting to put the tying run on base, the hurler's first pitch was straight down the middle. Dean pounced on it, knocking it up the middle of the diamond and into center field, scoring another run. Suddenly we were back in the ball game!

Chapter 34

CLIMAX

The Birnamwood team took the field entering the top of the sixth clinging to a narrow one run lead. Their hurler strolled to the mound with purpose in his step. Left. Right.Left. Right.

After their infielders finished infield practice, they whipped the ball around the horn, and the third baseman tossed it back to the pitcher.

"You can do it, man, you can do it," he said. "One. Two. Three!"

"*We need runners,*" someone yelled from the Kickapoo side of the stands.

Time was getting short for a rally. Filled with hope, the fans from the Kickapoo rose to their feet. The tension was so great that Clyde, who had been hustling about stroking his white beard, sat down for fear of a heart attack.

The Kickapoo Kids had come a long way, and we had faced and defeated most every style of team around, but to come back against this one would be tough.

Cletus, our third baseman led off the inning. Upon direction from Coach Duke, he choked up a few inches on the bat. After nibbling around the plate with a couple of curve balls, both just off the outside corner, the hurler worked him with a high and tight fastball. Anxious to get on base, he swung at the pitch and towered an infield fly to the first baseman. Dean worked the count to one and two before lining a deep drive toward the gap in left center, where the center fielder robbed him of extra bases with an outstanding diving catch. When the fielder excitedly jumped up after the play, I could see green grass skid marks across the front of his uniform.

With the possibility of defeat getting closer with each out, Enoch stepped to the plate. He never did things many other players do when the chips are down, when nervous time sets in. He did not bite his lower lip, take his cap off and replace it, or pound the dirt out of his spikes with his bat. He stared straight ahead—cocked his dark hickory bat—and took his statue-like stance in the box. To assume the pitcher had a pitch that would get Enoch out would be risky.

Behind by one run and with two out, the count reached one and one. When Enoch took an outside knee-high pitch that the umpire said nicked the corner of the strike zone, he glanced back at the umpire in disbelief. A sharp look spread across his face before he returned his attention toward the hurler facing him. The count reached two and two after he didn't bite on a curve in the dirt, and it temporarily stayed at two and two when he fouled off another pitch.

From the dugout, I glanced into the stands and noticed a little red-haired boy fiddling with what appeared to be a metal puzzle, paying no attention to his father's excitement. Reflection from the afternoon sun that was peaking its head in and out of the clouds temporarily blinded me. A radio hummed in the background, Earl Gillespie and Blain Walsh announced excitedly that Joe Adcock had just driven in Eddie Mathews with a double off the left-field wall in County Stadium.

Then the unbelievable happened. Guessing what the next pitch would be—Enoch wheeled on a curve out over the plate and drove a line drive over the brick, thirty-foot left field-wall.

"Get over it! Get over it!" I could hear him yelling as he ran toward first.

From the sound of the crack, the left fielder must have known it was gone—he never moved a foot. His body remained motionless, except for the sideways movement of his head as he gazed downward toward his feet. Then in a display of apparent unbelief, he pounded his glove, again and again, against the ground.

In a wave, we rushed from our bench onto the field. The sun temporarily burst through an overhanging cloud, and the cheering drowned out the chirping of a robin that was perched on the roof of the dugout calling for rain.

The shot should have tied the score, but in the excitement of the mobbing celebration, our jubilant team had somehow prevented Enoch from touching the plate. Recognizing this, the alert umpire threw his right hand to the side and high—his thumb protruding upward.

"Batter out!"

Hysteria and confusion were everywhere. The Birnamwood fans jumped with adulation for their team. Players shouted and whooped. Meanwhile, the Kickapoo fans, and their team, reacted with a mixture of shock and frustration.

—⁘—

Encouraged by their good fortune, Birnamwood rose to the occasion in the last of the sixth inning. Freddy had tired and they scored a multitude of runs. The lead was just too much to overcome for the Kids in the final inning.

The Kickapoo Kids walked over to the Birnamwood group of players and shook hands with every member of the team. I immediately thought of what Preacher said to us after our first season playing for the Sterling Orioles:

There'll be excitement and there'll be heartbreak. You'll beat some big teams and win some big games. But you won't win all of them. You'll win because you have character, and when you lose, you'll lose with character. We're going to have fun either way. You're the Kickapoo Kids and we're proud of you.

Although at the moment the experience seemed surreal, we all knew it had been great fun—but the ride was over.

There were no noses to be wiped with this bunch, we had won together, and now the entire team was responsible for our only loss. Win or lose, we loved to compete against the best, and we had done that to the limit of our ability.

We weren't lucky today, I whispered to myself.

As I was strolling off the diamond in a somewhat somber mood, I almost ran into a man who was approaching me, he grabbed me by an arm.

"Bones . . . isn't it? Remember me? My name is Kingman. I coach Menasha St. Luke's. I umpired at that Legion game you played in last fall in Viroqua."

"Oh yeah, I remember talking with you." His remark brought back happier memories and cheered me up a little. I smiled.

"You been sick . . . is that right?"

"Yeah I have."

"Too bad, I think you would have had a good chance of beating this team you played today if you would have been healthy. I tell my young men that adversity is not always a bad thing. It can toughen you for the trials that will come later on in life, I hope you'll remember that."

"Thanks, I will."

"I guess it turned out good for the other winner though," Kingman continued. "I know they wouldn't care to face Enoch tomorrow. You guys' got a good team."

—⚞—

By the time the Kickapoo fans left the park at around 8:45 that evening, the sun had fallen lower in the western sky.

"That's one thing I admire about that group of men you have, Coach," a scout for the Milwaukee Braves said to Coach Duke just before we entered our dressing room. "They have character and mental toughness.

I wish I had time to follow their progress in life after baseball. They're going to do well. They've won a lot, but not every one of them can play professional baseball. For most of us, there are greater victories and lessons learned in life by losing once in a while. Tell them that for me."

"That credit doesn't go to me," Coach Duke was quick to reply. "It's because of what they were prepared for by two other people. I hope they'll remember the advice those men gave them, and not get sidetracked by what the world has to offer."

"I'm going to invite Enoch to work out with the Braves at the stadium in Milwaukee. Tell him to ask your other pitcher to come with him. I saw him at the Legion tournament last year. I understand he's been ill."

"Hope to hear from you again," Coach Duke said.

The two men shook hands and went their separate ways.

The story behind the Kickapoo Kids was so captivating that it brought hope to a community during a time of adjustment after World War II and grabbed the attention of the entire sport of baseball.

In the team dressing room the press centered on Coach Duke and the rest of the team. No one made excuses.

"I'd like to say we came, we saw, and we conquered, but I can't," said Coach Duke, his voice somewhat forced. "It is what it is. We got beat today by a better team." Then Coach Duke laughed and added, "But we sure gave 'em a heck of a scare didn't we?"

By this time, the two buddies, Fr. Murphy and Pastor Johnson had arrived. My eyes followed them as they slowly walked to the back of the room and sat down on a couple of metal chairs. Everyone's attention turned to these two men of the cloth we all so very much respected.

After hesitating for a moment to collect his emotions, Fr. Murphy rose and stood beside his chair. The room became quiet. He cleared his throat and looked like he wanted to say something, but no words came out. Then he began . . .

"I believe everything happens for a reason," he said as he began to walk through the team with his head up. "Don't you agree with me, Gus?" He shifted his attention for a brief second across the room to Pastor Johnson, who silently nodded.

"Hold your heads up—you didn't win the gold metal but you've made history," the priest added. "You played the game as well as you could, that's all any of us can expect. The rest was not your business.

"Most likely the press will analyze this game in any manner they please as to who is the better team, and that's their right. But I just feel it in my bones that somewhere in time—perhaps fifty or sixty years from now—when your great grandchildren sit at your knees and ask if you did something memorable when you were their age, you won't have to shy away from the question, no sirree.

"Possibly, when most of us are dead and gone from this playing field we live in, somebody will write the rest of the story—the whole story as to what you Kickapoo Kids were all about. You've brought a lot of fun for a couple of old preachers—and hope to more people than you'll ever know.

"And most of all," he continued, "you've kept your values straight doing it. You'll always be winners in our minds, right, Gus?" Gus just smiled and nodded silently, his eyes red and moist.

"Wanna ride back to the hotel?" Coach Duke asked as he strolled slowly over to the two clergy buddies.

"No . . . we've kind of a mind to walking," Gus replied.

"Thanks anyway," Fr. Murphy added, as he reached toward Coach Duke and shook his hand.

—⟋⟍—

Rain began to fall as our bus left the tournament site for the journey home. Puddles on the slick black street reflected an artistic glow from streetlights, adding a yellow tint on the scene. Drops of rain splattered against the windshield of the bus and beads of moisture trickled like teardrops toward the wiper blades. The windows fogged from the inside, and street signs became barely visible. The ride was quiet. Although we tried to lighten the load with occasional chatter and laughter, our thoughts were at other places and in other times. From '46 to '53, much had happened, too much to escape the back reaches of our minds. Games, plays, ifs, ands, and buts were recalled in the most precise detail.

Scenery repeated itself. The bus radio strengthened and then faded as we traveled through the countryside from one town to another. No sooner did our driver settle on a clear station of country music than static drowned it out. The last few phrases of "Wheel of Fortune" dimly played as he passed through the dial.

A copy of *Sporting News,* a gift from our hotel, lay on the floor beside my seat. I picked it up and searched for the name of my friend, Rob, narrating along the way. There it was—listed in the minor league farm system contract offers for the following year, signed as a catcher for the St. Louis Browns / Baltimore Orioles.

"Hey guys, look at this!" I yelled with excitement to the rest of the team.

Suddenly the mist stopped, the fog disappeared, chatter circulated, and laughter filled the setting. *Way to go, Rob,* I thought. *Coach did not want you but the pros did.* Like Willie said, *"All you needed was a chance."*

After a little over a two-hour trip, we entered Millersville. On our way to the high school the bus circled past the river dam. Corky peered with intensity at a boy under a street light casting his line along the bank.

Things are already returning to normal, I thought.

As the bus curved into the school parking area, I could see Dad and Preacher standing beside our car. I stepped off the bus and walked directly to the passenger side of our automobile and entered. Although they both were inquisitive as to all the details of the tournament, I was in a rather melancholy mood and didn't say much.

"Well I'll be switched," Preacher piped up. "Just to satisfy my curiosity, if nothing else, I'd still like to take a week off and play them again," he said, with a big smile on his face. "Maybe the score would be different. I wouldn't bet against you."

I wouldn't either, I thought.

—ɯ—

As I walked outside our house in the evening before retiring to bed, an orange full moon was glowing overhead. From somewhere in the distant part in our woods, I could hear the howl of an adventurist coyote calling his pack to join him. *I'll bet it's the same guy I always hear at this time of night.* It wasn't long before his crew arrived, yipping happily with optimism for an evening of successful hunting.

The following morning I slept in. It was dreary and overcast. A light mist fell. The full moon of the early night was not visible. Nevertheless, it wasn't long before Ben, our Plymouth Rock rooster, began to crow. He was right on schedule to perform his duty. In spite of the darkness and threat of storm, that old bird knew a new day—with all its promise—was about to dawn.

Immediately I hopped out of bed, pulled on my clothes, ran down stairs and into our front yard. The sky in the east was beginning to brighten. An orange glow steadily forced its way over the hilltop. I surveyed the familiar surroundings, and uttered a deep sigh.

I'm only eighteen and my whole life is ahead—I wonder what the future brings ...

Chapter 35

CLOSURE

After the reunion banquet had concluded, the sportswriter I'd talked with earlier strolled back to our table, pulled out an empty chair, and sat down across from Dean and me.

"I was talking with some of your other teammates over there." His face became filled with expression and he leaned forward toward the two of us as he spoke.

"It was an honor being here today. Few people are given the privilege to sit down and chat with the past, face to face. That must have been a really exciting experience, the ride to the record and all. Didn't you guys ever think about the bigger teams you were facing?"

"No we didn't," Dean was quick to reply. His voice expressed certainty. "All we thought about was that their pitcher was just another kid out there throwing the ball. He threw it and we hit it—at least most of the time." Laughter circulated the table.

"I understand a number of the players on your team had offers to play pro ball," the writer said.

"After what my brother told me about the big cities," Dean replied, "I felt more comfortable just being around here. The Kickapoo Valley has always been my home. I think most of us felt that way, isn't that true Bones? We're sort of held captive by the Kickapoo. We may drift away for awhile, but there's something about the lure of this valley that can't be put into words, that keep's pulling you back—you can't ever escape it."

By this time Enoch, followed by Tim and Lance, made their way to our table and Enoch seated himself beside me.

"You can leave and move on to other surroundings," Enoch said, "you can achieve goals that were beyond your imagination, but in the backwaters of your mind, there're always be the good old days we shared together in the Kickapoo."

"We made some memories," Tim said. "On some of these cold winter nights I've got to admit that my mind still drifts back to the way it was."

"The Kickapoo Kids," I said to the sports writer. "That's what you guys called us."

"Well . . . it's good that you're all here today," the writer sighed as he spoke.

"This may sound like boasting," I sort of interrupted the conversation, "but looking back, I think almost every starter on our team could have been offered a pro contract if they would have expressed a desire. Heck, even our bat-boy played four years in the Baltimore farm system." There was more laughter.

"Too bad you never had a chance to meet PJ," Dean continued. "He and Shane, who was a mainstay of our attack and a strong part of our team, are gone now. There was a time . . ." Dean lowered his head and moved it from side to side with somber emotion as he spoke, but the sports writer sympathetically interrupted.

"Yes, I know," he placed a hand on Dean's shoulder. "You guys must have been something."

I noticed some of us old men at the table were starting to get a little misty eyed.

"PJ passed away just recently," Dean continued. "He was over ninety. It was harder to get into the big leagues when PJ played then it is now because there were only half as many teams and players. PJ was the best baseball player I ever saw. He was as good as any major leaguer. Better than my brother who played with the Tigers. We could never have done anything without his and Preacher's help."

"I feel like I know him already from what I heard from the other guys," the writer continued. "I understand he played against the famous Kansas City Blue Birds."

"When I was a kid, Dean, Shane, and some of us had a chance to talk with one of the Blue Birds' players when they were at the fairgrounds," I said. "His name was Willie. That's over sixty years ago now, I often wonder whatever happened to him."

The writer's face lit up and a look of curiosity spread across it . . .

"What did you say his name was?"

"We just knew him by Willie, that's all . . . why?"

"I'll just bet that's J.W. Ritchie! James William "Willie" Ritchie," the writer replied. "One of the best players for the A's when they were in Philadelphia. Everybody called him JW, sort of like your PJ."

"Is that right?" I spoke with wonderment in my voice. "I remember him saying to me that all either of us needed was a chance, remember that Dean?"

"I wonder why he said that?" the writer responded. "Do you know?" The question was innocent enough. I just smiled and glanced at my old teammate deep in thought . . .

"Well, I'm glad he finally got his chance," I said.

I rose from my chair, still in wonderment, and curiously walked to a corner of the bar area where an old colorful antique jukebox from the '50s was standing. As a result of the dust that had accumulated on its surface, it appeared no one had played it for a long time. *I wonder if it works.* I brushed dust off the frontal area to get a clear look at the menu. Pausing, I flipped through the list of tunes and artists that were available. Jo Stafford, Patti Page, Eddie Fisher, Mitch Miller, Guy Mitchell, Rosemary Clooney, Nat King Cole, Frankie Laine, and sure enough, there it was, "Wheel of Fortune." After fumbling around in one of my pockets, I found a stray quarter, dropped it in, and pressed G7. Turning toward our table, I walked back to our group—head down— deep in memory of a time so long ago. *I wish Shane was here . . .*

As Kay Starr started to sing the nostalgic ballad in the background, I noticed a far off smile sweep across the face of Dean and the other Kickapoo Kids at our table. I stopped and stood beside Dean's chair, and placed a hand on one of his shoulders.

"It's getting past my nap time old buddy, and I'll be switched if I've ever told you this before, but although Enoch was considered the star of our team, you may have been the best all around athlete."

"Thanks Bones, you weren't too bad yourself."

"Ha!" Dean yelled as he jumped to his feet beside me. "Got your glove with you?"

"It's in the trunk of my car."

"Wanna play catch?"

Epilogue

T he class of Millersville High School 1953 baseball team was forty-seven and four through four
years, and thirty-two and two in our junior and senior
years. The team played in the WIAA State Baseball
Tournament three out of four years our class was in
school, 1950, 1952 and 1953. During those years our
only loses were at the state. To do this one year would
be a major accomplishment—but for a division five
school to do this against division one opponents—is
nothing short of a miracle! After graduation—five players on this remarkable team were offered pro contracts.
Three played on a 1957 Soldiers Grove team that won
the Wisconsin Baseball Association Championship,
and two were members of a 1971Madison team that
won the AABC National Stan Musial World Series.

—⚹—

I return to that area along the banks of the Kickapoo River quite often. The high school building has been turned into a company that markets mushrooms. The ball diamond next to the school is a green barren field that has been partially filled with a condominium building.

After departing my auto I slowly walk across the field to where home plate must have been located.

My mind is a warehouse of memories ...

No monument is standing in dedication as to what went on here. There is no plaque attached to a pole to remember the team's accomplishment. I shake my head, and wonder how many people know just how good this team actually was—or if they even know the team existed.

I glance at the area where the pitcher's mound must have been and for a split second see Enoch release a twisting blur toward home plate at a speed in the mid-nineties. *Although he became famous, I know he still thinks about the good old days.* Then I step along the path of the ball I hit into the parking lot to win the game on "Shepp's Day," a game that advanced us toward the state tournament. One, two, three, I speak to myself while pacing off the steps. *My gosh, that must have sailed four hundred and fifteen feet, or more.*

Along the road north of Millersville, another school has been constructed that incorporated the

Millersville and Soldiers Grove high schools. The old grade school—in which some young pranksters led a cow on a cool Halloween night, still stands beside the river dam. Rather than preserving it as a landmark, I understand the new generation of the city residents decided to have it demolished. *Perhaps a forecast for many of us,* I think, *when we become unnecessary.* The bank building where an outhouse was elevated to rest on its roof on that same evening still stands along the main street. It is no longer a bank—but a tavern.

The Sterling Grade School has been reconstructed into a building used by the local government. I stop for a peek through a window, and for a brief period of time memories allow me to visualize kids at desks doing their schoolwork. As my stare becomes more trans-fixed into the now cluttered and empty room, I almost believe I see Earl and me setting behind our desks with yellow writing pads in front of us, even the ink wells and our writing pens.

The store in Sterling that PJ operated, and where the men from the neighborhood congregated to dis-cuss everything from the price of butterfat to the ball-game on Sunday has burned down. Nothing stands in its place. There are no outdoor movies anymore, nor the smell of popcorn and butter.

A way of life has passed. The farm Preacher owned has been sold to another neighbor. The field he carved out of his small acreage to start all of this is now patrolled, not by small lads in baseball uniforms with the name Orioles written across their chests, but by large Black Angus cattle. They graze peacefully unaware of the mystical figure of Dad and Preacher sitting side by side on hastily constructed wooden bleachers observing the action on the field. They are equally oblivious to the laughter of a group of kids that were destined for immortality—*to change record books—and make high school baseball history in Wisconsin.*

ABOUT THE AUTHOR

I n 1989, Paul and his wife Susan founded Alliance for Life Ministries (AFLM), a Christian ministry located in Madison, Wisconsin. Their effort is geared toward making a difference by taking God's Word and applying it to His Cultural Mandate.

Before retiring, Susan was a department supervisor for the Registrar's Office at the University of Wisconsin in Madison. Paul was self-employed as the founder and owner of Union Financial Services, an estate and financial planning organization that operated primarily within the Midwest.

After the sale of his business in 2002, Paul became free to devote 100 percent of his time to ministry work. What makes their ministry particularly unique is that they have actually done what most other organizations only suggest. Some other uncommon features of their organization are that they have never received any form of salary, wages, benefits, or financial reimbursements for their efforts.

In 1999, AFLM received the prestigious Salt and Light Award from The Center for Reclaiming America for Christ, as Outstanding Christian Organization in the United States. Paul's commentaries have appeared in publications and on the websites of ministries all over the world. His wife, love of his life, best friend, ministry partner and hero passed away in 2013.

The *Amazing Journey of the Kickapoo Kids* is his first novel.

Paul Lagan can be reached at:

P.O. Box 5102
Madison, WI 53705

Email: paulwlagan@gmail.com

Made in the USA
Middletown, DE
11 June 2016